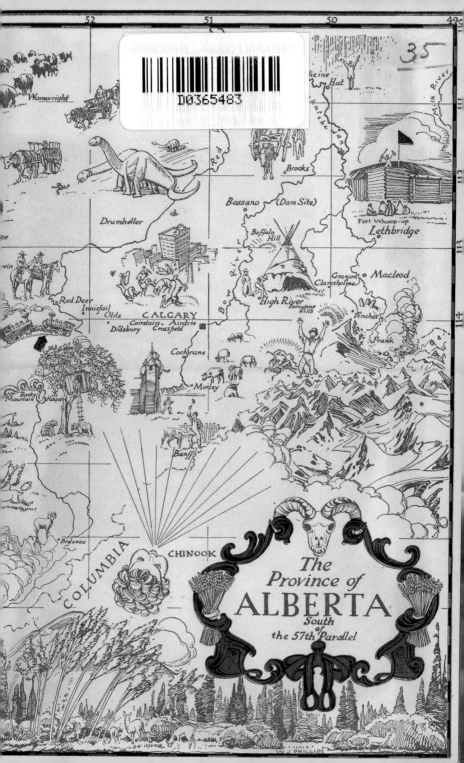

The
Province of
ALBERTA
South of
the 57th Parallel

To Molly and Max Ball
From Lilian and Ken
Christmas 1945

Remembering happy days in the
land of Johnny Chinook

(Didn't we meet
Johnny Chinook
between 1437 and 1943 ?)

Johnny Chinook

Tall Tales and True from the Canadian West

By ROBERT E. GARD

LONGMANS, GREEN & COMPANY
LONDON :: NEW YORK :: TORONTO
1945

LONGMANS, GREEN & COMPANY LIMITED
of Paternoster Row
43 Albert Drive, London, S.W. 19
Nicol Road, Bombay
17 Chittaranjan Avenue, Calcutta
36A Mount Road, Madras

LONGMANS, GREEN & COMPANY
55 Fifth Avenue, New York 3

LONGMANS, GREEN & COMPANY
215 Victoria Street, Toronto 1

JOHNNY CHINOOK

Copyright 1945

By LONGMANS, GREEN & CO.

First Edition June, 1945
Second Edition November, 1945

PRINTED IN CANADA.

WRIGLEY PRINTING COMPANY LIMITED
578 SEYMOUR STREET, VANCOUVER, B. C.

CONTENTS

CONTENTS—*Continued*

Introduction

By DONALD CAMERON

The Province of Alberta is situated on the third prairie steppe, its eastern boundary along the 4th meridian just west of the Missouri Coteau, a ridge of dirt hills rising 300 to 600 feet between Alberta and the plain to the east.

The distinctive physiographic features are the Rocky Mountains on the west and the drainage basins of two great river systems. The Saskatchewan with its two branches, the north and south, flows east in the southern and central part of the province, and the Mackenzie with its two great Alberta tributaries, the Athabaska and Peace, flows north into the Arctic Ocean. In the extreme south the Milk River, a tributary of the Missouri system, makes a brief loop in the province before swinging south to eventually join the father of waters. These rivers, their sources either deep in the glaciers of the Rocky Mountains or in the adjoining foothills, are swift-flowing and have cut deep channels through the surrounding prairie plains.

Occasional high ridges and hills stand out above the Alberta plain. The Milk River ridge projects many miles southeastward from the western foothills. The Cypress Hills, reaching an elevation of 4000 feet, about 35 miles southeast of Medicine Hat, provide a distinctly different type of vegetation and agriculture from that of the flat-lands. In the dry area southwest of Hanna the Hand Hills rise to a height of 3500 feet, 1200 feet above the surrounding countryside, and as a result of heavier precipitation provide good ranching country. Farther north and east the Neutral and Nose Hills form the northern edge of the short grass plains and also the northern boundary of the country where ranching is still an important industry.

Other scattered hills or mountains reaching elevations of from 3000 to 4000 feet can be seen south and southwest of Lesser Slave Lake where Beaver Mountain rises to an elevation of 4000 feet. The Swan Hills north of Edmonton and the Birch and Saddle Hills in the Peace River Country about completes the list of elevations, outside the foothill area, which mark the presently settled area of the province, and in one way or another influence the life of the settlers.

Generally speaking the southern part of the province, or the short grass area, is a country of few rivers, a light and sometimes drifting soil, high winds and bright sun. Its agricultural potentialities have been under question since Captain John Palliser and his colleagues made their survey of "that territory which lies between the Laurentian Shield on the east, and the Rocky Mountains on the west", for the British Government in the years 1857-60. The party traversed much of the territory we know now as the brown soil or short grass plains of western Canada. Palliser divided the land he saw into two classes. The northern, wooded, park country he called the "fertile belt", and the rolling, treeless short grass plains, the semi-arid desert or "true prairie". He believed that the northern "fertile belt" had all the requisites for maintaining a permanent agricultural population, but he did not think the "true prairie" was suitable for such purposes.

As a result of his explorations, Palliser foretold with remarkable accuracy what was to be the history of settlement in a large part of the country which has since become known as Palliser's Triangle.

Palliser's Triangle, as far as Canada is concerned, had its base on the 49th parallel from a point near Turtle Mountain in Manitoba, westward to a point on the international boundary, near the present port of entry of Carway in Alberta. From Turtle Mountain the Triangle, which was more nearly an irregular pentagon, angled northwestward through what is now the provinces of Manitoba and Saskatchewan to a point a few miles south of the present city of Saskatoon. From there the line angled mostly west by south, crossing the Alberta boundary near the site of the present village of McLaughlin and continuing to a point known as Bow Fort on the Calgary-Banff highway. From Bow Fort the line angled slightly southeastward again, until, just east of the foothills it cut the international boundary at Carway.

Actually, the territory that Palliser included within his famous Triangle is simply the northwestern extension of the great North American prairie plains. This region, in addition to the Canadian portion, includes parts of the six northern plains states of the United States. It includes the western four-fifths of the states of North and South Dakota and Nebraska, the northeastern corner of Colorado, the eastern third of Wyoming and the eastern two-thirds of Montana.

The people who have lived there for twenty, forty, sixty years or more have developed a distinctive way of life and a different outlook from that of the people who live on the Pacific Coast or in Eastern Canada and the Eastern United States. This distinctive attitude of the acclimated western plainsman is the product of the one outstanding climatic characteristic of the region—variability of rainfall.

Other regions have variability of rainfall too, but the reason it is different and more important on the short grass plains is because it is what has been called "variability near the margin". The total annual precipitation over the whole area seldom exceeds 20 inches, and in many years it varies from 7 to 12 and 13 inches.

In a region which receives over 20 inches of rain annually a variation of 3 to 6 inches may not be serious, but in a country that normally gets from 10 to 15 inches, that variation can mean the difference between 40 bushels of wheat to the acre and 5 or 6. It can mean the difference between adequate pasture on the ranges and gaunt, starving cattle in the spring. That is why the rancher and the grain grower, the two dominant types of settler on the plains, are the most weather conscious people in the world. They are people whose lives are lived in the speculative atmosphere of weather close to the margin—the margin which spells the difference between abundance and scarcity.

The story of Southern Alberta is the story of ranching from about 1870 to 1900, and of ranching and wheat growing from 1900 to the present day. Painful lessons have been learned, and in certain great areas of the short grass plains can be seen scars of settlement that should never have been. Thousands of acres of semi-arid land were broken up and sown to wheat in the years between 1906 and 1917, but were soon abandoned. The land in these worst drought areas has either returned to its original purpose of grazing, or new methods of conservation have been applied which have led to a new economy and a more stable agriculture.

The story of Southern Alberta is at once the most colorful and exciting of our western heritage, and the people who made it established the traditions and legends which have become a rich part of Canadian life. Probably in no other part of Canada have the elements of adventure and romance been combined so generously.

Calgary is the commercial center of the short grass country, and Edmonton is the capital city of the great part of the province known as the park belt region. From the standpoint of history the park belt region is the oldest settled part of Alberta. David Thompson and Alexander Henry made their separate ways to Edmonton in 1807 and 1809. Peter Pond, the trader, became Alberta's first farmer when in 1779 he cultivated a garden and grew grain on the south slope of the valley which rises from the Sturgeon River at St. Albert.

The region includes practically all the rich black soil land of the province. It is a country of gently-rolling hills, streams, lakes, and deep river valleys—a land of poplar bluffs and willow clumps. Stands of spruce, pine, tamarack, and birch dot the river valleys and the flat benches of sandy soil north of Edmonton.

From the time the voyageurs and courieurs de bois

made their way by canoe and trail up the valley of the Saskatchewan to the present day, this region has been a rich source of food and supplies. In the days of the fur trade, fish and game, including the lordly buffalo, provided sustenance for all. Today, millions of pounds of beef, mutton, bacon, butter and eggs are going forward from the region to feed a hungry world. Sixty percent of Alberta's farmers live within this fertile and productive region and in less than sixty years the land of the trapper, the trader, and the Indian has become a land of thriving farms and villages.

North and west from Edmonton a thin ribbon of settlement found along a single line of railway and a rough gravelled road, links the older, southern part of the province with the new and rapidly growing empire of the Peace River Country. Both railway and highway wind for more than 80 miles through forest and swamps along the shores of Lesser Slave Lake. From Smith on the Athabaska River to High Prairie at the western end of Lesser Slave Lake, is a long corridor—a great no-man's land with occasional high hills shouldering out of the forest. From this wilderness the road emerges into the gateway of the Peace River Country at High Prairie.

The Peace River Country is a vast new land of farms and great stretches of forest. The single dominant characteristic of the region is the Peace River. It separates the various folk; it batters and repels them, and at the same time unites them in a sense of community—the Peace River community. The people of the Peace country always speak of "going outside" when they visit Edmonton or Vancouver.

The river is at once a barrier and a means of transport and communication. Countless cargoes still go up and down its swiftly changing currents. Boats and barges go from Peace River town 250 miles upriver to Hudson's Hope and they go 300 miles downriver to the frontier settlement of Fort Vermilion. Cargoes of fur, cattle, pigs, and grain come upriver. Cargoes of machinery, supplies, and oil go down.

The ideals and traditions of the Peace River people are firmly rooted in the deeds of such early pioneers as Sir Alexander Mackenzie, Samuel Hearne, and David Thompson. In the exploits of a later day, men like Jack Hornby, "Peace River Jim" Cornwall, Fletcher Bredin, Twelve Foot Davis, and Sheridan Lawrence have all enriched the legend of the Peace River Country as they blazed the trails of a new civilization in the great Northwest.

The settlement of Alberta is no less interesting and varied than the geography. While the first settlers were slowly making their way across the western plains, a small group of determined men in Ottawa were facing the staggering task of building a railroad through a wilderness and across a continent. In spite of tremendous obstacles and with a vision beyond their time, they pushed the steel westward across 3000 miles of virgin land. Undeterred by swamps and muskeg through 1200 miles of Pre-Cambrian rock, across 900 miles of prairie, up and over the bastion of the Rockies and down to the Pacific Coast, they pushed the Canadian Pacific Railway, uniting Canada from coast to coast in the last great empire of the west.

Following the lines of steel came the settlers; lured by

the song of cheap, bountiful land. On and on they came with the migration reaching flood tide in 1911 and slowly receding until 1914. From the English counties and the glens of Lochaber, from Land's End to John O'Groats came Scotsmen and Englishmen, and Irishmen from Ulster and Armagh. From Austria and Bohemia and the plains of Moravia, from the Danish farms of Funen and Jutland, and the Swedish lands of Skane and Vermland, from the fjords of Bergen and the valleys of Asker and Aas, they came. From Holland, Belgium, France and Italy and from the black earth country of the Ukraine came thousands of settlers. These were joined by thousands more from eastern Canada and the United States, all eager for the new land.

They were a converging stream of languages and cultures welded together by a common desire for freedom and opportunity. Engineers and scientists, doctors and lawyers, artisans, traders and peasants, all came dedicated to the task of building new homes, opening up new land, building cities and towns on the Canadian plains.

On a September day in 1905, in a ceremony beside the Saskatchewan River in the hustling town of Edmonton, Alberta became a province. Today, 39 years later, over 800,000 people have found their homes in the cities and towns and on the thriving farms of a rich and tradition-filled land.

They have had much to learn. Coming from established communities in older parts of the world they naturally tried to impose on the new country those methods, forms, and institutions with which they were familiar. It has taken Albertans 30 years to learn that Alberta is the greatest "next year" country on earth, and both farmer and business man know that the margin of safety between a rich harvest and a poor one is never wide, particularly in the south. This knowledge makes people conscious of an element of risk which shapes not only the individual's outlook but his whole approach to social institutions. The people have learned that if they were going to conquer the elements on the western plains they would have to adapt themselves to the conditions they found, and not try to mould the western plains into a replica of an eastern or old-world pattern.

The people have become acutely aware of the Alberta sunshine, the hail, the rain, and the warm chinook wind with its mysterious arch in the west. Such things have had much to do with the creation of a distinct western spirit, an optimism that is at once hopeful and fearful, a sense of humor which is the source of many of the tales in the following pages.

DONALD CAMERON,

Director, Department of Extension,
University of Alberta,
Edmonton, November, 1944.

AUTHOR'S FOREWORD

The writing of this book was undertaken for the people of Alberta. Especially it was undertaken to perhaps encourage other writers to use the fine materials of the West. As a result of my year's work as Director of the Alberta Folklore and Local History Project there is, at the University of Alberta, a permanent file of materials pertinent to western backgrounds. This file is open to the study of any western writer interested in interpreting his region.

Many thanks to all the Alberta folk for their interest and assistance. My sincere gratitude is also due the Calgary and Edmonton Public Libraries, the Provincial Library at Edmonton, the Extension Library of the University of Alberta, the University of Alberta Library, the *Edmonton Journal,* the *Calgary Herald,* the *Lethbridge Herald,* the *Edmonton Bulletin,* the *Calgary Albertan,* the Canadian Broadcasting Corporation, the *Canadian Cattlemen Magazine,* the Ryerson Press, the Canadian Pacific Railway, and the members of the Alberta Weekly Newspaper Association.

My final thanks to Maryo Kimball Gard, A. M. Drummond of Cornell University, and to the Humanities Division of the Rockefeller Foundation.

Prologue

You know how it is. You get a feeling about a certain place. You can't exactly explain the way you feel except to say, "this place is different from any place on earth", or "there's a spell over this country", or "it's a mighty mysterious bit o' the land". You can't exactly put it into words, but you'd like to, and you'd like to be able to command a muse, or spirit, or some sort of supernatural being to help you do it. That's the way I happened to meet Johnny Chinook. I wished for him and there he was.

The first time I met Johnny he was standing on top of a high Alberta hill listening to strange music. After we got acquainted I could hear the music too: a far-off wailing that Johnny told me was the sound the old Red River Carts used to make as they crossed the prairies from Fort Garry. Along with the wailing was a dim, ghostly rumble, and this, said Johnny, was the forgotten thunder of the hooves of millions of buffalo.

Another time I met Johnny standing right out on the bald-headed prairie on a shimmering day in midsummer. He was watching a mirage, and when my imagination got sharp like Johnny's I could see what he saw: a procession of characters who made folktale history in Alberta. He pointed out Bob Edwards and Paddy Nolan, Nigger John Ware and Kootenai Brown, Twelve Foot Davis and

1

Kamoose Taylor, Father Lacombe and Crowfoot, Dave Cochrane, Baldy Red, and Jeff Davis.

It was a long procession and took a long while to pass. When the prairie twilight had dimmed out the last faint figure, I felt sad because I didn't know a single character in the whole long line. Johnny, however, said he could fix that for me and he did, for not long afterward I met him in the foothill country on a very blue day in autumn. It was remarkable how he became in turn the leading figures of the procession we had witnessed.

Johnny doesn't appear in person in the book except as a muse. He doesn't need to appear since he represents all the good storytellers in Alberta. I wouldn't mention him at all if I were the only one who'd made his acquaintance; but I find that almost anybody in Alberta can tell you about Johnny. Of course, they don't always know his name. Sometimes he's just known as a farmer, rancher, storekeeper, surveyor, schoolteacher, lawyer, doctor, politician, lumberman, rafter, bootlegger or any number of things. And there are lots of different descriptions of him. Some know Johnny as one per cent man and ninety-nine per cent straight liar. According to others, Johnny is a big fellow, something like Paul Bunyan, with a voice that on still days you can hear for twenty, thirty, forty miles. There are those, too, who'll tell you that Johnny is just a little guy with a big reputation—especially when it comes to spinning yarns. They'll tell you that you're likely to spot Johnny riding a Chinook wind as it comes puffing over the mountains, or that you'll maybe see him trailing the rains and the big snows in the cattle country. He seems to like violent weather changes, political disputes—in fact, any event that folks remember is likely to include Johnny.

To me Johnny is a personal figment, a certain feeling that represents Alberta. He represents the winds, hails, rains, mountains, prairies, rivers, and muskegs. He represents the average man who likes to relate the stories of the countryside, and my desire to hear them. He lives in the present and the past. A convenient figment, Johnny.

Being everybody, Johnny told me all the stories in this book, and being everybody he respects fact almost (if not quite) as much as he loves to relate fiction. Some of the yarns, Johnny assures me, are gospel truth.

However, maybe you know a different or a better version of a tale than the one Johnny told me. This is possible for these tales have echoed before around the campfire, in the bunkhouse, in the hotel bar, and across the dinner table. Johnny Chinook has lived a long while in Alberta.

PART ONE

SHORT GRASS COUNTRY

I

❧

Country Weekly

CHARLES CLARK, EDITOR OF THE *High River Times,* oracle of the foothills, was arguing with a Chinaman as I walked in the newspaper office door; and Mrs. McCorquodale, Mr. Clark's right-hand assistant, was furiously writing copy for the Wednesday paper.

Mr. Clark went right on with his argument, but Mrs. McCorquodale glanced at me over the top of her horn-rimmed glasses, said "hello" and made her pencil move faster than ever. After a while the Chinaman won his point and went away, and Mrs. McCorquodale impaled her copy on the hook.

"And now," said Mr. Clark, "what can I do for you? Don't believe I've seen your face before. Must be a stranger to High River."

"Yes," I said, "I—"

"Well," said Mr. Clark, "anything's likely to happen in this office. When people want anything they come in and ask for it. That's the way High River people do things."

"I've seen you some place," said Mrs. McCorquodale,

"but where? Oh, I remember you. You're the fellow who's collecting stories about Alberta."

"Stories!" said Mr. Clark. "Stories? Man, you've come to the right place. We've got stories here. Make 'em every day. You ought to visit the beer parlor—down the street two blocks and turn to the right. Anybody can tell you where it is."

"I was hoping you'd drop in," said Mrs. McCorqudale. "Bob Needham, up in Calgary, was telling me about you. You must think we're inhospitable. Come in and sit down. You see, tomorrow is our publishing day. I guess you know what that means on a country weekly."

"I do," I said. "I didn't know you published tomorrow or I wouldn't have—"

"Most of the work's done," said Mr. Clark. "Stay and chat awhile."

"We really treat strangers very well here in High River," said Mrs. McCorquodale as I sat down beside her desk. "In fact, I suppose we're about the most hospitable town in the foothills. That's a result of the old ranching tradition. But I must say we pick and choose our friends."

"Like Shorty McLaughlin," said Mr. Clark.

"Yes," said Mrs. McCorquodale, "like Shorty McLaughlin. Have you heard about Shorty?"

I said, "No."

Well in the old days the Indian tribes sometimes left their dead in a wigwam. The deceased was left in a sitting position facing east, and around him were neatly placed all his treasures and possessions. The tent door was then closed and the tribe moved on. Shorty Mc-

8

Laughlin once used this trait of Indian nature to get rid of a newcomer whom everybody disliked.

In the clearing back of Shorty's stood an Indian tepee, and in it was a dead Indian—a big chief. He had been braced upright, but, even so, he was quite dead—the toll of nature.

Shorty discovered this, and a great plan dawned. He led the newcomer out to a little target practice to prepare him for the inevitable day when he would be obliged to protect himself against the terrible red man. The stranger was nothing loath; for he had heard some scalp-raising tales. Shorty and the stranger edged off to the clearing, and Shorty suggested for a target a tree in the general direction of the tepee. Bang! went the revolver.

"You've got to be careful," warned Shorty, "you came pretty close to the tepee that time. We'd better have a look." They stepped over and Shorty lifted the tent flap. There was the chief, erect, but unmistakably dead! "Now you've done it!" groaned Shorty.

One wild look was all the newcomer needed. "Save me!" he cried.

"Well now," said Shorty, "I'll do all I can to hold the Injuns back, but you haven't very long. You better burn the trail as far and as fast as you can go. You haven't much start, so get going!"

That fellow lit out and he never showed up in High River again.

"We take people as they come nowadays," said Mrs. McCorquodale. "Have to. But it hasn't been so long since a man had to prove he had the right stuff in him before he got far in the ranching country."

"Mighty good people in this neighborhood," said Mr. Clark, "except maybe the Hutterites. In some ways they're a good people, but—"

"They won't fit in," broke in Mrs. McCorquodale. "They keep apart. They want to educate their children themselves and in their own way. Nowadays you can't be isolated as they want to be, and it's especially bad for the young folk."

"They're good farmers," said Mr. Clark, "but they're buying up all the best land. That's all right if they'd mix and be good citizens, but—oh, well, I've an editorial about them in tomorrow's paper."

"Stories!" mused Mrs. McCorquodale. "You must go to see Senator Riley. He's our grand old man here in High River."

"Get him to tell you the tale of the lost Lemon Gold Mine," Mr. Clark said. "He knows that yarn better than any man now living. He ought to. Spent enough time looking for it himself."

"One thing I want to ask you, Mr. Clark," I said, "I understand that the *High River Times* succeeded another paper here: the *Eye Opener*, edited by Bob Edwards."

"Oh," exclaimed Mrs. McCorquodale, "now you've really asked for a story!"

"The story of Bob Edwards," said Mr. Clark with a twinkle in his eye, "is undoubtedly the greatest tale in Southern Alberta, or maybe in all the West for that matter. Tell you what you do. You go over to see Senator Riley and get the story of the Lemon Mine. Then come back, and we'll let you see our file of the *Eye Opener*, and maybe we can tell you a tale or two about old Bob."

10

"Senator Riley lives straight down this street," said Mrs. McCorquodale. "You can't miss his place. You'll have to make a detour around the C.P.R. station—"

Mr. Clark was already on the way to his desk with a handful of copy. When I got my hat on and the door opened, Mrs. McCorquodale was making her pencil fly across a sheet of copy paper. As I went out the door, she muttered, "What in the world will I do about Women's Activities?"

1.—DAN RILEY

"Yes, sir," said Senator Dan Riley as I stretched comfortably in a chair in front of his fire, and he sat down in his favorite chair where he could watch the people passing on the sidewalk, "yes, sir, this is a good country, and some wonderful things have happened out here. You wouldn't believe it, but a friend of mine, Buckskin Williams, had the narrowest escape from rattlesnakes I ever heard of. One time Buckskin was pulling out of Milk River with a freight wagon and noticed that every horse on the near side was crowding the chain. When the near wheel horse reared, Buckskin saw what the trouble was: a big rattler had struck, missed the horse, and hit the wagon tongue. The tongue started to swell, and Buckskin had to saw it off mighty quick to save the wagon."

The Senator glanced at me, his blue Irish eyes twinkling. When I looked at him, I could understand why he typifies the fine traditions of courage, hospitality, and good humor of the ranching country. He has lived in the High River

11

District since 1883. His hospitality is famous throughout Southern Alberta, and you are likely to find a variety of people at his house. The Stoney Indians consider him their great friend and adviser. The old-timers like to come to swap yarns; townspeople are always dropping in; and many travelers going through High River stop off to visit the Senator. He is very proud of his Celtic origin, and in characterizing some individual whom he admires he is fond of saying, "He is a fine man. An Irishman."

"You should have come around here ten-fifteen years ago," continued Senator Riley. "So many of the real colorful figures of the region are gone now. A lot of folks call themselves old-timers nowadays that have no right to the name. Old-timer used to mean something in this country. You might pass a man on the street and say, 'Good morning, old gentleman', and he'd pass you right up; but if you said, 'Good morning, *old-timer*', he'd stop and know right away that you were one of the right sort.

"Time does slip by." The Senator was silent a moment, his eyes fixed on some point outside that I couldn't see.

"That's my son, George," the Senator said. "Just coming back from town. He and I batch here. I want you to meet him."

The front door opened and George Riley came into the room. He is a big man like his father and has the same twinkle in his eyes.

"George," said the Senator, "this fellow is collecting stories about Alberta."

"Read about you in the paper," said George Riley. "Say, you ought to tell him about Wild Bill," he said to his father.

"Don't remember much about Bill," said the Senator. "He was a queer customer. That's about all I do recall."

"Queer is no name for it," George said. "Nobody knew where the old cuss was from, and nobody in the world could have kept track of all the crazy things he did. He was likely to pop up anywhere, especially at dinner time. Wouldn't say a word, just come into a ranch house, sit down at the table and begin to stow it away. After a while, he'd get up and disappear."

George Riley laughed suddenly. "I know one time when he pretty near scared some women to death. Like I said, he was a strange customer. Well, God knows why, but one evening he went out to a fellow's cow shed and dug a hole in the manure just deep enough to bury all of him except his head. His hair was about two feet long, and he had a big beard, too. When he got himself buried in the manure, there was this God-awful head, just sticking out of the top of the pile.

"This rancher's wife and a friend of hers were out gathering the eggs when suddenly they saw this disembodied head sticking out. They dropped their eggs and ran a mile, I guess."

"Wild Bill had a way with horses," said Senator Riley. "It was a funny thing: somebody would have a mean horse that nobody could ride, and if Wild Bill happened along, he'd take that horse and ride him. Just throw a saddle on and ride away."

"That's right," George Riley said, "and he'd pop up in the most unusual places." He looked at me, "Don't know whether you know about range fires or not, but they're bad things in this country. Especially bad in the old days

13

when the grass was longer than it is now. One way they had of fighting range fires was to kill a calf, split it open, fix a rope to the head and one to the hind feet, tie off each rope to a saddle, and drag the animal right over the edge of the fire.

"Well, one day a fire got started, and some of the boys set off after a calf some little distance away. They'd just about come up to it, when suddenly Wild Bill stepped out of a ditch, shot the animal, had it split open, and had disappeared again before the boys got there."

"Yes," said the Senator, "but Wild Bill was kind of crazy. We really had some great figures out here."

"Nigger John Ware was one," said George Riley.

"Yes, Nigger John Ware, Fred Stimson, Johnny Franklin, George Lane—Howell Harris was another."

"Who was Howell Harris?" I asked.

"Harris was an Indian trader, buffalo hunter, and sort of all-round superman. In his later years he was a cattleman and manager of the Circle Ranch, one of the largest outfits in Western Canada. He built the first building of which we have any reliable record on High River, about 1865. The place was called Fort Spitze, about five miles from the present town of High River.

"Not long after Harris arrived at Spitze he made an enemy. A young brave, who had arrived only a few days before from some distant tribe, wished to avenge the death of his brother who had been killed by a white man. The brave decided that, as Harris was a big man, his brother's death would be avenged if he killed this white trader. This was the Indian custom: not necessarily the man who did the killing, but any white man's death would even up the score.

14

"This brave planned the manner of Harris' passing in the following way: before daylight the Indian would crawl to the roof of the low, log house immediately over the only door leading from Harris' room, and when Harris stepped out in the morning, he would shoot him in the back. It looked like a cinch, but you know how it goes—'the best laid plans of mice and men,' etc. You see, a certain woman to whom the Indian had confided his plans came to Howell in the night and gave him warning; and so instead of going out the door, as was his usual habit, Harris opened a small window in the rear, took his rifle, and slipping quietly around the corner, got a bead on the brave, and the Indian was soon on his way to the Happy Hunting Ground."

Senator Riley laughed silently. "I remember I asked Harris if the Indians didn't resent this. He said they did, but he squared it with a half gallon of whisky."

"Nigger Dan used to work for Harris, didn't he?" asked George Riley.

"He did," said Senator Riley, "and if there was ever a dead shot with rifle or revolver, Nigger Dan was that man. One time Nigger Dan aroused the enmity of a young Blackfoot brave named Lightning Streak. A woman was the cause of the fracas, as usual. The brave issued a challenge to mortal combat which was accepted by Nigger Dan.

"The agreement was: Winchesters at eighty yards. The combatants were to stand back to back. Harris, as referee, was to count: one, two, three. At the word three, they were to turn, begin shooting, and walk toward each other till one or the other went down, or their guns were emptied.

15

"It was unlikely that Dan would have far to walk as he was a dead shot. Sure enough, Dan killed his man at the first shot, losing, however, the lobe of an ear by the Indian's bullet. Immediately another young brave volunteered to take his brother's place, and after the preliminaries were all settled, the fatal words again rang out: 'One, two, three!' Again Dan whirled and killed his man—hitting him directly between the eyes. But the crown of Dan's Stetson was punctured by the Indian's bullet. That was that."

"Is that all that happened?"I asked.

"Oh," said the Senator, "the women mourned, and the tom-toms beat to celebrate the passing of the two braves, and probably their heroism furnished the subject of tales told round the campfires for years to come, by those who witnessed the duel and by their descendants."

"Mr. Clark said you might tell me the tale of the lost Lemon Gold Mine, Senator," I said. "I have heard—"

"The Lemon Mine," said the Senator, and he laughed all down inside him. "I ought to know the story of that. Enough of my time went into looking for it. And enough of my money, too."

"Are you comfortable? Have a cigar—"

2.—THE LOST LEMON MINE

THE HISTORY OF THE LOST LEMON MINE WAS TOLD ME BIT by bit, year by year, around many a campfire, by that old frontiersman, Lafayette French, as we traveled, pros-

16

pected, and camped in the vastness of the Rocky Mountains in the years that are past.

For a better understanding of this story, I will tell you who Lafayette French was. French was born in Pennsylvania in 1840 and came to the western states as a very young man. There he spent several years on the American frontier. He appeared in the Northwest Territory as an Indian trader and buffalo hunter in the pre-Mounted Police days. He came after the Lemon Mine had been found and lost by two prospectors he had previously staked in Montana. One, Blackjack, was dead—murdered on the eve of discovery by the other, Lemon, who was driven insane by his deed. Lafayette French came to this country to rediscover the Lemon Mine.

Sometime about the spring of 1870, a party of miners left Tobacco Plains in Montana to prospect the North Saskatchewan River, known even at that time to contain showings of fine gold. In the party were two men known as Blackjack and Lemon. The former had the reputation of being the best prospector in the West, having found some of the richest placer camps in the western states, and was the real discoverer of the famous Cariboo diggings in British Columbia. These two experienced prospectors were staked by French and traveled with the party to the Saskatchewan River. They found gold, but not in paying quantities, so in the fall they decided to leave the rest of the party and return to Tobacco Plains to winter.

They gladly availed themselves of the opportunity to travel south with a large half-breed party, headed by one La Nouse whom I knew well. This escort offered protection against the hostile Blackfeet and Blood Indians.

17

They traveled south by the old trail which lay along the foothills. La Nouse and his party were bound for Fort Stand Off; Blackjack and Lemon headed for Tobacco Plains (a large Roman Catholic Mission in Montana); so they separated.

The two prospectors were supposed to have gone up High River and over the mountains by an old and plain trail used by the Indians from Tobacco Plains who drove large bands of horses in to what is now Alberta every fall, and drove them back again loaded with pemmican. Blackjack and Lemon were passing the river as they proceeded. They followed showings of gold to the head of a mountain stream. There they found rich diggings from grass roots to bed rock, about five feet. They sank two pits, and in bringing their horses in from picket, accidentally found the ledge from which the gold came—a ledge of decomposed quartz.

French, who saw samples of this rock at Fort Benton, described it as resembling a body of gold with a little rock shot into it. The sample of this placer was coarser than anything ever found in the placer gulches of the western states. Is it any wonder that many men, then young and in their prime, spent the rest of their lives in a useless search for this Eldorado?

In the camp that night, the two adventurers had a disagreement as to whether or not they should stake the find and return in the spring. One favored this, the other opposed it. The argument finally terminated with Lemon killing his partner with an ax as he lay in his blankets. However much he might have wished to flee from the scene of the tragedy, he could not do so until daylight; so

18

he built a huge fire and with his gun under his arm marched back and forth all night.

Little did he think two pairs of human eyes watched him and had witnessed the entire tragedy. Two young Stoney braves, William and Daniel Bendow, had followed the pair, watched them sink the holes, and saw them panning the gravel. They were waiting for what those strange white men might do on the morrow.

As the night wore on, Lemon was half crazed with the thought of the terrible deed he had done in his passion; and with a dim sense of humor the Indians whistled occasionally to further distress the unfortunate prospector. With the first streak of dawn, he mounted the big roan horse that French had given him and took the trail across the mountains. The Indians packed up what was left: camp outfit, grub, rifle, etc. Taking the two remaining horses, they started to Morleyville to report to their chief, Bearpaw. He must have been much interested as he made the young braves swear never to reveal to any person the location of what they had witnessed. It is not uncommon for whites to commit perjury, but no Indian was ever known to do so.

Many of those in late years who endeavored to locate the Lemon Mine know how religiously those two sons of the mountains kept their oath. Many bands of horses and herds of cattle—fortunes in themselves to those people—have time and time again been offered, but that strange fear of the penalties prescribed by that terrible oath rose up before them, and they both died with the secret locked in their breasts.

I knew them both well and traveled and camped with

19

them in the mountains. They were splendid types of the old Indian chieftains, heads of a large following of their own progeny, ruling their little kingdom with kindness and with wisdom. How I admired this type of Indian: their dignity, their independence, their kindliness to their own people, their deep knowledge of nature. That book which is closed to so many contained valuable and interesting secrets.

But to go on with the story! Lemon arrived at the Mission at Tobacco Plains and at once confessed his crime to the priest whom he had known the preceding winter. He had with him the gold they had saved on the day of the killing, also a sample of the rock which they had found. He seemed half-crazed, and his crime weighed heavily upon him. There was at the Mission a half-breed named John McDougald, a man versed in mountain travel. The priest dispatched McDougald to the scene of the tragedy on instructions given by Lemon as to the location of it.

McDougald found the place, buried Blackjack, built a mound of stones over the grave to keep the wild animals from digging up the body, and returned to Tobacco Plains. Later the Indians reported to Bearpaw the finding of this mound of rocks. He at once dispatched William and Daniel with orders to tear down the mound and to scatter the stones. This they did, and the last trace of a bloody murder was removed from the face of mother earth. How well she has hidden her secret ever since in spite of all efforts to uncover it! The Indians were ordered to hunt no more in this locality nor to use the trail. Mountain trails that are not used soon become impassable and so this trail is not used today—unless it may be one of those opened up in later years by forest rangers.

Lemon spent the winter with his spiritual friend and, although he acted strangely at times, was for the most part sane enough. So during the long winter a party was formed and equipped to start in the spring to work the prospect. As soon as the snow made it possible to travel, a start was made. But they were not alone. All the miners who had wintered in that part of the country had heard of the rich find and were filled with hope of much gold to be found. They formed a large party—about seventy-five men—and followed Lemon and his men.

They stopped at Crow's Nest Lake, proceeded north from there where Lemon camped the party, somewhere about six miles from the original find. This was necessary in order to get grass for their large bunch of horses. Lemon and his party had camped some little distance from the main body, and early next morning, leaving two men in camp to look after it and to kill deer, they started, followed, of course, by the other party.

Lemon was unable to locate the place and, after a fruitless search, concluded he had taken the wrong gulch. This would not go down with those who had followed him, and they accused him of trying to throw them off and threatened to lynch him. Lemon mounted his horse and rode back to camp where he became violently insane. His own party stood guard over him all night and in the morning started back over the mountains. They reached Tobacco Plains, and Lemon, although he had lucid intervals, never fully recovered his reason. He lived for many years with his brother who was a cattle rancher in Texas.

So ended the first expedition and so have ended many more. Every one has been unsuccessful and many of them tragic.

Next year the priest outfitted another party from Tobacco Plains. This was to have as its leader, McDougald, the man who buried Blackjack. McDougald, who was at Fort Benton, was to meet the rest of the party at Crow's Nest Lake; they were to proceed north from there. McDougald left Benton to keep the appointment, but at Fort Kipp—a whisky trading post—he drank so much booze it killed him. The party at Crow's Nest Lake waited a week before hearing of the death of their leader. And so they turned back.

Next year another large party was equipped and got as far as the lake when mountain fires burned all the timber and grass, so they were forced to abandon the enterprise.

The year following, the priest sent a small party under the guidance of Lemon, but on nearing the place Lemon went mad again, and they were forced to take him back.

It would appear that the priest now gave up the quest, but it was taken up by others. One of these was a member of the first Lemon party, a man named Nelson; but after a summer's useless search, the party disbanded, and each man continued an independent search. Finally Lafayette French followed a lone trail. Once sickness overtook him back in the vastness of the hills, and he was barely alive when he finally reached my ranch on the head of Willow Creek. There he was nursed back to health, and the next spring saw him again ready and eager to renew the search.

22

It was about this time that my curiosity was aroused as to what French was looking for; slowly and gradually he told me the story. He began by showing me a rough pen and ink sketch of rivers and mountain ranges, and at the head of a stream with three forks was an X. He told me that the map was made by Lemon and that the mark was the Lemon Mine, the richest thing ever found in the Rocky Mountains. He told me that that was the reason he had come to Alberta and said he would continue the search as long as he lived. From that time until his death fifteen years later, I was associated either directly or indirectly with French in his prospecting.

From him I learned the Indian trails, the passes, and the camping grounds; learned to pack, to travel, and to love the silent mountains. And so, though I found no gold, I can truthfully say now that I have found something that gold cannot buy.

French went about his work methodically—he was, in fact, the most methodical man I have ever known. He spent some months in the '90's with the two survivors of the several expeditions that had come into the country. He even had one of them come by pack train to Crow's Nest Lake and then north in an endeavor to have this man identify some of the landmarks of the district traveled by the first expedition headed by Lemon. He kept La Nouse and his band of half-breeds through the winter of '83, so as to check in the spring and to discover where Lemon and Blackjack parted company with him—La Nouse having gone to Fort Kipp and the two prospectors to Tobacco Plains.

French fed William Bendow, the Stoney Indian, and

his retinue one winter at Lee's ranch on Pincher Creek and, in the spring, put twenty-five horses and twenty-five cattle in a pasture which would become Stoney William's, when he showed them the location of the killing. On the second day of the expedition William said he could go no farther—the terror of that oath came over him—and the expedition was abandoned.

Only a few years before French's death he made a bargain with the same William to show him the place he had looked for so long. William and his band were on their way to Morley and agreed to camp at the old George Sage place—an abandoned ranch on the middle fork of High River—until French could get George Emerson and myself to join them. That night William died suddenly. His people secured a Red River Cart and proceeded with his body to Morleyville. The night of their arrival, William's son-in-law also died without warning. Is it any wonder that the Indians believe there is a hoodoo on everyone who tries to locate that place? In fact, old Indians refuse to talk about it and literally freeze up when the name is mentioned.

French was terribly burned in a fire that destroyed the Emerson house on the night of his return from his last prospecting trip. On the evening of his return, he wrote me a letter and posted it at the Bar U Ranch. In it he said that he had at last located *IT* and was coming to High River the following day to tell me everything. On his arrival he was unable to talk to me before he died; so if he had really solved the problem which had occupied so many years of his life, the secret died with him.

Many attempts have been made since that time, the

most notable in 1929. Many there are who say 'nothing will be found on this side of the mountains,' but geologists designate a tract of country between Crow's Nest Lake and Mist Mountain on the head waters of the Highwood River as the disturbed area in which precious metals might be found. In my opinion, if the Lemon Mine is ever found, it will be in this territory which is really a trough of the Cretaceous Sea bounded on the west by the Paleozoic limestone of the main range of the Rockies and on the east by the Livingstone range, also of limestone. This trough is now a north and south valley, transversely cut by three watersheds of the Sheep Creek, Highwood, and Old Man rivers. The area is rich in coal, some low grade phosphate rock, and low grade deposits of iron. There are interrelated beds of conglomerate ash. a hard green rock occurring chiefly in the south and known as the Crow's Nest Volcanics. It is called the disturbed area because the beds of sandstone and shale, cradled between the ranges, are often found pitched on edge. The most remarkable feature, both within and without the mountains, is that both main streams occupying wide valleys flow on transverse strike lines rather than north and south. Yet nowhere on these streams have colors of gold ever been found, though it is safe to say every one has been prospected by someone at some time or other since the finding of the Lemon Mine.

If one were to give credence to stories that drifted down from the early days, the search for this Eldorado has claimed more than Blackjack's life. There is the story of a white man's skeleton found in the gap of the Old Man River and with it a bag of gold. There is the story of two men badly wounded stopping over night in the '90's at a ranch in the foothills. They carried gold dust and were fleeing from the West. They rode away next morning for Fort Macleod, but never arrived. Had they rediscovered the lost Lemon Mine and then been followed and killed by the Indians?

From time to time old mounds are found; the remains of cabins, old rusted muzzle-loading guns, and I. G. Baker tin containers date these. But a man in the mountains does not abandon his outfit!

3.—EXIT AN EDITOR

WHEN I RETURNED TO THE OFFICE OF THE *High River Times*, Mrs. McCorquodale was still writing copy. On being reminded that I wanted to hear a story about Bob Edwards, Mrs. McCorquodale took off her glasses and said with a twinkle in her eyes, "You know, Bob Edwards is a tradition here in High River."

"Then he published the *Eye Opener* here before he went to Calgary?"

"He most certainly did. In fact, he tried publishing a paper in several Alberta towns none of which really seemed to appreciate the honor."

"Where did Edwards come from?" I asked.

"He was born in Edinburgh," replied Mrs. McCorquodale. "On his mother's side, he was related to the Chambers family—you know, the famous publishers. He often said that if his *mother had been a gentleman,* he would have inherited the Chambers publishing business.

26

As it was, he was educated in France and Belgium, and eventually drifted out to the Western States.

"He started out to be a farmer, but farm life apparently didn't agree with Bob. The farmer he worked for was pretty unreasonable about working long hours, and Bob argued with him about it. Eventually Bob persuaded his brother to purchase the farmer's place, and as soon as the deal went through, Bob took great delight in booting the farmer off.

"When he finally came to Canada he wanted to start a newspaper out here in the West, so he began to tell all his friends that he was going to start a paper in Wetaskiwin and that he would call the paper *The Wetaskiwin Bottling Works.*"

"Why in the world did he choose that title?" I asked.

"Well," said Mrs. McCorquodale, "Bob explained it by saying that his paper was going to be a corker. And it certainly was! He tried publishing in Wetaskiwin, Strathcona, Leduc, and finally in High River."

"Why did he leave High River?"

"Well," said Mrs. McCorquodale, "old-timers of High River maintain that what put the finishing touches on Bob Edwards' journalistic career in High River was not so much what he said, as what he *did*—or was blamed for doing. They gleefully refer to the final outrage as 'The Incident of the Mixed Gramophone Records'."

It seems that a traveling salesman came to town with something very enticing in the way of gramophone records, choral music designed to take the place of choirs at church services. The salesman won the consent of the church management to try out his sacred music at the Sunday service next day. Flushed with success, the salesman shared the story of his almost-certain sale with the boys round the hotel. They were all hospitality and enthusiasm.

But, as a matter of fact, the salesman had two suitcases of records on hand, one strictly sacred and the other of a most dubious nature. While he was enjoying social diversions which kept him fully engaged till church time, busy hands were at work switching records from one suitcase to the other. You can have one guess as to whose were the busiest hands of all.

However, there is no admission of guilt, no hint of shame, in the bland report of developments which appeared in the next issue of the High River *Eye Opener*. Bob Edwards describes the catastrophe of the mechanical choir as follows:

On being told that there was just one Methodist Church in town, the stranger explained his business. He was a gramophone choir promoter. Having long realized the difficulties which small town churches experience with their choirs, he had devised a scheme which solved the whole cheese. All church troubles are traceable to the choir. If the minister eloped, it was sure to be with a member of the choir, and so on. His gramophone choir would put a stop to all that nonsense.

Through the kindliness of Dr. Stanley (the main pillar of the church), this rather scrubby-looking person obtained the promise of a fair trial for his gramophone choir on Sunday. Needless to say, the man kept going full blast all Saturday night in the room adjoining the bar, and when Sunday dawned the professor was in horrible shape from lack of sleep

28

and too much of Jerry's fine old Glenhorrors. Anyhow, when Sunday evening came with the fateful hour of his church appointment, he was not himself at all.

All High River was at church to hear the new gramophone choir, and the back pews were filled with the tougher classes. Sure enough, the machine was perched on a little table, with the professor capering round fussing with the records.

"Hymn Number 471," announced the preacher. *"Hark the Herald Angels Sing!* omitting stanza three."

"See here," protested the professor, "this here automatic choir omits nothing. I can't hop and skip in the middle."

The people were evidently charmed with the music of the Edison quartet, and even the preacher looked gratified.

The next hymn announced was *Nearer My God to Thee,* and the congregation looked forward expectantly. Preliminary coughing and settling drowned out the gramophone announcement, but the machine had not taken many turns till it was realized that the heavenly choir was singing *Just Because She Made Them Goo-Goo Eyes.*

The professor hastily stopped the machine and started another record, but the minister stopped him. "The resignation of the gramophone choir is accepted," he said. "Let us pray."

Next morning the scrubby-looking professor might have been seen ambling to the depot on his way to Macleod. His records must have got mixed on Saturday night. He was a failure at church, but a brilliant success at the bar.

So that was what happened. Suspicion, not too surprisingly, centred on Bob Edwards as being a foremost promoter of the dirty work. And present survivors of that dark hour in town history are generous enough to

29

admit that the plan of switching records was Bob's. They merely plied the professor with red-eye.

At any rate, Bob's doom was sealed as an instrument of evil, and in an issue immediately following comes the stark announcement:

> The Presbyterian Church has asked us to remove the notice of services from its cozy corner abaft the locals. And they got it for nothing, too! Feeling must be strong.

And an exasperated tone can be detected in the same issue:

> These small towns are awful. Wetaskiwin threw us down. Leduc threw us down. Strathcona, being dead anyway, shook its shriveled finger at us. High River is passing us up. Ye gods! That we should have lived in such places and whooped them up free of expense.

So with this parting shot, Bob departed for the tolerant and generous atmosphere of Calgary.

❧ ❧

II

Leaves From a Notebook

*Give me your magic double sight, Johnny Chinook, to
see old Fort Macleod and Medicine Hat and Calgary. Let
me see Indians, whisky traders, Mounted Police, ranchers,
remittance men and all the others. Let me hear the
cracking whips of the bull-team drivers, the clanging iron
of the railroaders, the laughter of the tricksters and the
wits. Let me feel the spirit of the West. Tell me a tale,
Johnny Chinook.*

As THE BUS STOPPED IN MACLEOD, I TOOK OUT MY NOTE-
book and glanced over the stories I had heard about this
historic spot of the West. Mounted Police had arrived
here in 1874 . . . established a fort; purpose: to chase
down whisky traders from Montana who were plaguing
the Indians. Macleod . . . named after Colonel Macleod,
in command of the first Mounted Police detachment to
arrive. Colonel Macleod: a fine man, generous, understanding of his men. There was a good story about
Macleod. What was it? . . . I remember!

Colonel Macleod and two men, a sergeant and a

corporal, were on liquor patrol. Corporal saw something suspicious in a badger hole by the side of the trail. He dismounted to investigate. Found a keg of red-eye. Took it to Colonel Macleod and saluted. "Sir, shall I knock the bottom out of this keg and empty it?"

"Wait a minute," said the colonel, " we don't know what's in the keg. Tell you what you do; you open it and give me a cupful. I'll taste it and see."

Corporal opened the keg, took a cup out of his saddle-bag, gave the colonel a cup of what was inside. Colonel tasted it, finally decided to empty the cup. Then he said to the corporal and the sergeant, "Bless me if I know what this is. You'd better taste it, Sergeant."

So the sergeant had a cup of the stuff.

"Know what it is?" asked the colonel.

"No, Sir," said the sergeant, "it's a new one on me."

"Well, let the corporal have a taste," said the colonel.

So the corporal drank a big cup, too. "I don't know what it is either," said the corporal.

"Well, I'll have to taste it again," said the colonel, and he did. So did the sergeant. So did the corporal. Finally the colonel said, "Boys, sure as I'm born, that stuff's whisky!" and then the corporal knew that it was time to pour the rest of the keg of red-eye out on the ground—

Colonel Macleod was an understanding man? I'll say he was!

Story about the missionary and the bull team driver— Missionary was once riding with a bull team from Benton to Macleod. Team got stuck in a mud hole. Out of respect for the missionary, the driver spoke gently to the bulls. They refused to budge. Finally the driver turns

32

to the missionary and says, "You'll either have to cover your ears or else we stay here all day!" The missionary covered his ears; the driver spoke to the bulls in his ordinary language. They went on their way.

The Macleod Gazette—wasn't it the second oldest paper in Alberta? Yes—the *Edmonton Bulletin* was the first. *The Gazette* was started in 1886. Paper had the unusual distinction of being printed by Indians. A cylinder press had been brought from Fort Benton, but there was no engine; and until one could be installed, the power to turn the heavy press was supplied by Indian braves. The Indians would enter the press room, peel off most of their clothes, and stand in line by the handle of the press. When the press was ready to churn out the paper, an Indian would dash up to the handle and set it turning. After a few turns he would be exhausted; then another would take his place, and so on until the edition was printed.

The old Macleod Hotel. Once almost the most famous hostelry on the continent; rough, ready, typically western. In its palmiest days it was run by Harry Taylor, known far and wide as Old Kamoose. Kamoose managed in his lifetime to be both missionary and whisky trader. His sense of humor is a legend throughout Alberta.

Outside Kamoose's hotel was a sign which said: MACLEOD HOTEL. Underneath was the picture of a gun pointed at a man's head and the following inscription: "No Jawbone—In God we trust. All others cash."

And Kamoose had some very strict hotel rules which he laid down in the early 1880's:

> Boots and spurs must be removed at night before retiring.

33

Every known fluid (water excepted) for sale at the bar.

Special rates to gospel grinders, and the gambling profession.

Towels changed weekly. Insect powder for sale at the bar.

No kicking regarding the food. Those who do not like the provender will be put out.

All guests are requested to rise at six a.m. The sheets are needed for tablecloths.

No checks cashed for anybody. Payments must be made in cash, gold or blue chips.

The bar will be open day and night. Day drinks, 50 cents; night drinks, $1.00. No mixed drinks will be served except in case of a death in the family.

Valuables will not be locked in the hotel safe. The hotel has no such ornament.

Baths furnished free down at the river, but bathers must provide their own soap and towels.

When guests find themselves or their baggage thrown over the fence, they may consider that they have received notice to quit.

To attract attention of waiters or bellboys, shoot a hole through the door panel. Two shots for ice water, three for a deck of cards.

Hotel life in Macleod was extremely rigorous. A guest who often stopped at the hotel arrived one day and saw a rancher sitting by the stove thawing the icicles out of his whiskers. Sympathetically, the guest asked the rancher, "What room did you have last night?"

Guests fresh out from England would sometimes leave their boots outside the door of their room in the vague hope that in the morning they would find them shined. The hotel's response to this gesture never varied. The boots, as soon as they had been put outside, would be hurled back through the transom with a barrage of oaths.

*The dining room at the Macleod Hotel was in charge of an American named Jim Collins who had a taste for practical jokes. One day while the guests were waiting for dinner, Jim appeared carrying an armful of empty soup plates. He gave one to each diner, then returned to the kitchen and emerged with a huge garden syringe loaded with hot soup. He simply squirted some soup into each plate. One or two of the guests complained that they didn't want any soup. Collins then put the syringe in their brimming plates, pulled back the piston, and sucked in the unwanted soup.

Just who was Kamoose Taylor who ran this famous hotel? Well, my friend, Norman Macleod—who is a nephew of the famous Colonel Macleod—an early resident of the town, gave me the low down.

Taylor's Indian name was Kamoose, meaning thief, though how he got it I cannot imagine, as he was one of the most kindhearted men I ever knew, and would give the shirt off his back to anybody who needed it. In fact he was too kind for his own good and finally lost his hotel though he was allowed to operate it until his death.

Kamoose was born on the Isle of Wight and came to the west coast as a missionary. Later he came over the mountains to what is now Alberta. He was intelligent and well-read—probably the result of his training for clerical duties—and was always well informed on current affairs, as far as our then limited means of communication permitted.

*From *When the West Was Young*, by J. D. Higinbotham, Ryerson Press, Toronto, 1933.

After arriving in this neighborhood, he must have degenerated rapidly, at least in the opinion of legal and moral professors, for he was the first victim of the persecution (?) by the Mounted Police after their arrival in Macleod. Kamoose and his friends were caught a few miles north of Macleod with a mixed cargo of whisky and buffalo robes. The whisky and robes were confiscated and stiff fines imposed. Thereafter, whenever Kamoose saw a policeman wearing a buffalo coat, he would remark, "Look at that d—d— (unmentionable) wearing one of the buffalo robes he stole from me!"

Kamoose was about five feet, six inches tall, but with a chest like a prize fighter, and must have weighed nearly 180 pounds.

Fred Pace, another Macleod old-timer, ran an establishment similar to Kamoose's hotel, and Fred's place was right across the road. Fred and Kamoose were deadly rivals, principally over the respective merits of Fred's hop beer and Kamoose's raisin cider. Both of them could become pretty deadly when fortified with a shot of something stronger than water.

Kamoose was not what might be termed a particularly natty dresser. The only clothes I ever saw him wear at Macleod were a pair of overalls, a heavy police knit undershirt, and a pair of heavy police brogans, often without socks. In the winter if he had to go out, he would commandeer an overcoat from one of his many perennial free boarders.

Owing to his small height and large circumference, it was impossible to fit him with ready-made overalls, so the lady of the house would have to make the necessary alterations, and, as she was not known for her tailoring abilities, the results were often rather marvelous: one leg above the ankle and the other dragging under the heel, the seat— owing to Kamoose having to sit so much—was always the first to give out and would be patched with anything that was handy, no matter what the material or the color.

One day Kamoose and Fred Pace were standing before their respective doors enjoying the sunshine. Pace called to Kamoose, "Mr. Taylor! Come over and enjoy a glass of my beautiful beer!"

Harry turned around and displayed the seat of his overalls with a faded blue patch on it, and retorted, "Your beautiful beer! Look what your damned beer did to me the last time I drank it!"

Kamoose was the subject of many tales, but he also told the odd story himself. Bob Edwards wrote in the *Eye Opener*:

> There used to be a great character in the early days named Kamoose, who ran the Macleod Hotel. He was a great hand for telling stories. Here is one that he told on himself. His chicken coop was being robbed every night of one or two chickens. Kamoose got a new lock put on the coop and used every precaution against further depredations, but still he kept on missing a chicken every morning. There was a little window about a foot square in the coop, which, of course, nobody could climb through. Finally he decided to sit up all night and watch. It being winter time and very cold he only stepped outside about once every half hour. In the wee sma' hours he went out and what do you think he saw? An Indian sitting over a little fire behind the chicken house warming

a long pole. Kamoose waited to see what he would do next. When the pole was sufficiently heated the Indian gently opened the little window and shoved it in alongside a row of hens. Of course the hens left their cold perch and stepped on to the nice warm pole which Mr. Indian quietly drew out. The story stopped there. What Kamoose did to the Indian was left to the imagination of his listener.

1.—JEFF DAVIS

A story of the Macleod neighborhood I particularly like is the tale about Jeff Davis. I don't mean the Jeff Davis who was President of the Confederacy during the American Civil War, but the Jeff Davis who was a simple bull whacker for the I. G. Baker Company—the big trading firm which once supplied provisions for so much of Southern Alberta.

Jeff was born and bred a teamster. He loved the great creaking wagons, but even more, he loved the oxen he drove. That the oxen were his one concern in life is perhaps demonstrated by the fact that he apparently lavished no care on his own person—was seldom known to endure the indignity of a bath—and wore, winter and summer, one boot and one overshoe. Beneath this soiled exterior, however, beat a great heart filled with sentiment and tenderness.

The time came when the railroad was built into the south, and transportation suffered the inevitable change. The old gave way to the new. The message that Jeff had been dreading came through: "Dismantle all bull teams. Shipping will henceforth be done by rail." And the message further stated that the oxen previously used for freighting were to be taken to the Strong Ranch some ten miles from Macleod, there to be fattened and sold for slaughter.

You can imagine how Jeff felt. He sat on his wagon-seat and thought the matter out. The oxen symbolized his whole life, the plodding, the twelve-miles-a-day treks across the prairie, the camp at night, the slow, sure progress that Jeff could understand. It seemed to Jeff that his life had ended.

But Jeff had to endure a still further bitterness. The company gave him the job of driving his beloved oxen to the Strong Ranch, and acquiescing to this final blow, Jeff set the bulls plodding on their last trek.

During the trip something happened to Jeff. When he got to the ranch, he didn't stop but kept right on driving the animals until he had them some ten miles south of where they should have been. He then returned to the ranch and told the foreman that he hadn't been able to reach the ranch that day but he'd drive the oxen in the following day. The next day, instead of driving the oxen back to the ranch, Jeff drove them some ten miles farther south toward the American border.

The ranchmen were very busy just then and didn't pay a great deal of attention to what Jeff was doing. So each day Jeff would ride out early in the morning, drive the steers a bit farther south, and return to the ranch. Eventually he had his pets some fifty miles south and east of the ranch, in good pasture and with good water. When he thought the oxen were safely hidden, Jeff told the foreman that the bulls had drifted away in the night and that he was unable to find them.

The foreman now began to take a keen interest in what was going on. He was responsible to the company for the steers, and the loss if they were not discovered might be considerable. He put his men on the job and they combed the hills and valleys for days but could find absolutely no trace of the missing oxen. When the men finally returned with the news that they couldn't locate the steers, Jeff Davis was happy. His pets were safe.

The foreman was angry, but there was nothing to be done. The oxen, meanwhile, were enjoying the fat of the fine grass country along the Milk River, and I suppose, they might have lived out their lives in this happy way had it not been for the sentiment Jeff felt for them. Jeff simply couldn't leave the oxen alone. In the dark of night he would take a horse from the ranch and ride out to be sure the steers were safe. Night after night he did this, and finally the inevitable happened.

The men at the ranch noticed that often one of the saddle horses would appear very tired in the morning, as though it had been ridden hard all night. The men started keeping watch. On the first night of their watch, Jeff appeared, saddled a horse, and set off toward the south. Of course they followed him, discovered what he was doing, and the next day the missing oxen were rounded up, brought back to the ranch, and to the fate which Jeff for a time had helped them escape.

Jeff became a blacksmith in Macleod after that, and lived there for a long while, but I am sure that he believed his life really ended when the bull teams were dismantled.

2.—THE BULLS

But forgetting Jeff's sentimental regard for his oxen, there is evidence that the bulls, when fattened, made fair eating. Norman Macleod told me that he once took a load of bacon to the Blood Indian Reserve and that while there the Indian Agent told him there was an old friend of his on the reserve who would be around to dinner.

"There were only two places laid," said Mr. Macleod, "and I asked the agent where the old friend was. He replied that the friend would be around presently. As we sat down, the cook appeared with a big roast—the first four or five ribs of the fore quarter, known as the hotel roast. I finished my first helping and passed my plate up for another. The lull brought the old friend back to my mind so I asked again where he was.

" 'You've just eaten him!' replied the agent. 'This is meat from one of the I. G. Baker Company's lead oxen!' "

Mr. Macleod makes life with the bull teams sound very entrancing. All the Baker lead wagons were big, six-inch skein Murphys, with hind wheels between six and seven feet high. It was a sight worth beholding to see a well organized train traveling over the prairie, stretched out for probably a mile. Six teams to the train, twelve yoke to the team, with the three wagons swinging and creaking along behind, and the sixteen-foot bull whips popping like pistol shots.

The crew consisted of the wagon boss, six bull whackers, the night herder, and last but not least, the cook. He was the supreme chief, had a private coach all to himself, coupled behind the three lead wagons.

The grub! Man! First, coffee. The real test of coffee

41

is when it will float a four-bit piece. Then there was bacon —commonly termed 'sow belly'. Beans always accompanied the bacon. The first thing the cook did when the teams pulled in at night and he had the fire going was to place a huge tin kettle of beans on to boil. The weary bull whackers gathered round the table—no! excuse me— each on his hunkers on the ground! The bean pot was placed in the center, and each one ladled out a huge plateful of beans, each kernel in its original shape, soft, delicious—ecstasy!

But that was not the supreme peak. The last duty the cook performed was to dig out his Dutch oven—a big, flat iron pot about two feet in diameter and eight inches deep, with a heavy lid having a high rim to keep the ashes and coals from falling off—and place it before the fire to heat. Then he dug a hole about two feet deep, shoveled in four inches of coals and ashes, carefully lowered the oven full of boiled beans into the hole, then the lid, covered the whole with more ashes and coals, and left the beans to simmer all night.

Breakfast! If you've never tasted Dutch oven beans, you've never lived! Of course, the whole seance is interlarded with huge chunks of sour-dough bread. If I had not already exhausted all my superlatives, I might have told you something of this! Then more beans—no, desert! consisting of fried apple sauce. Oh, to be young again! Beans!

3.—WHOOP-UP

One of the first things I did when I arrived at Lethbridge was to go out to the site of old Fort Whoop-Up.

42

This famous whisky trading post was built in 1867 by adventurous fellows from Montana who managed to carry on an extremely good business in contraband goods.

Whoop-Up was snugly built on the flats at the forks of the St. Mary's and Belly rivers by Healy and Hamilton, two rough and ready characters who were very proud of the fact that their establishment was the only thriving trading post between Edmonton and the International Boundary.

Hamilton, indeed, gave the fort his own name, and Fort Hamilton became Whoop-Up—so the story goes—when a trader returning to Fort Benton in Montana was asked how things were going at Fort Hamilton. The trader replied, "Oh, we're whoopin' on 'em up!"

And Whoop-Up was an apt name. One trader at the fort is said to have written to a friend: "Dear Friend, Bill Geary got to putting on airs and I shot him and he is dead. My potatoes are looking fine."

The trading was conducted through a wicket in the heavy door. One tin cup of whisky bought a fine buffalo robe. A quart of the stuff bought a fine pony. This was hardly a fair exchange, especially when one understands what the *whisky* consisted of. As nearly as I can discover, it was mixed in a wash tub to the following specifications: one gallon of high wine—a mixture of alcohol and water —to three of water with tea leaves and a plug of tobacco thrown in for good measure. Down in Kansas, the traders used to throw in a rattlesnake head, but I have not heard that this was done at Whoop-Up.

Whatever the mixture contained, it ruined the Indians and was the chief reason for the arrival of the Mounted

Police in 1874. When the police finally appeared, they found the Stars and Stripes flying above the fort. The traders had all vanished with the single exception of a man with a wooden leg who greeted the police with the greatest good nature.

There isn't much to see at Whoop-Up these days. When I walked out to the place with Hod Seamans, director of the Entomological Branch at Lethbridge, we even had a little trouble finding the location. There is a filled-in well, some bits of the old chimney, and several depressions which may have been root cellars. But the glory of Whoop-Up is past. The elements are finishing the work started by the Mounted Police, and unless the Historic Sites and Monuments Board decide to erect a cairn, even the site of Whoop-Up will sink into oblivion.

4.—ALBERTA TRICKSTER

There have been many humorists in Alberta, and a good deal of their humor seems to have taken the form of trickery. It takes a real master trickster to be pleasurably remembered by his victims, and there was one really great master in Southern Alberta. His name was Dave Cochrane.

I wanted more information about the slippery Dave, so I cornered Norman Macleod—now living in Lethbridge—and demanded that he tell me some Cochrane tales. Macleod chuckled; thought the matter over.

"Well," he began, "anyone hearing the name 'Cochrane' would naturally conclude tha⁺ Dave was of Scotch descent, but I am sure he must have been Irish, for he was always ready for a fight or a frolic. In the few fights I saw him in, he was always laughing and fighting at the same time. More than that, he managed to win all these encounters.

"When I arrived at Macleod in 1880, Dave had left the Mounted Police and had squatted on the Blood Reserve. When the Indians were moved to the Reserve and the Agency established, Dave managed to laugh the Indian Department into paying him $3,500 for this land, although he had no legal claim to it.

"With this cash, he later moved to the Porcupine Hills to plague Dr. MacEachern, manager of the Walrond Ranch (which later became one of the largest and best managed ranches in the West). I presume Dave's reputation had preceded him, as the doctor accused him of stealing the Walrond calves and tried to induce Dave by every means except remuneration to get out. I am not prepared to make affidavit as to Cochrane's guilt in this case, because it is so different from his usual procedure of stealing from one to give to another.

"Anyway, he proceeded to make life miserable for the poor doctor by deviling him whenever possible—all in a pleasant and neighborly manner, of course.

"Matters reached a climax one day when the doctor and Dave met, and, as usual, the doctor commenced his abuse. Dave did not make any reply but went on quietly loading his pipe, and when this was completed, he pulled out a match, lit the pipe, and dropped the burning match. The grass was very dry, and away went the fire! It took the strenuous efforts of the doctor and Dave to extinguish the blaze. This could hardly have improved the

45

harmonious relations between the two, especially on the doctor's part.

"But, as I said, it was usually for the other fellow that Dave stole—sorta like Robin Hood, you might say—and he was always ready to give assistance.

"An instance of his readiness to help was back in—1881, I think the year was. We had quite a time keeping the I. G. Baker store at Macleod in supplies. Stock-taking started January second and was completed by the end of the month; the orders for supplies were then forwarded from Benton. The first of these supplies would commence to roll into Macleod sometime in July, after the rivers had subsided enough to permit the bull teams to cross. But often after a long winter, some of the staple lines would be sold out before spring, and we'd have to borrow supplies from other communities. This particular year our supply of sugar ran out, and a four-horse team was sent to a neighboring place to bring back some sugar. On the return trip, two of the horses gave out on the Blood Reserve not far from Stand Off. The driver, Henry Devons, walked over to Dave Cochrane who was plowing in a field near his house and told him his trouble. Without any hesitation, Cochrane unhooked two of his horses and turned them over to Devons. When Devons thanked Cochrane and promised to send them back, Dave promptly said, 'Oh, don't bother, they'll come home by themselves.'

"Another instance of Cochrane's generosity in providing for the helpless was for a long time a standing joke on Dave himself.

"He had brought in a load of hay for Kamoose Taylor and had unloaded it in the corral at the rear of the restaurant, then nad gone in for supper. Afterwards, while strolling around Dave met a friend who had broken his doubletrees and could not replace them. 'I'll fix you up in a minute,' said Dave, and he led his friend into the corral where most of the country visitors were in the habit of keeping their teams and wagons, took the doubletrees off a wagon, and gave them to his friend so that he could get home that night.

"On going to the corral in the morning to hook up, much to his surprise Cochrane found someone had moved his wagon before his raid and that he had generously stolen his own doubletrees to give to his friend!"

I thought it was about time to throw in a yarn about Dave myself, so I said, "That reminds me of the story I heard about his helping a fellow find a wheel-nut for his wagon.

"It seems that Ed Maunsell, a rancher, was once about to buy a buggy from J. B. Smith, a neighbor. Smith told Maunsell to go to Dave Cochrane and see if, among the junk he had collected, Dave couldn't dig up a wheel nut. Maunsell went, and he and Dave hunted high and low through Dave's collection, but no nut! However, good old Dave told Maunsell to wait ten minutes and he would *get* him a nut. In ten minutes exactly, Dave returned with the very thing. Maunsell paid Dave a dollar and started back to fit the nut on his rig.

"On the way, he met the mail carrier who had lost a wheel off his buckboard and was stuck in a slough. Maunsell stopped to offer assistance to the dismayed mail carrier who couldn't see how a nut could have come off his wheel, let alone not be found anywhere in the dirt near the scene of the accident! Maunsell had a good idea that Dave Cochrane was responsible, so he told the mail carrier to wait where he was until he could attend to a little business.

"Maunsell then returned to Cochrane's and, not wishing to hurt Dave's feelings, said that the nut he had purchased didn't seem to fit his buggy wheel. Then Maunsell went back and told the mail carrier to go up to Dave's place and see if Dave couldn't find a nut that would fit the buckboard. The mail carrier went, and sure enough, Dave had one! He sold the mail carrier his own nut for a dollar!"

"Yes," said Norman Macleod, "that's Dave Cochrane, all right; and there's another yarn about Dave that showed his cleverness, though perhaps not the same spirit of generosity."

"Kamoose Taylor had brought in a billiard table for his restaurant. After unpacking it, Taylor carefully piled the cases in which the table had come in the corral, intending to use them in building some much needed shelves for his kitchen, since finished lumber was practically unprocurable.

"George Rowe, who shortly before had left his packing job for the C.P.R. at Rogers Pass, had come to Macleod to go into partnership with Taylor. One evening while he was out looking for their milk cow, Rowe met Dave Cochrane driving home with the much valued packing cases on his wagon. Cochrane told Rowe that Taylor had given them to him.

"Hurrying home, Rowe commenced to upbraid Taylor for doing this, as they had agreed the kitchen needed those

48

shelves. Taylor was as indignant as Rowe, and the two vied with each other in calling Cochrane all kinds of a thief. Rowe then climbed on his horse and hurried out along the trail where he at last caught up with the wily Dave, who was calmly jogging along, perfectly confident in the belief that his story of the gift had been accepted.

"After a great argument, Rowe made Cochrane turn around and return the cases to Taylor's corral. Then he watched until Dave was across the slough and well on his way home.

"In due time, Rowe and Taylor returned to their well-earned slumbers, certain that they had at last out-witted Dave Cochrane. Much to their disgust, however, the next morning they found the cases gone again. Rowe started out, riding directly to Cochrane's place, but a strict search of the buildings and surrounding country showed no sign of the missing cases nor of Dave Cochrane. He must have cached them somewhere intending to pick them up when the atmosphere had cleared or had already given them to some good friend who he thought needed them more than himself. Anyway, Rowe and Taylor never had their kitchen shelves out of those cases!"

I think the most ingenious trick Cochrane played was when he saw a shiny stove and decided that it should be his. The stove had just arrived for the winter use at the Mounted Police Barracks and had temporarily been put around back out of the way. Dave coveted the stove and finally figured out a plan to, more-or-less, legally own it. Therefore, when he went into town, he would take back home with him a piece of the stove: a lid, a leg, a part of the door, or an ornament. Soon the stove had been stripped of everything, and only the bare framework remained. Dave knew he couldn't try to sneak out this framework without arousing suspicion, so he got a bucket of water and tossed it over the stove. He waited until he thought the stove had gained a covering of rust and then went to the Mounted Police officer commanding the post.

Dave calmly inquired whether he might haul a load of junk which was cluttering up the back yard of the Barracks. The Commanding Officer told him to go ahead. So along with the junk, Dave lifted the new stove, now rusty and mostly dismantled. He hauled it home, reassembled it, took off the rust, and made it shine like new again.

Not long after this, the police officer paid a visit to Dave's cabin, and saw the fine-looking stove. "Where did you get that new stove, Dave?" asked the Mountie.

"Why," said Dave, " it was amongst the junk you told me to haul away from behind the Barracks!"

"The last time *I* heard directly of Cochrane," said Mr. Macleod, "was while I was with the Hudson's Bay Company at Nelson, British Columbia. I used to make quarterly trips over the territory. One of these took me up through the Lardeau to Trout Lake, from there to Thompson's Landing, and home by the Arrow Lakes. I stayed one night at Trout Lake, and in the evening was chatting with the hotelkeeper, named Madden, who had just returned from the Yukon. After talking on various subjects, he said he had met a man from my country—Alberta—but could not remember his name.

"Madden said he was coming out over the Dyea Pass in

the middle of winter and had the bad luck to smash up his sleigh. As it was getting dark and very cold, he was worrying about what he could do. Fortunately, the mail carrier, who was on his regular trip in, came along and suggested he come with him a short way back on the trail where his regular camp was located. There they could spend the night and in the morning see what could be done with the damaged sleigh. Much relieved, Madden did this, enjoyed a good hot supper, and spent a comfortable night in the well-built shelter. In the morning after another good meal the mail carrier took him to a nearby cache where, as Madden said, he appeared to have a little of everything in the world.

"He proceeded to fit him out with a better sleigh than his own had been originally and offered him anything else he saw; nor would this generous host accept a cent in payment for the sleigh or entertainment.

" 'I wish I could think of his name,' said Madden. After considering for a moment he said, 'It was something like "Coburn", but I know that's not it.'

" 'It was not "Cochrane", by any chance?' I asked.

" 'That's the man!' said Madden, *Dave* Cochrane'."

"Yes," sighed Mr. Macleod, "Just the same old Dave Cochrane. Wherever he may be, if he is still alive—which I doubt as he was much older than I—I'll bet, while his bank balance may not be very big, he still has a substantial cache somewhere nearby where you or I or any other friend may, like Madden, have our choice of whatever we may select without payment at all. And he'll always give it with that same old cheerful smile."

5.—THE BIG ROCKS

One of the famous stories of the Macleod area is the good natured yarn about Napeo. Napeo was known as the Old Man, and was reputed to have lived on Big Chief Mountain since the time it was just a hole in the ground. This is probably true since Napeo is reputed to have built Chief Mountain up to its present height. Of course, Napeo is an Indian legendary figure, but he was real enough to have a river named after him, the Old Man River.

About ten miles west of Macleod near the road leading to Pincher Creek and the Crow's Nest Pass are three large stones. The following is one story of how these rocks came to be where they now stand. Norman Macleod says this is the true story, and his word is good enough for me.

Napeo had a young and beautiful daughter who was ardently courted by a Northern chief, probably from Edmonton or Rocky Mountain House. Apparently the young chief's qualifications did not measure up to Napeo's expectations—in other words, his horse-stealing abilities were not sufficient to ensure enough ponies to equal the value placed upon the young princess.

Napeo awakened one morning after a strenuous night of poker—or its equivalent—played with members of the local Indian Y.M.C.A. to find that in the night, the bird had flown—his beautiful daughter had vanished.

Rushing out of his tepee, Napeo turned his attention toward the Land of the Midnight Sun—that being the direction from which the suitor had come. Napeo's suspicions were confirmed when he beheld, far in the distance, the eloping pair jogging along, the young chief trying to force a little more speed out of his struggling cayuse by vigorous applications of the whip, while the dusky bride shouted scornful words at her pursuing parent who was dividing his verbal expressions equally between the fleeing pair and his erstwhile friends of the Y.M.C.A. who had trimmed him in the card game the previous night.

At last, realizing the futility of words, Napeo grabbed his bow and commenced showering arrows on the couple with no success, until, his supply of arrows exhausted, he turned to nature's own weapons, the handy rocks, still with no better results. Finally he saw his daughter and her chief disappearing into the wavering light of the Aurora Borealis.

So that is how the great rocks came to be standing near the Crow's Nest road. And, as Mr. Macleod says, "Since no one actually saw them arrive in any other manner, the story must be true." However, on world-shaking problems such as this, there can be no uniformity of opinion. There are, for instance, some carping critics who claim that the three great rocks were deposited there during the glacial period. But to all such critics, Mr. Macleod replies:

"The Old Man River still flows quietly; the three rocks are still in the same place; and Chief Mountain seems to occupy the same place and appears just the same as it did when I first saw it over sixty-three years ago!"

There are many good tales relating to the Macleod-Lethbridge area. It is difficult to select among them and difficult to stop wanting to tell them. I would like to tell the full story of Al Martin who deserves a place in folk history with Billy the Kid, Wild Bill Hickok, and Wyatt

Earp. Al was probably the best revolver shot ever known in Southern Alberta, and without doubt, the most dangerous gunman.

I would like to take time to make leisurely observations as to where Button Chief, of the Blood Indians, got an old blunderbuss which bore all the marks of having been used in the Spanish invasion of Mexico.

Certainly one of the famous tales of the South is the saga about Village Boy, the race horse brought from the East to run the Indian ponies into the dust. Poor Village Boy couldn't accustom himself to the high altitude and suffered most ignominious defeat at the hands of a shaggy little Indian cayuse. Village Boy's owner, Fred Kanouse, put him out on the range where he contracted a severe dose of mange from the Indian horses. In the spring, Fred brought Village Boy in, treated him with a heavy application of coal oil and sulphur, and started for Dick Kenneficks' Blacksmith Shop. Fred left the miserable beast on the road while he went into the shop to heat the branding iron at the forge. In a little while he came out, applied the hot iron, and immediately the whole horse was in flames. Fred pulled his gun and shot him.

This tale has ever since been known as the "burning horse of Macleod," and there have been many interpretations of it. In one version, poor Village Boy unleashed his once great speed in a last frantic and heroic dash across the prairie, spreading a roaring prairie fire. According to Norman Macleod who saw the whole thing, this tale is without foundation, but I have always felt that Village Boy, who was such a great horse in the East, deserved a more heroic and spectacular end than that accorded him by cold fact.

54

Not long ago a young pilot-in-training at the air station wrote a little verse about Macleod:

On and on the time is ticking
But to me the time has stopped;
For the dead and lonely cities
Old Macleod has got them topped.

But Macleod is not dead. On every side are the ghosts of the past, and to me, these ghosts are living and real—symbols of a tradition and a history unequalled in Southern Alberta.

III

❧

Chief Mountain Horse

I HAVE TOLD A NUMBER OF INDIAN STORIES AND LEGENDS, but from Chief Mike Mountain Horse of the Blood tribe I have received the most complete set of legends and tales. Chief Mike has written these down himself in an effort to inform everybody about the lore of his people.

I first met Chief Mike in Lawyer Hogg's office in Lethbridge. Neither of us was present under duress of the law but simply to chat and, on my part, to hear Mike tell some of his tales.

I had no part in taking down these legends which, Mike assures me, are not simply Blood Indian legends but are typical of the whole Blackfoot confederacy.

I like these tales, and the story Mike tells of Charcoal, that strange man, is especially full of high dramatic interest. I think you will like Mike's stories, too.

1.—IN THE BEGINNING . . .

The following Indian legend—our Genesis—was known to the Indians many, many years before the advent of the white man. While making no attempt to explain its similarities to the Bible story, I maintain that it is the true Indian version and has not been changed in any way since the Bible story was introduced to the Indians.

A long time ago there was a great flood. Water was everywhere, and no living thing was left except one super-man called Nahpi and a solitary muskrat. Nahpi, realizing his responsibility as the only man to survive the great disaster, said to the muskrat, "You must dive to the bottom of this water and bring up some earth."

The muskrat accordingly dived, but the distance to the bottom was so great that when he returned, it was as a floating dead body. Upon examination, Nahpi discovered that he had reached the earth, for in his claws there was soil. Nahpi took this soil in his hands and commenced rolling it; as he rolled the soil, it multiplied and fell and blew and scattered from him until the present earth's surface was formed.

Having restored the earth, Nahpi picked up some of the soil he had generated and formed animals and birds which, after giving them breath of life, he freed to habitate the land and air.

Then after long solitude Nahpi realized his need of a human mate. Picking up more soil, he took a rib from his side and from these materials constructed the form of a woman into which he breathed life. This woman became his constant companion, and together they had much enjoyment in the ruling of the world.

One day Nahpi and his woman were sitting on the river bank in deep meditation as to ways in which to improve the earth. Naphi arose, picked up a buffalo chip from the ground, and said to his companion, "I will cast this buffalo chip into the water. If it floats, I will cause the coming generations to rise again on the fourth day following their death."

But the woman restrained him saying, "Not so, for by this means the earth would soon become overpopulated. Rather let me take this stone and cast it into the water. If it sinks, people will die forever, but if it floats, life will be eternal." And so, through the woman's logic and influence (superior as it has proven even to this day) death came into the world as the Indian understands it.

After a time, owing to the heavy business of governing and arranging for the future of the world, Naphi and the woman separated, and for many moons were not together.

Naphi, in order to carry on his projects, had created many men to help him. One day when he and his band were hunting for buffalo, Nahpi became separated from the rest and went south alone as far as the Highwood River. Standing on the edge of the east bank, he observed below him in the valley a number of tepees, all of magnificent workmanship. Their chalky whiteness could be seen from afar, and the neatness and orderly fashion of the settlement greatly impressed him. He began to shout and wave to attract the attention of the owners. To his surprise he discovered that the inhabitants were the woman he had created and several women companions who had been created by her.

The woman came to meet him and explained her activities. Nahpi, deeply impressed by the resplendent encampment and the obvious advantage of having an amalgamation with the women who had made it, said, "I

58

have created many men who are without women companions. Let us align my men on the bank of the river, and from them your women can select husbands." This the woman agreed to, and the men were accordingly aligned on the bank of the river, Nahpi standing with them.

Then the chief woman retired secretly and removed her fine clothes. She unbraided and disarrayed her hair, donned dirty rags, and was the first of the women to go forth to choose a husband. Thus disguised she walked up to Nahpi and seizing his wrist announced her choice of him as a husband. Nahpi, however, seeing but an unkempt hag and having in mind his own woman as mate, would not be led away.

So the woman returned to her tepee alone. Gathering the others around her, she instructed them to go up to the bank and choose their husbands, but on no account was any of them to select Nahpi. The women did as directed: all chose husbands, and Nahpi was left standing on the bank alone.

The chief woman again arrayed herself in her finery, combed and rearranged her hair, painted her face, and came forward to Nahpi. Shaking her fist at him she said, "You have made me ashamed in the eyes of all other women by not coming with me when I chose you for a husband. Now you will remain standing on that spot, but not as Nahpi for I will prepare a charm which will turn you into a pine tree."

And this huge pine tree is still standing in solitude somewhere along the banks of the Highwood River.

So runs the tribal legend of the formation of our earth

59

and of the subsequent development of its life, a story, to my mind, similar in many respects to the Genesis of the white man.

2.—THE DIPPER

"The Seven" is an Indian name for the Dipper.

There was once a certain warrior who was very fond of hunting. Occasionally on his return home from these expeditions, he suspected that his wife had not stayed home to her domestic duties and was probably meeting someone during his absences. "I will obtain tangible proof," he thought.

The next day, after his hunting trip, he returned without disclosing himself to his wife and observed her engaged in the task of tanning a hide. After a short while, she laid it aside and, going into her tepee, came out again with a flint ax and a rawhide rope. Her husband followed her into the nearby brush. Reaching her objective, an old hollow tree stump higher than a man, she struck the stump, whereupon a serpent crawled out from the top and transformed itself into a handsome man.

The warrior waited until his wife had departed for home. He also returned only to pick up an earthern bowl and depart again. Arriving once more at the old stump, he proceeded to tap on it with his knife, whereupon the reptile emerged from the top. With one tremendous blow, the warrior cut its head off with his knife, and holding the bowl close to the headless body, let the blood drip into it until it was filled. He then returned to his lodge.

"Will you make some soup out of this buffalo blood?" he asked his wife. The woman complied, and when the soup was ready, she filled a bowl and offered it to her man. "Put it aside and let it cool," he said, "and you had better have some yourself."

After his spouse had finished her portion of the soup, he said to her, "You have drunk your sweetheart's blood."

Wailing loudly for her lover, she returned to the stump, only to see the headless body of the serpent hanging from the top, blood still dripping from it. She returned to her tepee and yelled to her husband as she approached, "You will die, too!" But he was waiting for her and chopped off her head with his ax before she could enter. He laid his wife's body on one of the skins she had been tanning and went back to the main camp. "I am now bereaved," he told the Headman. "My wife died of sickness while I was out hunting with her."

Her brothers, suspicious of her death, went out and located her dead body. They decided to remain with the body for an indefinite period. On their numerous hunting trips, they usually left their youngest brother in charge of the camp. When they returned, they frequently found that some stranger had been there and cooked their meals.

One day while the brothers were in the tepee talking, someone outside spoke to them in a wailing voice: "Don't look out. I am your dead sister. My husband is responsible for my death. The ax he used you will see lying on the ground when you come out."

On another day, the brothers again went hunting and, as usual, left the same boy to watch their camp. On this occasion the sister appeared in person to the boy. "I am

61

appearing to you, my brother," she said, "because of the great affection I have always had for you." The boy told the others of this incident and declared that he was afraid to be alone with the spirit of his sister.

"Hide yourself under the robe and when she comes again try to discover the source of her supernatural powers," they instructed him.

The boy did as he was advised, and the sister again appeared at the camp. She was observed to pull out a buffalo robe, the border of which was partially ornamented with human scalps. The boy heard her say, "My brothers' scalps will complete the center decoration."

This the boy recounted to his brothers. After further consultation, the lad was advised to hide once more and steal her bag containing the ornamental robe and other belongings. The boy did as he was told and managed to steal the following articles from her bag: a porcupine tail used by medicine men for doctoring face paint, quills for decorative purposes, and buffalo sinews used for sewing. With these possessions, the boys fled from the camp in fear of their sister's spirit.

On discovering her loss, the sister immediately started in pursuit. After traveling some distance, one of the runaways looked behind and saw her approaching. "Look, there she is!" he cried to the others. She was gaining on them rapidly.

"Throw away those porcupine quills so she will lose time in picking them up," one of the brothers suggested. The quills were thrown out and scattered to the wind. Then more distance was covered.

"There she is again!" another cried as he observed her again appearing over the horizon.

"Throw away the paint." This was done, and the sister stopped to gather her paint from the ground. It enabled the boys to gain on her.

"She's coming again," one of them panted as he observed her figure at a distance.

"Scatter her thread!" This was done, and after awhile, the porcupine tail was also discarded.

About this time the lads had reached a tree which they proceeded to climb, the oldest one at the bottom, the youngest at the top. Here their sister came upon them.

"I am going to kill every one of you," she cried. She then climbed up and knocked down one after the other, until she reached the sixth brother.

Just then a bird was flying by and screeched out to the one occupying the highest perch, "Shoot that feather in her hair or else she will kill you, too."

The lad took careful aim, and letting fly, hit the feather, splitting it in twain; whereupon the woman fell from the tree dead.

The lone survivor then descended from his perch and laid his six brothers side by side on the ground. Taking his bow and arrows, he shot upwards, calling out loudly as he did so, "Look out, my brothers! An arrow is coming down. It may hurt you. Jump up!" He repeated this performance four times. On the fifth, his brothers responded by jumping to their feet.

A consultation was then held as to their next procedure. Some advised returning to the camp, but the youngest brother said, "No. Our sister is supernatural. She may rise again and kill us. Let us ascend to the heavens and form a part of the stars."

This was agreed to. The seven brothers stood in the form of a dipper. "Now shut your eyes and don't open them until I give the word," the boy told them. They followed his instructions.

Upon the word being given, the brothers opened their eyes and found themselves in the heavens.

They are still standing there in the form of a dipper.

3.—CHARCOAL

It was haying time on the Blood Reserve in the year 1896. One morning Charcoal asked his wife to accompany him and assist him in the hay field. "I am not well this morning. I don't want to go," replied Pretty Kangaroo Woman, and was accordingly excused by her husband.

Charcoal came home unexpectedly from his work that day and found his wife entertaining in a fashion too hospitable even for an Indian hostess, a young brave who was one of her distant relatives. Charcoal admonished his wife's paramour in somewhat the following words:

"Young man, listen to me. My wife is your relative. Discontinue these meetings and don't gossip. This will be a secret among the three of us. I have no inclination to let people know that I discovered you two; they would have a very poor opinion of me, if they knew. So I will do nothing further."

The lovers, however, refused to heed this warning. The young brave again had the temerity to intrude on Charcoal's household, and was again discovered. No second warning was issued by the wronged husband. The Indian prides himself on his stoicism and ability to conceal his emotions at all times. Thus Charcoal managed to hide his feelings.

One morning, shortly after the second episode, Charcoal again requested his wife to accompany him to the fields. "Come with me and tramp the hay down in the rack as I pitch it up," he said.

"I have a severe headache," his wife replied. "I do not think I can go."

With his suspicions aroused, Charcoal went to his labors alone, and hitching his team to his mower, commenced cutting hay. About a quarter of a mile away, he observed the rival for his wife's affections engaged in the task of raking hay. He kept an eagle eye on him and his suspicions were augmented when the watched one made a sudden disappearance.

Charcoal had arrived at the extremity of his endurance. His pride was stabbed with murderous hate, and who shall say that this condition, under similar circumstances, could have existed only in an Indian's breast?

Believing that the young man was once more visiting his wife, Charcoal decided that he would definitely and finally ascertain just what was going on. To unhitch his team and make his way home was but the work of a few minutes. On his arrival at his tepee, he was informed that his wife had repaired to the river bottom to fetch wood. With still greater ire and jealousy—for he remembered the "severe headache" of the morning—Charcoal armed himself with a rifle and rode to the river bottom.

In a clearing by the bushes, he spied his wife's horse grazing about unattended. Farther on was another horse bridled with a harness bridle, also grazing unattended. Proceeding through the surrounding brush in search of his wife, his face contorted with vicious purpose, Charcoal came to a half built log stable. Peering through the openings between the logs, he discovered his wife in sinful tryst with her lover. Without any preamble, Charcoal fired through the chinks of the log structure and hit the young man. Severely wounded in the head, one of his eyeballs hanging from its socket, the Indian sprang with the swiftness of a rattler to attack Charcoal. Fighting like maniacs, alternately beating each other down, falling under and rising again to deliver savage blows, the fight continued. The younger man had the advantage of youth and strength, but this was more than offset by his terrible wounds. Charcoal, spurred on by mad fury, finally managed to beat his adversary into complete insensibility and left him for dead.

Next morning two women, meeting at the scene of the late conflict, heard moans coming from the log structure, and their investigation disclosed a man lying on the ground inside. "Tell my brother to come for me," he said. "I am wounded. Charcoal is the man who shot me."

But the message as given was never delivered, for Charcoal, either hearing or surmising that his work was incomplete, returned and finally dispatched his enemy.

Police patrols and Indians visiting the scene of the conflict later found signs of a bloody struggle. Their visit took place after the discovery of the corpse by an Indian catching horses close to the log stable and his report of the gruesome find. It was decided by the police that this was a clear case of first degree murder, and immediate steps were taken to apprehend the killer.

66

Strangely enough, Charcoal did not fall under suspicion during the early part of the investigations. Another Indian, Eagle Shoe, who, it was discovered, had had a quarrel with the slain man, was the first to be suspected. Charcoal, however, anticipating discovery sooner or later and apparently giving way to desperation, was the first to strike.

Making a nocturnal visit to the home of Mr. McNeil, a former member on the Reserve, Charcoal shot through a window and wounded McNeil in the side. Only the deflection of the bullet by a flower pot, and the ministrations of Mr. Robert Wilson, whose rudimentary knowledge of surgery enabled him to cleanse and dress the the wound, saved McNeil's life.

This was only one of the many escapades performed by Charcoal from his hiding places in the days following his flight from justice. Instead of appearing before the police and attempting to vindicate his actions, or going to the Indian Agent and letting him hear his story, Charcoal had sought refuge in flight. Six persons accompanied him: his two wives, Pretty Kangaroo Woman and Sleeping Woman, the mother of one of his wives, his grown daughter, and two boys.

Pitching their tent in close proximity to Chief Mountain, Charcoal made many nightly excursions to the surrounding country in quest of food and other commodities. Once he visited the Mounted Police detachment at Cardston and appropriated some of the officers' equipment—I believe it belonged to Inspector Davidson. On this occasion he was surprised during his raid and took cover behind a watering trough which Sergeant Armour (since retired on pension) approached, a lantern in his hand, to water his horse. Charcoal fired at the officer, grazing him, and the sergeant promptly retreated to a less valorous but much safer position.

One morning in a frenzy of despair Charcoal walked to the top of a hill near his tepee, and gazing out over the Belly Buttes, the scene of his boyhood days, he sang his battle song. Then thinking of his friends, old associates, old customs, and his life before he became a fugitive, he wept aloud. What terrible suffering, what torture his soul must have undergone, as he looked down at the territory where he had always known liberty, respect, and never fear. These tribulations will never be appreciated by anyone who has not thoroughly known the red man's love of wandering and free existence, and his comparatively happy life on the Blood Reserve.

On his return to his tent his daughter, seeing the tears on his face, wept also. "My father," she sobbed, "I wish that I might kill her," indicating her stepmother, the faithless wife of Charcoal. "She is the cause of all our misfortune. You have been a good husband to her, but she has never appreciated your kindness. Let me kill her."

Charcoal would not listen to such talk. "My child," he said, "you must not talk so. I know what is going to happen to me. But you are still young. You must go on with your life."

Now snow had begun to fly which made tracking a great deal easier, and police patrols and Indians trailing the refugees discovered the exact spot of Charcoal's camp, having noted the smoke from his fire. A depot was established by the pursuers. Men were left to care for the horses, and the main company went a tedious journey on

68

foot through the timber, reaching the fugitive's camp at break of day. Chief Scout Green Grass warned both police and Indians not to shoot until the tepee was surrounded, when a general attack was to be made at a given signal. No sooner had these instructions been given than Charcoal came forth from his tepee, his rifle in one hand, the other shading his eyes as he carefully scanned the wooded area that lay before him. Always on the alert and scenting human presence, he stepped back into his lodge. The attackers concentrated a barrage of shots on the top of the dwelling and then, from the front, rushed their objective. They found that Charcoal, his two wives, and one of the boys, had escaped. The mother-in-law, the girl, and the other boy were caught and taken into custody.

Reports as to Charcoal's flight from this time on vary, but his depleted family party made their way back to the Blood Reserve where they stole two horses—presumably police mounts—which were subsequently found by the Peigan Indians at the river bottom where the town of Brocket now stands.

Meanwhile, Charcoal continued to the timber right of the Peigan Indians at the Porcupine Hills, and from this place of refuge made many stealthy trips to their Reserve for food. When he left his camp, he tied each of his wives to widely separated trees, being suspicious—and rightly so—that they were only too ready to effect their escape.

One night when raiding the Peigan encampment for the purpose of procuring a fresh mount, he was surprised during his selection of a horse by a resident brave, Coming Door, who asked, "What are you doing? Are you Charcoal?" ⁄ For reply, Charcoal fired at his discoverer but without registering a hit. The fire was returned, but Charcoal also escaped unscathed, and by the time Coming Door and his friends had organized a pursuit party, darkness concealed the trail.

On a later nocturnal visit to the Peigan Reserve, his destination was the Old Agency, and Charcoal's small son accompanied him. Leaving the boy at the river bank with instructions to wait for him, Charcoal rode across the river. On the way he met two boys coming from the Old Agency, but having drawn up the hood which was attached to his blanket cloth, they did not recognize him. In his own words, when he related the experiences of that night to other Indian prisoners in the Macleod guard room at a later date, he said, "I went up to a hand game that was being played in a tepee and stood among a crowd of boys. No one recognized me. I looked into the tepee and saw a Kootenay Indian sitting there. I got ready to shoot him but remembered I had left the boy on the opposite bank of the river. This prevented me from firing."

When Charcoal returned to the place where he had left the boy, he found that he had escaped or had been captured. What had actually occurred was that the boy had gone to the home of Woodman, a Peigan Indian, who took him to the Mounted Police detachment located about a mile away. Police, interrogating the boy that night, were informed of the whereabouts of Charcoal's haunts in the Porcupine Hills.

Next morning, in company with Mounted Police and Indians, the boy directed the officers to his father's place of hiding. In the interim, the refugee had not been idle.

70

Anticipating that the boy might bring the police to his camp, he moved his location northward about a mile, and, watching his previous site, saw the horses approaching it. "There is my son guiding the police to where we camped," he called to his wives. Thus, once more, he was able to evade his pursuers.

As previously mentioned, whenever Charcoal left his hiding place in quest of food, he invariably tied his women to trees, far apart. He omitted part of this procedure insofar as he tied only their hands behind their backs, their legs together, and then left them some distance apart on the ground. Before taking his leave, he informed Pretty Kangaroo Woman that he had decided to kill her when he returned.

Sleeping Woman observed Charcoal's departure and when he had gone some distance, she cried to her sister in distress, "How has he tied you?" On being told, she suggested that they roll toward each other. This they did with great difficulty, after which they contrived to loosen their bonds. Sleeping Woman first released Pretty Kangaroo Woman's hands by using her teeth on the cords, and Pretty Kangaroo Woman then released her. The women had barely gained the protection of the encircling wood when Charcoal returned and discovered their escape. Going to the edge of the brush, he called to them, and while one expressed a desire to return, the other exhorted her not to do so. The two then made their way to the Blood Reserve and after days of hardship arrived there with terribly lacerated feet. They were made captives by Rides-at-Door, a Blood Indian, who handed them over to his chief and the Indian Agent who, in turn, committed them to the care of the Mounties.

71

And now the case narrowed down to the pursuit of a lone fugitive. One night, with more snow on the ground, Charcoal rode forth on a food hunting expedition, choosing as a likely destination some Indian camps and houses on the north side of the river, just east of the Peigan Agency. Knocking on the door of Jack Spear's house, he cried, "Whose house is this?" There were numerous Indians in the house gambling, but no one answered his call, for all were aware of his reputation of shooting on sight. Instead, they busied themselves trying to get under cover. Some leaped behind the big cast iron stove, others utilized an all-too-small table, and one generously proportioned lady — tipping the scale at approximately 300 pounds—attempted vainly to do a disappearing act into the sideboard. Finally, one fellow, more intrepid than the others, ventured to answer Charcoal's question.

"Where does my friend Running Crow live?" came the second query.

"At the next house," came the reply, and the hiding places disgorged their relieved occupants as Charcoal rode off in the direction indicated.

On arriving at Running Crow's house, Charcoal, still sitting on his horse, called out requesting that food and necessary commodities be given him. But Running Crow decided to prepare a trap for him. Stationing himself behind the stove, armed with a rifle, and placing his two wives, armed with axes, on either side of the door, he invited Charcoal to dismount and enter.

Again the fugitive's sense of impending danger warned him, and, taking a short cut, he jumped his mount over an old root cellar and fled. Immediately after, two

Mounted Police arrived at the camp from the opposite direction and were informed that Charcoal had just left. Pursuit was delayed, however, until the following morning when eight Indians took up the easily followed trail in the snow. At the same time Big Face Chief, a Peigan Indian, was dispatched to Pincher Creek to inform police there of the discovery and direction of the flight of the wanted man.

Charcoal struck south, breaking into a farm house where he stole food. His trailers came upon him in the act of making a fire in the vicinity of Chipman's Creek. On sighting the posse, Charcoal remounted and galloped off, his desperation now seemed to change to a hysterical joy of combat, for as he rode, he sang his battle song. The Peigans followed in hot pursuit.

Many Chiefs (now one of the Counselors of the Peigan Indians) shouted to him, "Come back, my friend! No harm is coming to you." Charcoal pulled up and looked back. But his momentary confidence was dispelled when Coming-Door, another trailer, screamed at him, "Charcoal, you are now going to find out that it does not pay to be foolish!" On hearing these words, the fugitive galloped off again.

Jack Spear, riding a gray horse, fastest and hardest of the mounts of all the Peigans, closed in on the fleeing criminal. Charcoal merely turned and looked at him, and the look alone sufficed to make Spear draw up and retreat to a greater distance. Twice the gray drew near Charcoal, and twice Spear hauled into a retreat on Charcoal's turning in his seat to glare at the pursuer, though the glare turned to derisive mirth as the retreats were made.

73

Tail Feathers, noted scout of the North West Mounted Police, requested Spear to trade mounts with him. John Holloway, interpreter for the police, made the same request, but both were ignored by Spear, even though he well knew that their horses were exhausted and could not gain on the pursued. And to this day that gray horse of Jack Spear's is spoken of as Runaway Gray by the Peigan Indians. Some of the pursuers, whose horses were played out by the long race, held onto the tails of the mounts of the other scouts in order to keep in the running.

At this stage of the pursuit, Charcoal turned and addressed the Indians, begging them to keep away as he was not on the offensive against his own people. But Sergeant Wild had just arrived from Pincher Creek with a fresh mount, and riding hard, rapidly overhauled Charcoal. However, the daring officer made a bad mistake. I do not mean to criticize too harshly the action of this intrepid young officer, but I do believe better judgment could have been employed, for he took the suicidal course of riding on the *left* side of the elusive one. As he came alongside, the sergeant shouted at Charcoal, asking his name and attempting to seize hold of the fleeing Indian.

Twice Charcoal motioned him away, then, when he saw that the officer could not be dissuaded, he shot him from his saddle and rode a short distance on. He came back and circled around the fallen figure, singing his war song; shot the body again, took the horse and ammunition of the vanquished, and continued his flight. Then, in his frenzy, he motioned the Indians to follow him; for his terrible deed had held them in their tracks.

But the horses of the scouts were entirely played out by

74

now, and to follow Charcoal, mounted on a fresh horse, was out of the question. Scout Tail Feathers, his anger aroused at seeing his superior shot down, mounted the horse Charcoal left and kept on his trail. The others took the body of Sergeant Wild and conveyed it to the farmhouse of John Dipadore, a Frenchman who lived nearby, whence it was transported to Pincher Creek.

Many and varied are the reports that have been chronicled as to the final capture of Charcoal, but I believe the following is the first disclosure of the actual facts of the event.

In his last wanderings, Charcoal, as always seemed inevitable, rode back to the Blood Reserve to the home of his brother, Left Hand, who had previously promised the police that he would aid in the capture of his brother. Knocking at the door, the fugitive asked that it be opened and that he be given food. Left Hand, recognizing his brother's voice, quietly directed his wives to assist in the capture, then, raising his voice, he invited Charcoal to come in. After feeding him and giving him a smoke (doubtless to disarm suspicion), Left Hand signaled one of his wives, a woman weighing nearly 300 pounds, who bore Charcoal to the floor. With Left Hand's help, the captive was held down till the other wife had summoned other Indians who came and tied him fast. He was then placed on a bed, and word of his capture was carried to the police. In the interval Charcoal attempted suicide by pricking an artery with an awl, but his act was detected in time to prevent his bleeding to death. The police came and took the prisoner away to Macleod where he was subsequently convicted of the murder of Sergeant

Wild and executed on the scaffold there on February 10, 1897.

For his part in effecting the capture of Charcoal, Left Hand was officially awarded a Chieftainship by the Department of Indian Affairs, but the Indians themselves never recognized his authority. In fact, they all adopted a particularly belligerent attitude toward him, believing his act to be unbrotherly to the extreme.

After the execution of Charcoal a large number of the red men congregated at the Catholic Mission to pay their last respects. Following the ceremony, Gambler, a childhood friend of the deceased, approached Left Hand, and after hurling at him all the vile names he could think of, proceeded to thrash him thoroughly with his whip. Others were about to repeat the punishment but were stopped by timely intervention.

Thus ends the story of Charcoal, a wronged man bent on protecting his honor, and through ignorance of the law, becoming more and more involved in deeds of desperation.

This story of Charcoal first published in *Royal Canadian Mounted Police Quarterly*, July, 1941.

IV

❦

The Cottonwood Black

IT WOULD BE A PITY TO WRITE ABOUT SOUTHERN ALBERTA
without telling the tale of a famous horse—a black horse,
a coal black horse named Midnight.

*In 1915 Jim McNab left his ranch on the Cottonwood
(not far from Macleod) and went to war. While he was
away, a number of colts were foaled on the ranch, among
them the coal black offspring of a thoroughbred mother
and a Morgan-Percheron sire. From the mother the colt
inherited speed and courage, from the father strength and
size. As the youngster grew, he developed such spirit and
love of independence that the boys on the ranch often
commented that he would develop into a great range horse
—*if* anybody could break him. They called him Midnight.

When Jim returned to the Cottonwood, Midnight stood
fifteen and a half hands high, a magnificent young horse,
completely wild, ready to be broken; and there was much
speculation among the ranch hands as to whether the boss
would attempt this job.

*Adapted from articles in the *Lethbridge Herald* and *Canadian Cattlemen.*

McNab, however, was eager to get back into the routine interrupted by the war, and one of the first things he did on his return was to set about breaking the young horses raised during his absence. He knew that Midnight would probably offer the biggest task of all the young stock, and McNab decided that he would break the other horses first. The boys thought maybe Jim had forgotten how to ride, but he showed them that he still knew the tricks and had very little trouble breaking a number of the young, green horses. Finally it was Midnight's turn.

Midnight was driven into a small pasture with a number of the tame horses, and when the horse had finally been cut out and into the corral, Jim knew that he was facing the struggle of his life. Midnight was roped, saddled, and at last it was time for Jim to mount. The boys had long been looking forward to the contest, and they knew, as did Jim, that if Midnight could buck as well as he looked, the chances were slim that the boss could stick him.

Jim mounted, and when the blind was jerked, Midnight paused a moment, perplexed by the human weight on his back, then he headed for the open corral gate and the friends grazing outside in the pasture.

The boys said afterwards that they had never seen such a bucking. Jim lasted exactly five jumps, was thrown off, and hit hard.

The boys were watching the boss, wondering how he would take it, but Jim said, "Get him back in here."

Once again, the black was driven into the corral, roped, and once again Jim climbed aboard. This time he lasted a couple of jumps longer before he was thrown with such terrific force that the boys ran to see how badly he was hurt. But Jim wasn't hurt. He got to his feet, gazed after Midnight who had once again rejoined his friends in the pasture, and said, "Boys, that black will be the greatest horse in all Canada. Just drive him back in here."

This time, before mounting Midnight again, Jim sat with the other men and discussed the young horse's technique. Midnight resorted only to straight bucking. He didn't sun-fish or fence-row as so many bucking horses do in order to get rid of their riders.

Jim was thrown a third time, and now the boys expected the boss to resort to unfair tactics in order to break the spirit of the black, but Jim refused to do this. If the horse played fair, Jim would also play fair. On his third attempt, Jim lasted a few more jumps, and he believed that eventually he could ride that black devil.

At the end of the day both Jim and Midnight were worn out, but Jim had ridden Midnight without breaking the spirit of the big black horse.

Midnight learned fast after that. He became one of the best cutting horses in Jim's outfit. But only Jim could ride him. If any other cowboy tried it, he was promptly bucked off and with such force that he didn't care to attempt the job again.

Between Jim McNab and Midnight grew a strong friendship, but even Jim had to be careful. If the black fancied himself mistreated or his natural love of freedom threatened in any way, he would buck, and when he bucked even McNab was not able to ride him.

The horse had never been extended nor his bottom tested, so when Jim had to make a trip to a ranch some

79

ninety miles away, he rode Midnight. When the time came for them to leave, Midnight started out proudly, head high, and never stopped once for the whole ninety miles. Nor did Jim have to use spurs.

Jim McNab was very proud of Midnight. He was certain that no man except himself could ride the black. Many persons urged him to enter the horse in various stampedes, and finally Jim entered Midnight in the stampede at Macleod held to celebrate the fiftieth anniversary of the coming of the old Royal Canadian Northwest Mounted Police.

Jim led Midnight into the arena, and there are many who remember what a magnificent horse the big black was that day. He towered above the ordinary stampede horse and really "stole the show" though he gave the two riders who had drawn him very little satisfaction. He piled them both in short order.

As time went on, Jim entered Midnight in other stampedes at local points, and always he bucked off any rider who was brave enough to climb on him. Jim feared that punchers gouging Midnight with spurs would make him an outlaw, and that is what happened. But Jim could not resist seeing the big horse spill the arrogant riders of the Red Deer and Medicine Hat outfits who claimed they could ride Midnight.

Under repeated urging, and taunted by the boasts of would-be conquerors of Midnight, Jim entered his horse in the big Calgary stampede of 1924. Interest ran high, and many excellent riders, drawn by the large purse and the fame that would come to them were they able to ride Midnight, entered the contest. The contest was to last three days, and McNab deeply regretted having consented to enter his beloved Midnight, well knowing the punishment the horse would receive. But Jim had given his word and took the horse. Midnight was plainly displeased with the whole proceedings. He showed the strain particularly when he was tightly cinched, placed in the narrow chute, and surrounded by strangers.

McNab stood by and watched the struggling throng as horses were liberated from the chute with riders up. He had been pleased when he had learned that one of the most boastful riders from the Red Deer outfit had drawn Midnight, but Jim was also regretting his decision to enter the horse. For Midnight was excited. He had been taken from the quiet Cottonwood, away from his friends, and placed here among strange men who prodded him through the bars of the chute.

Finally Midnight's turn came. It was plain that the horse was insulted and mad clean through. The Red Deer rider took his seat, touched Midnight with the spurs. The signal sounded, the gate flew open and Midnight leaped. On the third jump he spilled the boaster—almost busted him, for the man lay still and had to be helped out.

The other great riders were not so confident when they actually beheld Midnight in action. The horse was heroic. In the entire three days not a single rider was able to stay on his back. Midnight was acclaimed the champion bucking horse of Western Canada.

But Midnight played fair. Not once did he try to kick or jump on a fallen rider. He appeared satisfied when they were bounced off his back, and sometimes he even turned and placed his nose on the fallen man before he trotted back to the chute.

During the Calgary stampede, McNab had many offers to sell Midnight, but Jim loved the fearless black and refused them all. He took Midnight back to the Cottonwood and let him rest from the exciting struggle. But the relationship between them was changed. Midnight would still come to McNab's whistle or call and in other ways still showed affection for the boss; but he never forgot nor forgave the cruel treatment he had received at Calgary. When McNab tried to ride him, he was quickly bucked off.

McNab had feared this would be the case. He didn't blame Midnight but was deeply grieved that he had consented to the maltreatment of his great friend.

Possibly it was his grief that led Jim to sell Midnight; for the horse was now an outlaw and fit only for the arena. He was sold to Peter Welch, of Calgary, who toured Canada and the United States with his string of rodeo horses.

And now began Midnight's great career as a rodeo horse. His fame spread. He became one of the most renowned horses in America.

One of the best riders in the United States came to grief at the hands of the Canadian champion. Bobby Askins of Ismay, Montana, came halfway across the continent to ride Midnight at Toronto in 1926. For four successive days Askins watched Midnight buck his men off in the preliminary contests. On the night before the final day Askins expressed the hope that he would draw the big black in the finals. Askins drew Midnight, and 20,000 fans crammed the huge stadium at the Toronto Exhibition grounds to see the ride.

It was a good ride but a short one. When the chute gates opened up, Askins spurred Midnight right behind the ears. The black horse was so astonished that he stood stock still. The packed grandstand roared with laughter as the big horse walked out of the chute with short, mincing steps.

Pete Knight, who was perhaps the greatest rider in the world at the time, whispered to a friend, "I wouldn't want to be up there right now for all the money in the world!"

But Midnight was already in action. Down went his head, and on his first terrific leap he almost shot the Montana cowboy out of the saddle. He clawed his way back desperately, but to little avail. On the eighth jump Midnight tossed Askins high in the air, and then for another four jumps he pitched so high and so hard that one of the stirrups smashed in two as it hit its mate over the saddle.

"He's even better than they told me he was," said Askins as they helped him to the first aid tent.

Two weeks later at Montreal, Pete Knight and Midnight staged the greatest tussle in the memory of the cowboys of the period. Although Pete was still aboard at the conclusion of the ride, he stated that it was the most terrific ride he had ever experienced. This was one of the very few times Midnight was ridden in his thirteen years of rodeo competition.

Midnight was not the wild type of outlaw. By nature he was gentle. He would do anything for a few lumps of sugar. He grew to love the competition of the arena, but he never resorted to tricks to unseat his rider. He simply put his head down and bucked, higher and higher at every jump, until on the fifth or sixth jump he would give a little twist which seemed to catapult the rider out of the saddle as though shot from a gun.

He loved to travel, and when he was sold to Eliot and McCarty of Johnstown, Colorado, he got a chance to travel from Calgary to Fort Worth, from Cheyenne to Madison Square Garden, and finally to Europe.

Midnight died at Eliot and McCarty's ranch at Johnstown in 1936. He was twenty years old. His owners placed a gravestone over his resting place as a tribute to his courage and love of liberty, and on the stone, they inscribed this verse:

> Under this sod lies a great bucking hoss,
> There never lived a cowboy he could not toss.
> His name was Midnight. His coat was black as coal.
> If there is a hoss heaven, please God, rest his soul.

And Jim McNab, who was the only man Midnight really loved, is said to have stated:

> I miss you Midnight, since you went away;
> The once blue skies have turned to ashen gray—
> Seemed to dim the sunshine from the range—
> But fond memories of you will never change.

V

Such a Curious Name

THE NAME MEDICINE HAT HAS EXCITED CURIOSITY THE world over. It is perhaps the most famous place name in Alberta since so many persons have wondered about its origin. Yet, did you know that at one time Medicine Hat folk thought seriously of changing their town's name?

Rudyard Kipling heard about their plan and wrote a famous letter. He wrote:

> To my mind the name of Medicine Hat . . . echoes the old Cree and Blackfoot tradition of red mystery and romance that once filled the prairies. Also it hints, I venture to think, at the magic that underlies your city in the shape of natural gas.
>
> Believe me, this very name is an asset. It has no duplicate in the world. It makes men ask questions, and as I knew more than twenty years ago, draws the feet of young men towards it. Above all it is the lawful, original, sweat and dust won name of the city, and to change it would be to risk the luck of the city, to disgust and dishearten the old-timers, not in the city alone, but the world over, and to advertise abroad the city's lack of faith in itself.

Many papers the world over reprinted Kipling's protest, and perhaps for the first time, the Medicine Hat folk really began to believe in the name of their town.

Like so many places in the West, Medicine Hat owes its name to Indian legend, and no one can be certain which legend is the correct one. The Blackfoot name of the town is Saamis, meaning head dress of the medicine man, and many Indians and old-timers declare that the town got its name following a battle between the Crees and the Blackfeet.

Blackfoot warriors are supposed to have attacked the Cree camp. After a fierce fight the Blackfeet slowly drove the Crees toward the South Saskatchewan River. The squaws and the medicine man fled, swimming their horses across the river, while the men stayed behind to cover their retreat. Near the middle of the river a gust of wind caught the medicine man's hat and carried it away. The Cree warriors, seeing this accident and believing it to be a sign of anger from their gods, lost courage and were driven from their camping grounds. The victorious Blackfeet named the spot "the place where the medicine man lost his hat."

There is another legend which, if not so apt to be true, is nevertheless much more colorful.

Many years ago, before the name of paleface was known in the land, when the buffalo covered the prairies like a huge black blanket and the Indians were lords of the land, the Crees and the Sioux, who were hereditary friends through countless ages, made one of their organized attacks upon the Blackfeet, the Peigans, and the Bloods. The Crees and the Sioux lived to the north of the South Saskatchewan River, while the Peigans and Bloods and the Blackfeet roamed the plains and the hills all the way from Calgary to the International Boundary.

Whenever the medicine men came to the conclusion that a war would be a good thing, they intimated the will of the Great Spirit, as revealed through them, to the chiefs of the tribes. From this revelation there was no appeal and war always ensued.

On one occasion the Crees and the Sioux contemplated making their customary raid into the southern country. They were ruled by an illustrious chief, the hero of a hundred fights or so, by the name of Kin-o-so-ta who, among all the great chiefs of the two tribes was held in the greatest honor for his prowess, his valor, and his general character. Among the many warriors who served under Kin-o-so-ta were a number of young chiefs, the rising men of that day, to whom in due course would fall the leadership of the people.

Among these lesser lights was one named Kaus-ke-to-o-pot, meaning the Black Sioux. Although young in years he was already a marked man. He had fought many battles. He had obeyed the traditions of his people. He was brave, ambitious, and skilled in the wisdom of the council, and was looked upon as the logical successor to the old chief in time to come. Incidentally, he possessed two wives. One, the wife of his youth to whom he had been wedded by command of his father, did not arouse his interest. Being allowed a larger latitude in matrimonial matters than is accorded to white men, he sought for another mate. He eventually found his affinity, a maiden named Wa-pa-soos, daughter of the great Kin-o-so-ta. The marriage took place with all the ceremonial rites suitable to such occasion. For a short time all was love and peace, but eventually their happiness was rudely

87

broken up. War was declared, and the warrior had to leave his tepee to lead his men against the enemy.

After many forced marches in the dead of winter the tribe arrived upon the site of the present city of Medicine Hat. The river was frozen over except at one spot which, owing to under-currents or other natural causes, never froze. Because of this peculiarity the Indians of the Cree tribe had a tradition that in this place dwelt the Great Serpent.

Kaus-ke-to-o-pot took his horse to drink at this magic spot and while the animal quenched its thirst, the Great Serpent rose up from the icy waters and spoke to the young husband, demanding of him a great sacrifice and holding out to him a great reward: "Bring hither your bride, Wa-pa-soos, and throw her to me that she may be mine. Do this, and I will show thee where lieth the medicine bag, and thou shalt become a great chief."

Swiftly Kaus-ke-to-o-pot returned to camp. Within his breast, love and ambition waged an awful battle. To Kin-o-so-ta, he told the story.

The old chief remained silent for a long time. At length he replied, "It is for Wa-pa-soos to say."

Wa-pa-soos did not hesitate an instant. "Throw me to the Great Serpent," she cried, "and so, my husband, be great."

The struggle in the heart of Kaus-ke-to-o-pot was terrible. The wife continued to plead, and for a long time he resisted her pleadings. At length, the combination of her entreaties and the promptings of his own ambitions were too great for him. Seizing his bride in his arms, he hurried to the river and hurled her into the swirling waters. They closed over her in an instant, and she was gone.

The young chief sank to the ground and for many hours he remained motionless, his head sunk in his hands. As the day waned, the waters of the rushing pool were cloven apart, and once more the head of the Great Serpent appeared and spoke to him.

"Thou hast obeyed me, Kaus-ke-to-o-pot, and now I will keep my promise. Go up the river above the camp for half a mile, and you will see a small coulee with a clump of maple and cotton trees growing therein. Under a fallen cottonwood tree by the spring you will find a medicine man's bag (or 'hat', for the same word stands for both in the Cree tongue). This bag contains all the charms which are necessary to make you a great Medicine Man and the greatest warrior of your tribe. These charms will insure the success of your present expedition against the enemy."

Kaus-ke-to-o-pot having secured the medicine bag, there followed a great powwow and a war dance. During these rejoicings the Blackfeet came upon them unaware, and the Crees and the Sioux were forced across the river. Night came. The Crees and Sioux held a conference and decided to lay an ambush for the Blackfeet. With all the ingenious characteristics of their race, they hit upon a striking and original plan. Out of stones and earth they built seven figures and stuck feathers in their heads. In the space between the figures they built a campfire. The whole deception was placed so that the Blackfeet could see it. Then they withdrew a little way and ambushed themselves in the willows which the Blackfeet would have to pass in going toward the make-believe men around the fire.

The Blackfeet came; the Crees and the Sioux attacked them, killing many. The Blackfeet were driven out of the coulee and across the river, followed by the victors. This great battle between these hereditary enemies was the last great fight that took place between them.

Of the subsequent career of Kaus-ke-to-o-pot, we know nothing. The story goes no further. The site of the Cree camp is the site of the old Royal North West Mounted Police Barracks, and the spot where the Indian medicine bag was found is marked today by a small spring overgrown by maples and cottonwoods. From that time on the entire district was known as "the place of the medicine hat (or bag)."

༺~~༻

VI

Rainmaker

KIPLING HAD GOOD REASON TO CALL MEDICINE HAT "THE town . . . with all hell for a basement," for the city stands directly upon immense fields of natural gas. It is possibly the feeling of standing directly over the volcanic forces which leads to an airy speculation among Medicine Hat folk—a speculation which lends itself beautifully to the general Alberta willingness to try anything once, maybe twice.

I can think of no better demonstration of this philosophy than that found in the peculiar tale of Hatfield the Rainmaker.

*They still remember Hatfield in Medicine Hat, especially on hot, dry days in July; for it was during a mighty dry period that they dickered for Hatfield's services. Their signing of the contract with him is viewed, even yet, as one of the greatest moments in the city's life. Just how successful the experiment turned out to be still is a matter of conjecture. But the records prove that during the period in which Hatfield was hired the Rainmaker managed to fulfill all the requirements of his contract.

*From the *Edmonton Journal*.

In the years before 1921 the southeastern corner of Alberta had been hard hit by drouth. Farmers viewed the new year with much the same welcome as a small boy has for a dose of castor oil. It meant putting in another crop for the sun to toast over its gigantic bonfire. But the early spring of 1921 brought with it the dawn of a new hope. From the U. S. had spread the fame of Charles M. Hatfield. Organizing under the name of the United Agricultural Association, the Medicine Hat farmers decided to grow a bumper crop again with the help of this famous man.

Charles Hatfield was born in Fort Scott, Kansas, in 1875, received a public school education in Minneapolis, and then moved to California with his family. Being interested in the study of the production of rain by artificial methods, he went to the Los Angeles Public Library and obtained all the books on the subject. With this information coupled with his own theories, he began his life's work.

His claim went unnoticed until 1904 when he bet several Los Angeles businessmen he could break a drouth that was ruining the district. He set up his apparatus in the foothills of the Sierra Madre Mountains, sixty miles from the city. Three days later, 1.64 inches of rain had fallen. He collected his wager. During the next seventeen years the Rainmaker successfully filled forty-two contracts.

Most famous of his rainmakings was in 1916 at San Diego, California. The council of that city agreed to pay him $10,000 if he could produce enough rain in one year to fill the Morena reservoir—a large natural basin from which the city obtained its fresh water supply. Thirty-three hours after setting up equipment the rain began. A rainfall of 9.8 inches fell during the first month, giving enough water for five years. But still the rains came. Over the top of the spillway poured a four-foot stream of water. Every stream was flooded and 110 bridges were washed out. The Otay Dam collapsed, drowning twelve persons and causing thousands of dollars in damage.

When Hatfield went to collect his money, the council refused to pay on the grounds that there had been no written contract. His financial loss was more than repaid, however, in that his reputation was made. Hundreds of offers were made for his services. No matter what district he chose, the rain followed. With such fame it was no wonder that he was idolized by the farmers of Medicine Hat.

On January 29, 1921, a representative of the United Agricultural Association signed a contract with Hatfield to come to Alberta. The agreement provided that Hatfield build a rain precipitation and attraction plant, that it be operated from May first to August first and that he endeavor to bring about the largest possible increased precipitation in that portion of Alberta within a 100 mile radius of Medicine Hat.

In exchange, it was agreed that "for all the rain falling from May first to August first in the described district, Hatfield should be given credit for one half of the precipitation, at the uniform rate of $4,000 per inch up to four inches or fraction thereof. The maximum consideration under the contract to be $8,000 for a four inch rainfall." There was to be no charge for all rainfall over four inches.

So it was that the Rainmaker arrived in Medicine Hat on April 20th. He was accompanied by his brother and assistant, Paul. The fact that a light rain was falling as they stepped off the train was considered a good omen. At a luncheon held in his honor Hatfield promised "a rainfall such as you have not seen in five, six, seven or eight years."

On April 22nd, with a cook-car and two wagon-loads of equipment and chemicals, he went out to Chappice Lake. This spot twenty-two miles northeast of the city was the site chosen for the experiment. He promised rain within three to six days after May first.

So closely guarded was the actual working procedure of the apparatus that no persons in the district ever discovered the secret. From reports the method seemed to be to erect either two or four large towers, twenty to thirty feet high, around a large body of water. They were to be built on the highest points of land in the area. On the top of each tower were galvanized iron tanks. A series of trays of specially prepared chemicals were placed in the tanks. The chemical was believed to be copper sulphate. Each tray was connected to the ground by wire, supposedly to create radio activity, although local engineers were of the opinion that there was nothing more than galvanic electricity. Hatfield claimed that the apparatus created an artificial vortex or water-spout.

True to his prophecy, the rain began on May 2nd. It was only a slight shower, but everyone was happy. On the 4th a heavy shower came. On the 5th an all night rain had brought a total of one inch. As each day passed, more rain fell, and all records for precipitation for the same

94

period were broken. Fields were so muddy that the farmers were unable to plant their crops.

Completely pleased with the results of their expenditure, the farmers laughingly appealed to Hatfield to turn off the rain. Telegrams came from all over the district. One read: "Rain enough. Stop for a few days." Another had the message: "Better take a holiday for ten days, giving us a chance to get our land seeded. Past ten days had plenty rain to do us for six weeks." The Rainmaker could have had any part of Medicine Hat for the asking —at that time.

On May 20th the Provincial Treasurer, Hon. C. R. Mitchell, on a visit to Medicine Hat, proclaimed that the "whole district is like a vast garden."

On May 25th a motion picture company from Toronto took pictures of the Rainmaker at work.

In all other parts of Alberta where rain had been lacking there was a heavy demand for his services. But that demand was to cease later.

As in other years, the dry weather came at the beginning of June. On June 6th, to relieve the minds of a few anxious farmers, Hatfield promised "lots of rain before June 13th." It was not until June 17th that the rain of 1.1 inches fell. It restored the crop to its former good shape, and a bumper yield was expected.

But within a week the joy had faded. Temperatures soared to 100°, and the crops withered. A meeting of the association on June 25th demanded action, to which Hatfield replied that "moisture conditions were very poor, but unless the signs were all wrong there would be a good rain before the end of the week."

The week arrived and passed, but it did not bring any rain. By some peculiarity every part of Alberta was getting rain except the district around the Hatfield tower. A few light showers on July 12th gave the crops a breathing spell, but that vanished under a real hot spell from the 17th to the 24th.

A good rain on July 25th achieved two purposes. It definitely gave the farmers some sort of a crop—not a bumper by any means. But it also brought the total precipitation to 4.24 inches, or just a shade over the amount for which the contract had been drawn.

August 1st found Hatfield taking down his towers at Chappice Lake. He met the executive of the United Agricultural Association and offered to reduce his guarantee by $2,500 because all sections of the district had not been benefitted equally. The committee obliged by asking him to return the following year.

The next agreement provided that the Rainmaker was to receive $4,000 per inch for each inch of rain over three and up to six, with a maximum payment of $12,000. Hatfield insisted that he be allowed to choose the site to place his towers the next time. He planned on a spot about sixty miles northwest of the city.

The train next morning carried away the Rainmaker, his brother Paul, the mysterious chemicals, and the towers. But they never returned. Whether it was because many of the farmers thought that it would be a waste of money, or whether it was because Hatfield had more lucrative offers elsewhere, no one seems to know. At any rate, since then, as before, the Medicine Hat district has to rely on the powers that be for moisture.

96

Surprisingly, the rains come about the same time each year, and the hot weather dries everything up about the same time each year. Maybe the Hatfield towers made a lasting impression on the skies.

~⚬~

VII

Foothill Capital

Johnny and I stood on the hills above the foothill capital. The fall air was sharp and clear. The mountains, eighty miles away, seemed near enough for a fifteen minute walk.

"This is it," said Johnny Chinook, "this is my town. This is Calgary!"

THE STORY GOES THAT NO ONE EXCEPT AN INDIAN NAMED Running Weasel foresaw a great city on the site where Calgary now stands. So completely was Running Weasel obsessed with the idea of Calgary's future that, as a dying request, he desired to be buried on the highest bluff around the Bow Valley so that he might see the city grow at his feet. One of Running Weasel's tribe, a brave named Starlight, buried his friend on the bluffs of what is now known as Mount Royal.

The Mounted Police, returning from a chase after whisky smugglers, could not know that the crude box they found on the bluff contained the bones of a true prophet. They took the box and buried it in a far corner of potters field. A prophet it seems, is without honor in Alberta, just as in Palestine many hundred years ago.

Running Weasel would be pleased. Calgary, darling of the C. P. R., Mecca and Medina of many a cowboy's dream of Saturday night, joy point of twenty thousand service men and women, is bursting with life. Anything can happen in Calgary and has. Calgary people are the children of change. They're used to ups and downs, violent changes in the weather, and fascinating and wondrous events. One winter there was a change in the government at Ottawa, and the weather man got fired. Just to be a contrary old cuss, he hid all the weather records with the result that all points west of Winnipeg were forgotten. That year the prairies had no summer at all. Next year they had summer all winter. And this state of affairs has been going on ever since.

But even in the coldest winter the chinook wind is likely to come stealing out of the mountain passes to melt the snow and make the old-timers think that once again they are inhabiting the *banana belt* of the North. During one particularly bad spell of weather when Calgary was very young, the drifts covered up the general store and the Methodist church, the two largest buildings in town. The mail carrier missed Calgary altogether and was halfway to Cochrane, twenty miles west, when a chinook came suddenly out of the mountains and he had to swim back.

Old-timers tell me that the early inhabitants of Calgary wore tin ears. This interesting fact was explained to me and after I heard the explanation I didn't, of course, doubt the truth of the statement. You see, it was like this.

Years and years ago newcomers in Calgary frequently went about in the wintertime without covering their ears. As a result a lot of these greenhorns had their ears frozen off. Now these poor fellows didn't dare go about the countryside without ears, so the local blacksmith, who by the way was also the dentist, was commissioned to make a flock of artificial ears. He tried leather at first, but this was unsatisfactory. The leather got soft and the wearer couldn't go near a horse without being nuzzled. Finally the blacksmith hit on the idea of tin ears, and they were a huge success, except in a hailstorm when the noise was terrific.

Calgary has always been a fascinating place. An old-timer named Theodore Storm tells how he came to Calgary in 1886. He looked over the town with a couple of friends, Fred Farrow and Charley Hammer. After they had walked a little way Fred said, "If there aren't any women here this must be hell!" Charley Hammer, who didn't care for women, said this was the place for him, and he would stay.

"They asked me what I thought about it," said Mr. Storm, "and I told them it didn't concern me much. This Fred Farrow said that if there weren't any girls to kiss, he was going right back to Eau Claire, Wisconsin. I advised him to stay and told him that kissing girls was a bad habit anyway. It was like eating soup with a fork; you never got enough!"

"But," continued Mr. Storm, "there is always a way around if you look for it, and in this case it was easy. We had the native daughters of that day. There were many of them and they lived in Elbow Park, too. They painted themselves, just as the women of today do, but they didn't wear silk stockings. They always kept themselves rolled up in a blanket. These blankets had black stripes on

100

them, some having just one, others two, three, or four. The more stripes these girls had on their blankets, the higher they were in society. So if a fellow could make friends with a girl who had four stripes on her blanket, he knew he had the cream of the land."

Calgary is a city of schemes and dreams. The man on the street is in a hurry, and it's my own personal opinion that he's hurrying because he has a hunch that if he gets somewhere soon enough, he may be able to get in on the ground floor of a bubble. For there have been plenty of bubbles blown in Calgary, and plenty of bubbles burst, too.

Even in the very early days Calgary citizens had their eyes on the rainbow. For instance, in those earliest days Calgary was infested with stray dogs. Mongrels, apparently belonging to no one, roamed the streets causing considerable annoyance. To rid the young city of these pests a reward of twenty-five cents was offered to the boys of Calgary for each stray dog brought to the city hall. The business acumen displayed by the youth of the city and the enthusiasm with which it entered into the chase soon made inroads into the city purse. Every dog that was found running loose was dragged to municipal headquarters on a piece of string, and dogs that were chained were unchained in the dead of night and captured as strays the next morning. The boom in homeless dogs became so absorbing that the city was compelled to rescind its resolution authorizing this canine bounty, if it would escape civic bankruptcy.

The whisky traders were among the most acute of early Calgary businessmen. Their business was always good.

101

Sometimes the Mounted Police would catch up with them, but the traders had a simple way out. They would merely toss their kegs of whisky into the Bow River and rescue them later as they floated downstream.

There were, of course, certain elements of town society that frowned on honest enterprise. Among these groups were the Prohibitionists.

One day Theodore Storm went down to the river to get water and saw a nice yellow keg floating there. He went out and got it, and sure enough the contents proved to be whisky. When Theodore got the keg to camp, one of the other men offered him fifty dollars for it. This fellow thought he'd take the keg into town and make a nice profit. There were, however, several in camp opposed to liquor of any kind. The boss was one of these. A conference was duly held to decide what was to be done with the whisky, and the Prohibitionists decided that it should be poured down a gopher hole. Mr. Storm earnestly felt that it would not have done any harm to let him have the fifty dollars and responsible human beings the whisky, instead of drowning innocent gophers with it.

In 1912 the real estate boom reached its height. The rainbow was very clear and near that year. A million souls were shortly expected to inhabit Calgary. A dream city was projected, and an English architect named Thomas Mawson was hired to transfer the dream into concrete plans.

Caught up in the wild enthusiasm, Mawson planned a city hall costing $5,000,000. He changed the course of the Bow River to make a proposed lake of magnificent extent. In fact he planned a whole set of municipal edifices unequalled anywhere in the world. It was a rotten shame that the bubble burst before these things came to be.

So dynamic was the enterprise of the boom that Bob Edwards felt called upon to write about it in the *Eye Opener*. His iconoclastic pen sketched a scene worthy of Aristophanes.

> The real estate boom in Calgary, *wrote Bob Edwards*, is reaching new heights. Everyone has a lot in mind—some desirable property. He wants to sell it or he wants to buy it.
>
> Scenes such as we are about to present occur with some minor variation constantly in Calgary — in homes, offices, hospitals, hotel portals, asylums, yea, even to the threshold of the churches.
>
> Actors in the drama are: the man who wants to get some teeth out, Dr. Scrunchem the dentist, Dr. McMurder and Dr. Slaughter attending physicians, the nurse.
>
> The scene, a Calgary hospital.
>
> A well-known man about town decided to have his "uppers" removed. The operation is to be under chloroform and in due course all parties concerned meet in the operating room. The victim is tastefully attired in a long nighty and jauntily swinging his legs and watching preparations.
>
> The dentist, Dr. Scrunchem, created a playful diversion by pretending to extract one of the nurse's beautiful teeth. There ensues a merry scuffle.
>
> Finally one of the doctors says: "Well, old cockalorum, stretch out on the slab and let's get it over. How's your heart?"
>
> "Oh, my heart's fine. Clap on the chloroform and get busy."
>
> "Well, in any case," says Dr. McMurder, "we'll let Dr. Slaughter look after your heart. Oh, I say Slaughter, did you ever sell those Elbow Park lots?"

"No, McMurder, I have them yet. Scrunchem here has been trying to trade me with corner lots on Seventh Ave. and Fourteenth Street West. But that's pretty far out."

"Indeed," says Scrunchem tartly, "I refused an offer of $30,000 for those lots. If those Elbow Park lots weren't so far out—"

"Say Scrunchem," says McMurder, "I'll bet you $50 my Elbow Park lots are not two blocks from the car line. I've got blue prints downstairs to prove it. Let's go down and look at them."

And off went Dr. McMurder and Dr. Scrunchem to settle their bet.

"The poor fellow," exclaims the nurse bending over the patient.

"What's that?" asked Slaughter. "Oh, the patient! Now let me tell you, sister, those Elbow Park lots are fifteen blocks from the car line. But I have some nice lots to sell not nine miles from the post office."

"But the patient—his teeth," cries the nurse.

"Oh yes, the operation. By jove I almost forgot this stuff I'm using. I wonder if I've given him an overdose of chloroform." With his ears against the patient's chest, Dr. Slaughter laughed heartily and then said:

"Well nurse, these fellows may be away quite a while. Let's see, the fellow's here to get his teeth out. How about whiling away the time taking out his appendix. We can fix it up with him later. That $250 will make a nice second payment on those lots of mine on 21st Avenue. Throw another bucket of chloroform over him and let's go at him."

Whereupon Dr. Slaughter produced a lancet from his vest pocket and plucking a hair from his head to test its edge, he gave a magical flourish and plunged it into the stomach of the unconscious man.

"Now I think of it," mused the doctor, prodding

104

thoughtfully round, "McMurder did pick up some fairly good lots at Elbow Park. Confound it, what's become of this blighter's appendix?"

At this point Scrunchem, the dentist, and Dr. McMurder appear. "Well McMurder won his bet," declares Scrunchem. "Those lots of his were close in after all."

"Oh that's all right," says McMurder. "Say Slaughter, what are you cutting up the patient for?"

"Ha, ha," laughs Slaughter. "I thought I'd just take out his appendix while we waited. I needed $250 anyway to meet my 21st Avenue payment."

"But Slaughter, my dear fellow," protests McMurder mildly, "you've cut him open on the wrong side."

"By jove, so I have," exclaims Slaughter. "You know I got to thinking about Elbow Park. Oh well, I'll just stitch him up again and we'll get on with his teeth."

"Say, Slaughter," interjected McMurder, "get on with your sewing. I want to show Scrunchem some property that might interest him. Scrunchem, why not yank out the teeth in the meantime?"

Prying into the victim's mouth Scrunchem got to work with such rapidity that he kept a tooth in the air all the time. An exciting race ensued between surgeon and dentist, the air filled with flying teeth and Slaughter stitching for dear life. Scrunchem won by a tooth.

"Now," says McMurder, reaching for his coat, "let's get out to Elbow Park."

Half an hour later the patient awakened feeling terrible. The nurse sat by his side with strained face.

"Say, nurse," he gasped, "I feel weak. A queer feeling in my stomach. Did they pull the teeth out of my stomach? Say, nurse, could I interest you in some choice Seventh Avenue property?"

105

Dashing madly at the heels of the land boom came the oil boom. In 1914, when oil was struck at Turner Valley, about thirty-five miles southwest, the wildest speculation prevailed in Calgary streets. The oil that caused this terrific furor came from a shallow sand well yielding about six barrels of crude per day, but it was oil! Everybody was going to get rich, and a lot of people set the golden wheels rolling. The *Calgary Herald* for May 18, 1914, carried the interesting item:

> On every available space in the downtown section, curb traders and agents have set up stands, and broker's offices spring up like mushrooms in hotel lobbies, barber shops, cigar stands, drug stores and out on the streets.
>
> Many tales of wonderful luck and fortune are already circulating freely and are being used by street brokers to persuade people to buy stock.
>
> At the lunch hour the scene of conflict was somewhat diverted to the eating houses where, across tables and while paying the cashier, future oil kings figured on their new seven seaters.
>
> Anybody who is not "in" is looked on almost as an outcast—one with whom conversation is almost an impossibility.

Spurred on by tales that the discovery well was a gusher, the man on the street dug down deep for his dollars, his dimes, and his pennies. Over five hundred oil companies were organized to drill for the liquid gold. Calgary's staidest citizens engaged in an orgy of speculation which reached such fantastic heights that some brokers used waste baskets as temporary containers of money eagerly offered by purchasers of oil stock—most of it entirely worthless.

Meanwhile, the C. P. R. eying its darling with an indulgent eye, was going about the pleasant task of opening the fine Palliser Hotel. A list of regulations to be observed by lobby armchair well drillers was published in the *Herald*:

1. No well shall be drilled before 6 a.m. or after 3 p.m. Operations at that time are liable to disturb the paying guests while in the midst of beautiful dreams of vast wealth and permanent gushers.

2. No more than one well shall be drilled in each leather chair, or sofa, during one time interval. It is exhausting to the furniture.

3. No well shall be drilled in a tone of voice which is audible within the three-mile zone, and causes the sky-light to flutter.

4. No well shall be drilled nearer than one foot from any door, window, or passageway, and no disputes shall be indulged in, or any lease located in such areas.

5. No dry holes will be tolerated in the lobby. All wells brought in must be in the thousand barrel class, or larger.

6. All shares offered are of the gilt-edge variety. No need to call for the prospectus of the company. Just throw your money up and get your receipt. You can later pass it on to your friends for a better consideration.

7. No well drilled in the lobby shall stop at shallow sand. Every well must run down to deep pay, and represent an outlay of not less than $100,000.

And then one morning in 1914 the United Kingdom was at war, and for the time being the oil boom was over. Summing up the big boom the old-timer, Theodore Storm, says: "It has been mentioned to me by different parties on several occasions that if they had been here in the early days they would have a million dollars by now. Getting a million is a big job. I knew several that started out to get it, but they didn't succeed very well. Some of them went to jail, some to Ponoka, and some hurried on into eternity, and the gophers are now using their valuable holdings as a playground. Well, I haven't got a million, but I have what is better. I have always been able to pay my way, and I still enjoy the best of health. I have a clear conscience and a proud mind, as I haven't got anyone's money."

A lot of Calgary people feel the same way.

VIII

A Chat in the Dark

I walked east on Eighth Avenue in Calgary with Bob Needham, daily columnist for the *Calgary Herald*. We walked slowly, enjoying the mild November night and the hundreds of service men and women who crowded the movie house doors or just walked along the street, glad for a little holiday and looking for a good time.

As we went east on Eighth, the noise quieted down, the crowds thinned out, and the buildings diminished in height. The shops were smaller. The darkness closed slowly around us.

"This is a street of ghosts," Needham said. "Back the street there—is today. Along here there's still a faint memory of yesterday."

We stopped in front of a secondhand store, one of several bunched all together, while Needham lighted his pipe.

"The cowboys and farmers like these secondhand stores. I doubt that they hang around this part of town just because it might recall the old days. But it's nice to think about it that way." He pointed to a magenta-colored shirt boldly displayed in the window. "You can't

109

tell a cowboy nowadays from anybody else, except that some of them still like these gay colors."

"The Alberta Hotel stood along here somewhere," I said.

"Yes," said Needham, "it was the real hangout of the old ranchers. A lot of the ranch boys hang out at the Queen's Hotel now, but in the old days it was always the Alberta."

An old-timer named Zack Hamilton told me a yarn about the Alberta Hotel. The story concerns Fred Stimson of the old Bar U Ranch—a really extraordinary character. Fred was a native of Montreal and affected an exaggerated English accent that was not at all in keeping with his somewhat rough and ready character nor with the western clothes he wore.

The occasion of this yarn was the usual late afternoon gathering of Southern Alberta worthies in the rotunda of the Alberta. The usual talk of the open range, outlaws, roundups, and fat steers was shuttling back and forth between hard-bitten Alberta riders and ranchers. Fred Stimson was there in all his glory, dressed in a buckskin coat, chaps, and Mexican spurs with dingers. W. H. Heald, then a well known sportsman of Calgary, was among the company, as were such Calgary characters as E. H. Hodder of the viking mustache; J. J. McHugh, one of the very earliest pioneers and ranchers of the district; John Lineham of High River; Goddard of the Bow River Horse Ranch, whose handsome wife was as good a rider as any cowboy; George K. Leeson of mail contract fame; W. R. Hull, a gigantic Englishman who found time to amass a comfortable fortune in the cattle business while cultivating an unnatural Oxford accent; Pat Burns, whose cattle were then beginning to appear upon "a thousand hills"; and a number of others. Paddy Nolan, the famous lawyer, was in a chair with his arms crossed, snoozing away the effects of his morning libations. The conversation of these worthies was salty and to the point, although it probably would have been reprobated at any gathering of the Y. M. C. A.

Surveying this assemblage from a seat in the window embrasure, were two tall young Englishmen garbed in correct British riding costume, apparently new arrivals in the country, and who looked down with great disdain upon what they obviously considered their vulgar surroundings.

In a very audible voice, one of them remarked to the other, "I have been out shooting the strange variety of grouse they have in this country which are named, most inaptly, prairie chickens. They are not at all to be compared with the Scottish grouse among which I did great execution last autumn as a guest of the Duke of Argyle. His Grace was kind enough to compliment me upon my marksmanship, although, of course, I was much too respectful ever to attempt to wipe his eye."

The other Englishman came back in a high penetrating voice somewhat as follows: "I fancy that the Argyleshire moors are good, but for birds and really sporting shooting give me the moors of the Duke of Sutherland. I have been his guest at Dunrobin Castle on several occasions."

These young men, speaking in their clear English voices, were easily heard above the hum of casual conversation that was going on about them. Fred Stimson fixed a penetrating eye on the two boasters, and then in a voice that easily dominated all other talk called out to E. H. Hodder, who was sitting some distance from him, remarking, "Oh, Hodder—"

"Yes Fred?" said Hodder.

Other talk was at once stilled because the company knew from experience that Stimson was about to say something.

He continued, "You remember, Hodder, last year when I took a consignment of five hundred fat steers to Liverpool, I did some visiting in England before I returned?"

"Yes, Fred," rejoined Hodder, "I remember it well."

"Well," went on Stimson, "as soon as the steers were disposed of, I made a little journey up to London and registered at the Cecil Hotel, intending to engage in a little diversion. However, by some means or other, the Old Lady of Windsor found out that I was in town, and she sent for me and insisted that I take up my quarters at the Castle. It was an honor, of course, but exceedingly stuffy and there was nothing much to do. They didn't even allow cards to be played in the Castle, but the Old Lady was quite friendly and her daughter, Miss Beatrice, was particularly so. A very fine person indeed, Miss Beatrice.

"There was a sort of pavilion on the grounds and on occasion I used to go there and sit around with Miss Beatrice and teach her to play euchre which she learned with great aptitude. One evening, when we were going to the pavilion, the Old Lady herself announced that she would accompany us, which she did, attended by a gigantic footman.

112

"We passed an exceedingly pleasant evening, and the Old Lady took quite a fancy to the game. However, about nine o'clock she stood up and said, 'It is my bedtime, Mr. Stimson, and I must go home. I will leave my daughter in your charge!' and she departed with her footman and umbrella because it had commenced to rain.

"Miss Beatrice and I passed an exceedingly delightful evening. The time went rapidly and after playing several games, we suddenly heard the clock in the tower of the Castle strike midnight. Miss Beatrice stood up and said, 'Oh, Mr. Stimson, it's midnight. Whatever will Ma say!'

"She quickly put on her wrap, and I escorted her to the portals of the Castle. The great building seemed wrapped in slumber. Not a light glimmered and the front door was locked. I attempted to ring the bell, but the only result was to pull about one hundred yards of wire out of the place that had been prepared for it and there wasn't an answering tinkle. I then walked up to the door and producing my six-shooter—the one, Hodder, with which I killed the 'rustler'—and with the butt of it I banged on the door which gave forth a hollow reverberation.

"For a minute there was no response, then the window over our heads was thrown open, and somebody called out, 'Who's there?'

" 'It's me, Ma,' said Miss Beatrice, with a fine disregard for grammar.

" 'Yes indeed, I know that, Miss,' responded the voice, 'but who have you got with you?'

" 'Oh, it's only old Fred Stimson from Pekisko.'

" 'All right,' said the voice, 'just wait for a minute until

113

I put my crown on and I will come down and let you in!' "

At the conclusion of the ridiculous tale, the young Englishmen snorted and took themselves from the scene.

When I had finished telling this tale, Bob Needham said gravely, "I've never been able to figure out whether it was the Alberta land that inspired the story-tellers, or whether the story-tellers have made Alberta seem like a fantastic country where anything can happen. If a story sounds logical and convincing out here, people scarcely believe it; but if it's fabulous and extraordinary, they know it has the ring of honest truth. For instance, you were asking about our Calgary weather. We really have fine weather here—pile up an awfully high number of sunny days per year—but we're not content to say that our weather is good. It has to be more than good. It has to be extraordinary. To help make the weather extra-ordinary we make up lots of tales—

There's the one about the Easterner who was visiting one of our ranches out here. At the entrance of the ranch he saw hanging from the limb of a tree a great log chain with really heavy iron links. "What's that for?" asked the Easterner.

"That's how we measure the wind," replied the rancher.

"How come?"

"Well sir," said the rancher, "it's like this. You see that chain—now when she rattles a bit, it's a breeze. When she swings, it's a wind. When she lays out flat, it's a gale!"

114

But of course the old-timers will tell you that we haven't had anything a serious-minded person would call a wind in recent years. Back about 1880 they had a wind that beat anything the old-timers ever saw. This wind blew for forty days and forty nights without stopping. No record was kept of the results, because they had no census at that time, and the missing were just carried away quietly without any publicity.

This wind started in the summer and kept on going until the fall of the year. When the wind finally stopped blowing, folks quit crawling around on all fours and ventured to walk upright. Soon as they did so, they noticed that quite a few of the old settlers were unaccountably absent. They had just been quietly blown over to Saskatchewan, and according to the foothills people that is how Saskatchewan got its start.

The wind also brought in a few strangers—hard-looking pilgrims who had blown in from the West and lodged in the coulees roundabout. Many of these strangers showed an unaccountable liking for fish, and from this it was deduced they had blown clear over the mountains from Vancouver.

And along with these tales of the high winds go the sagas of the marvelous, clear sharpness of the air of southern Alberta. People gasp with wonder when they first see Calgary, because every building looks as if it had been cut out of cardboard and set neatly on a clean stage with an unbelievably blue sky for background.

Sometimes on the bald prairie, you'll see a mirage—a group of elevators up in the sky or the reflection high in the air of a whole village. But even without the mirage distances are deceptive. You look at the mountains on a bright, clear day in the fall, and you'll figure you could go over and touch them. But they're likely a hundred miles away.

One time a stranger arrived and stood admiring the scenery to the west—the great, ragged hump of the Rockies.

People asked him to guess how far the mountains were from where he stood. He guessed twenty miles. He was astonished to learn that they were over three times that distance.

Well the stranger thought that over a while, then turned to a man who was standing nearby and said, "What a stupendous country!" The man he spoke to happened to be stone deaf so didn't hear the remark. The stranger looked at him fixedly a moment then shrugged his shoulders. "How dumb of me," he said to himself, "I should have realized. That guy is probably fifteen miles away."

We walked for a little way in silence. I was trying to think of some remark to match this flow of eloquence. Finally I said, "You Calgary people are proud—"

"Proud," Needham cut in, "you're damn right we're proud! When I was in Winnipeg some days ago, I got talking to a man about the weather, and he foolishly asked me what the weather was like when I left Calgary. I told him the simple facts without any glossing over or exaggeration. This man shook his head with doubt and said, 'You Calgary people are worse than the Californians!' Pride? Of course we're proud. Pride's a good thing. I'm told that there's more pride growing up now than there

116

ever was. In the old days a lot of people came out here just to make money and go away. They don't do that anymore. They just stay here and feast on their pride. You go into one of our neighboring towns, and they'll tell you proudly, 'This town has the highest flag-pole in southern Alberta.' Another will tell you, 'This town has the second-biggest herd of pure-bred Holsteins between Calgary and Moose Jaw.' And so on. Every town has its own record. They are all unique. The town of Bassano, for instance, which is located near the big irrigation dam, proudly calls itself: 'The best in the West, by a Dam Site'."

Several girls passed us, walking rapidly toward the brighter lights of downtown Calgary. They were giggling and looking over their shoulders at a couple of Air Force lads who were keeping just the right distance behind. Bob Needham nodded his head. "Plenty of girls here in Calgary now. Fifty-five years ago, in the foothills of Alberta, a woman was more precious than gold—an unmarried one, that is. And she didn't stay unmarried long. There were plenty of bachelors only too anxious to get themselves hitched. At one time it was stated there were only four unmarried girls between High River and the International Boundary—that's an area roughly the size of England. So you can imagine that in those days everybody waited for the train or stage to arrive to see whether there might be some unmarried girls coming to town. The old-timers down at Macleod tell me that the arrival of the stage was the big moment for every bachelor in town.

"Some of these more ardent bachelors would climb to the top of houses and watch with field glasses, to see if

117

the stage was approaching. As it grew nearer, they could look inside and study the prospects. When at last it drew up in front of the hotel, there would be a regular stag line of awkward, sun-tanned men, every one of them wondering whether his fate, his destiny, his future might not be stepping down to the wooden sidewalk.

"Mail-order marriages were common in those days. And they still are today. We often carry little ads in the Calgary papers which end with the fine, old, familiar words: *Object Matrimony*. But in the old days, when a wife was harder to come by, mail-order marriages were much more common.

*"A regular newspaper was published in Chicago just for the purpose of bringing together western bachelors and spinsters, and it had quite a few subscribers in the Alberta foothills. The name of the paper was *Heart and Hand*; and as soon as an issue reached the ranching country, it was eagerly passed around.

"In some cases *Heart and Hand* got results. First, of course, the ranchers would sit down and write a letter to the lady whose charms were advertised in *Heart and Hand*. Then she would reply. Soon there would be a complete description and inventory on both sides. Finally, with luck, the lady would leave her home wherever it was and make her way up to Alberta.

"Even officers of the North West Mounted Police were not immune to the marriage contagion. In one case the bridegroom-to-be was a Mountie officer who went to great trouble to avoid being disappointed.

---

*The source of this story may be found in *When the West Was Young*, by J. D. Higinbotham, Ryerson Press, Toronto, 1933.

"His bride was due in on the train. But he wasn't going to meet the train—no! He stationed himself on the hillside near the station with a powerful pair of binoculars. At last the train pulled in, and the bride-elect stepped down. Finding no one to meet her, she walked up and down the platform.

"Meanwhile the Mountie had his glasses trained on her and was giving the lady a very careful study. At last he decided she wouldn't do. He dispatched his orderly with a note of regret and sufficient funds to send the woman back to her home."

"Yes, there are plenty of girls here now. I suppose any man can get married if he wants to make even a little effort. Two or three years ago there were three young men farming near Castor in the prairie country. They felt the need of a woman around the place to do the cooking and to wash the dishes. But they weren't very energetic about going out to get themselves wives. They just knocked together a couple of pieces of wood and stuck up a notice by the side of the road. The notice simply said: *Wife Wanted*. I don't know whether these fellows got any answers. If they did, they didn't deserve them."

Looking back, I saw that the pretty girls had stopped and were now talking to the Air Force lads. I wondered whether this lent point to Needham's story. Possibly it did.

We walked for quite a long way. I had no idea where we were, but presently we had entered a park. Suddenly something huge loomed in the darkness ahead of us.

"There he is," said Needham. "Life size. They've found quite a few specimens not far from Calgary. Put

119

this up to help us remember our natural history. How do you like him?"

I caught my breath, for there ahead of us stood—head, tail, and all—a great dinosaur. In the starlight I thought I saw him lift his head, shift a little to get a better view of the valley.

"The kids love him," said Needham, "and I confess to a real affection for him myself. But there's been many a man with a few drops too much to drink who's been scared out of a year's growth by coming on him suddenly in the dark."

I was sure now that I saw the dinosaur move. In fact he arched his head around, looked at me, said, "Hello there," and got back into his position, staring down the valley.

Which simply goes to prove that wonderful things can and do happen in Calgary.

IX

Some Calgary High Spots

I WAS STANDING IN THE LOBBY OF THE PALLISER HOTEL IN Calgary. The lobby was packed with six hundred old-timers, their sons and daughters and their grandchildren.

The courage, bone, and blood of the ranching country was well represented. These were strong men and women. They, or their fathers or grandfathers, had dreamed, lived, and fashioned the southland upon a prideful heritage—a heritage of honesty, forthright speech, courteous manners, and pride in the sweep of the broad land.

Some of them dreamed tonight. Their eyes were silent and far away. Others talked rapidly and loudly, hoping to entice the past into the Palliser lobby.

Behind me, two old-timers were arguing about which had come first into the country. They made their argument sound important. Apparently one of them thought it was very important, for I heard him say that just as soon as he went and found a little refreshment he'd be back and settle the argument in the good old-fashioned way. The way he scooted off, I knew that he was at least serious about the refreshment.

The other old-timer muttered a slighting remark, eyed

me for a moment, then came over to where I was standing.

"I'm going to tell you something," he remarked, "and I want you to see whether you can guess the point of this story."

"Shoot," I said.

"That old coot I was talking with doesn't believe me, but I came here in 1883," said the old-timer fingering his badge. "That's a hell of a long time ago, isn't it?"

"A lot of things have happened since 1883."

"You're damned right," snapped the old-timer, "especially since he didn't come till 1890! And now I'm going to tell you something." His eyes moved from group to group around the lobby. "Charlie!" he yelled suddenly. "Come over here. You too, Tim! Bring old Harry with you!"

When Tim, Charlie and Harry had gathered around, the old-timer said, "I'm going to tell this young feller something."

"Guess I could tell him something myself," Tim said.

"You keep out of this, Tim. I'm doin' the telling."

"You need to wet your whistle,' Harry said.

"Maybe I do."

"You tell him something first," Tim said.

"All right," said the old-timer. "You boys know how it was out here in 1883, don't you?"

The boys nodded.

"It was a tough country. Injuns? God, there were a lot of Injuns! Good people, too, till the whisky traders got 'em filled up with booze."

"I recall," said Tim, "once—"

"Shut up!" ordered the old-timer. "Well, one time I

122

was out along the river bottom when I heard a hell of a banging noise. Wham! Wham! Wham! Wham! Couldn't figure it out so I decided to scout up and see what it was."

'I recall," said Tim, "once—"

"Shut up! Well sir, when I got up behind a big tree where I could see, what do you think I saw?" He looked at me. "You know?"

"No."

"Didn't think you would," said the old-timer scornfully.

"Do you other boys know what I saw?"

"Sure," said Tim.

"Then shut up till I tell you to talk."

The old-timer came very close to me and took hold of one of the lapels of my coat. "I saw two Injuns. One was lying flat on the ground. The other was beating the hell out of an old oil can with a club. Now, young feller, what do you suppose they were carrying on like that for?"

"I could make a guess," I said.

"Don't guess," said the old-timer. "You might guess right, and this is *my* story. Well, I watched for a while, when suddenly I saw somethin' like a cloud, or steam, rise up out of the Injun that was lyin' on the ground. When he saw that steam, the feller with the club beat that can about ten times harder. In a minute or so the steam that was risin' out of the Injun turned into the form of a devil with horns and scooted away into the bush as hard as it could tear. Now—" The old-timer looked at me very seriously, "now you can tell 'em what you think the Injun with the club was up to."

"Well," I said, "it sounds to me as if he was driving out a devil."

123

"You're too smart," said the old-timer as he let go of my lapel. "That's just what he was doin'. Devil simply couldn't stand the racket, so he took himself off. Last I saw of the Injuns, the feller on the ground had got up and was mounting his cayuse."

"I've seen something better than that," said Tim. "I've seen the Sun Dance in the old days when it was the real thing."

"I've seen it, too," the old-timer said.

"You never saw it done like I did."

"I certainly did," said the old-timer.

"Well," said Tim to me, "I guess *you* never saw the real old-time Sun Dance, did you?"

"No."

"It was really somethin'. You know, it was a custom the Blackfeet had to show how their young men could stand pain. They'd take a knife and nick through the muscle of a man's breast. Then they'd put a stick through the hole, tie both ends of the stick to rawhide thongs. Then they'd tie the rawhide thongs to the limb of a tree or the pole of a big tepee. The idea was that the brave'd dance until he pulled the stick right through the muscle. I've seen it."

"There was a lot more to it than that," said the old-timer. "It was a whole ceremony—not so much to show how they could stand pain as it was a kind of medicine dance—"

"Oh, I know that!" said Tim.

"I've seen 'em do it," said the old-timer. "You know, they'd get pretty worked up when that dance was goin' on. I was standin' watching it one day, when a big brave

124

came running up at me with a rifle. Thought at first it was me he was after. But he stops right in front of me and says, 'I'm brave, too.' Then he stuck that rifle right up against his chest and shot himself straight through the heart."

The old-timer who had needed refreshment came ambling up to us, looking very satisfied with himself.

"1883, eh?" he said. He stuck his thumb under his badge and shoved it out. It said: 1881.

"Where'd you steal *that*?" yelped his companion. "1881! You didn't come till '90, an' you know it!"

But before he could square off, it was time to go in to dinner.

Yes, I heard many tales that night at the old-timer's dinner. I heard about Cappy Smart, the famous Calgary fire chief and how Cappy once, long ago, met the Duke of York. The Duke was visiting Calgary and was being escorted around by the Mounted Police, but Cappy, dressed in his splendid fire chief's uniform, was also present as added protection. Cappy, however, had not been introduced to the royal visitor.

A meeting with certain Indian chiefs had been arranged, and when the Duke's party met the assembled chiefs they found some of them dressed in colorful uniforms not unlike, indeed, the uniform worn by Cappy Smart. The Reverend John McDougall was acting as interpreter for the Indians, and seeing that Cappy wanted to be introduced to the royal guest, said: "Your Royal Highness, permit me to introduce Chief Smart." The Duke turned to McDougall, and in his high English voice replied: "Dr. McDougall, of what tribe is this splendid savage?"

I was told about some of the high spots of Calgary's history: the arrival of the Mounted Police in 1875; the naming of Calgary by Colonel Macleod, and the explanation that Calgary in the Gaelic means clear running water; the rumors of a railroad in 1881 which brought adventurers of all kinds to the Bow Valley, and their settlement on what is now known as Brewery flats.

So certain were these early settlers that the advancing railway would locate its depot on the level reaches of East Calgary that they squatted on every available inch of land and sat tight, mentally subdividing their holdings into townsites. But the advancing steel crept on and on, until one day it passed the squatters by and for reasons known to itself the Canadian Pacific located its station on its present site. The first train actually arrived in Calgary on August 27, 1883.

There was the scare that young Calgary received in 1885 when it was feared that the Blackfeet would arise and slay every white settler in southern Alberta; and in 1886-87 came the terrific cold which drove cattle right into the Calgary streets.

In 1890 there was a big celebration in Calgary when they turned the first sod for the Calgary and Edmonton railway; and in 1893 Calgary became a city.

And I also heard high spots in Calgary's folktale history. The tales that stick closest to my memory, I have written down.

X

Temperance Crusader

TO FULLY APPRECIATE THIS STORY IT MUST BE UNDERSTOOD that Bob Edwards liked a drink as well or better than the average man. In fact, when the urge came upon him, Bob was apt to forget friend, foe, and his family journal, the *Eye Opener*, whose more-or-less irregular appearance punctuated Bob's lapses.

It must also be understood that Bob Edwards was the great champion of the underdog, the little man, a fact which certain downtrodden individuals and knights battling in lost causes had good reason to remember. When, for instance, Bob went one morning into a Calgary cafe to have breakfast, he noticed one of the waitresses had been weeping.

"What's the matter, Rosie?" asked Edwards. "Who stole your scone?"

The waitress told him she had bought two worthless lots from a Calgary real estate man, investing all her savings.

"It's all right, Rosie," Bob said. "You leave everything to me."

Bob went to the real estate man and told him to refund the girl's money.

"Who the devil do you think you are?"

"I'm the *Eye Opener* man."

"I don't care if you're the devil himself. Get out of my office!"

Edwards went. But the next day the *Eye Opener* told the whole tale, and in a little paragraph at the end Bob had written that in the next issue he would reveal the real estate dealer's name.

A day or so later, Bob went again to the same cafe. The girl was happily smiling. Bob knew that everything was all right.

It was 1915. Calgary had weathered the land boom and the oil boom and now had decided to settle the liquor question. For a long while there had been a growing sentiment in Calgary for some restriction of the liquor traffic. The hotelmen, who ran all the bars, were getting nervous, for at last a vote on the prohibition question was coming up.

They had good reason to be nervous. A group of smart young men had taken up the cause of prohibition and had conducted their campaign so successfully that they needed only one good stout blow to turn the tide.

The Calgary hotelmen were even more frightened when news reached them one day that Bob Edwards might turn against them. This news was unbelievable and cataclysmic. For years Bob had been one of the steadiest customers at the Calgary bars. Many of his closest friends were bartenders. None of the hotelmen had noticed a coolness on Bob's part toward his friends of the beer taps and whisky bottles, and they simply couldn't understand the rumor. They picked a delegation and sent them to find out the truth.

"Yes," said Bob, when the delegates had gathered in his office, "I don't like what you fellows have been doing. You call yourselves hotelmen, when most of you have no rooms a dog would sleep in. I don't like it. The hotel business is suffering, and so is the liquor business. It's getting so that when you go in for a drink, you're not sure whether it's genuine red-eye or snake poison."

"But Bob," protested one of the delegates, "we all know you and—"

"Sure," said Edwards, "I've been a good customer, but I've always paid for my fun. I don't owe you a thing, and I think a change is called for."

"Look, Bob," said another delegate, "if the Prohibitionists win out, it'll be horrible. You won't be able to get a drink anywhere. You'll be up the crick then!"

"I know that," replied Bob, "but it's all right. Maybe it'd be good for me to go on the wagon. Anyway, I'm tired of the bad stuff you've been putting out."

Then one of the craftier delegates spoke up. "Bob, you could use some money, couldn't you?"

"Certainly."

"Maybe you could use a lot of money."

"I certainly could."

"All right. We'll give you fifteen thousand dollars if you'll support the hotelmen in this vote. That'd keep you going for some time."

Bob thought a moment, then he stood up.

"Gentlemen," he said, "you can leave my office. I've never sold the old rag yet, and I never will." He held open the door.

"All right, Bob," said one of the delegates, "it's your choice. I only hope you won't be sorry."

"I won't be," Bob replied.

That same day Bob entertained a delegation from the prohibition interests.

"We need you, Bob," said one of the delegates. "If you turned against the liquor interests, it would swing the vote. How about it?"

"Well, gentlemen," Bob replied, "I don't know. A lot of those fellows are my friends." He thought for a moment. "They offered me fifteen thousand dollars. That's enough to get back at one grab most of the money I've spent with them. How much will you fellows offer?"

"We haven't got a dollar, Bob."

"It's a good thing. I won't be bought or sold. Friends or no friends. I'll tell you what I'll do. I've told those fellows how I feel, and I'll back my play. This is Monday. The *Eye Opener* comes out on Saturday. I'll write an article in support of prohibition for the Saturday paper."

"Thanks, Bob," said the delegates.

"Don't thank me. This is a matter of principle. If the barkeepers had shot square with the public and with me, I'd have stuck by 'em. Let's see what you can do!"

So Bob Edwards wrote in a new rôle—the champion of prohibition. The article he penned that Monday night was strong stuff. He drew the readers attention to the fact that if they voted for prohibition, it would injure the hotelkeepers. He asked that they pause and think about that, but he also asked that they consider the drunkards who squandered their money on bad whisky, the hardships of drink on women and children, and ended up by saying: "Now gentle reader, if your vote on Monday will help dash the glass from a drunkard's lips, support the bill!"

And having written this epistle, Bob Edwards went to bed sober.

The Calgary daily newspaper, *The Albertan,* was at that time printing the *Eye Opener. The Albertan* was edited by one of Western Canada's really great newspapermen, W. H. Davidson. Mr. Davidson, out of courage and friendship for Bob, had taken on the job of printing the *Eye Opener.*

On Tuesday, Bob sent the article over to *The Albertan* to be set and had no reason to think about it again until Thursday. On Thursday a couple of the bar-boys went around to see Bob and took him a few bottles of first class, grade A, bottled-in-bond. Bob was never one to refuse a drink, and this polite gesture was one he could deeply appreciate. The first drink led to a second, and so on until Bob was left sitting at his desk in no fit condition to battle anybody's cause. Anyone knowing Bob would have realized that this was the start of one of his famous bats, which might last from two, three days to a week. The hotelmen simply stood by and waited.

That afternoon, Charley Taylor brought from *The Albertan* the proof of the *Eye Opener's* front page for Bob to proofread. Bob was still sitting at his desk quite drunk, unable to focus his eyes, and not caring anyway. He took one bleary look at the copy, grabbed a pencil and marked a big X right across the whole front page. Thereafter, he said and did nothing more. A couple of his friends came and bore him sorrowfully to the hospital

131

where Bob kept a room for just such occasions as this while Charley Taylor trudged back to *The Albertan* with a canceled front page and a heart full of grief.

The prohibition people had heard by this time what was going on and had rushed to salvage as much of the wreckage as they could. They sought the advice of Mr Davidson who said, "Well boys, Bob told me to print five thousand copies of the *Eye Opener*. So far I haven't seen or heard an order countermanding that."

"But Bob canceled the front page! It hasn't even been proofread!"

"That's all right," said Mr. Davidson, "I'll proofread it, and we'll get the paper out just the same!"

The prohibition people went away feeling fine.

Possibly they wouldn't have felt so fine had they known what was going on in the Edwards office.

Bob had a girl working for him, and her job was to count the papers, check them out to the newsboys, and keep a general eye on things. When Bob was carried out, she was left to hold the fort.

On Friday morning she was visited by two of the hotel-men.

"We want to buy five thousand copies of the *Eye Opener*."

"The papers haven't come up yet," said the girl. "Anyway you couldn't buy them all like that. Mr. Edwards wouldn't like it."

"We want five thousand copies," the men said, "and don't argue about it. We'll pay the full retail price."

"I don't know," said the girl. "If you come back—"

"When will those papers be here?"

132

"They usually come up late Friday evening."

"We'll be here," said the men. "Five thousand. Don't forget."

Naturally the prohibition boys heard the news of this new threat. Once again they sought Mr. Davidson's advice.

"Well," said Davidson, "we'll break up that scheme. The paper's ready now. We'll mail all the out-of-town *Eye Openers,* then we'll lock up the rest of the issue right here in the vault."

So the *Eye Opener* containing Bob's attack on the liquor interests never reached his office. But Bob's prohibition friends, fearing an attack by the hotelmen on his premises, crouched in the *Eye Opener* office that Friday night fully expecting that some time before morning they would be engaged in actual war. However, the hotelmen, probably learning of the whereabouts of the papers, never showed up.

Bob Edwards meanwhile slept peacefully at the hospital.

On Saturday morning the *Eye Opener* was on the Calgary streets.

When the vote on prohibition was counted, the Prohibitionists had won by sixty thousand to forty thousand. One of Bob's friends went to the hospital to tell him the news. Bob was still wobbly but got up, dressed, and went down to his office. The Prohibitionists were having a big parade, and when it passed Bob's office, the whole parade stopped. People cheered and cheered. Bob smiled, a bit puzzled by the whole affair but glad to see the people happy.

The hotelmen, of course, were very angry. They had

bought nearly a whole page of the *Eye Opener* for an ad, and for this space they never paid a cent.

Bob always felt bad about that.

XI

❦

*Bob Edwards and Peter McGonigle

WHEN SIR JOHN WILLISON, EDITOR OF THE *Toronto Evening News,* opened a strange little newspaper mysteriously left on his desk, he choked a cry of excitement. For there, staring up at him from the front page, was a story which began:

> A pleasant banquet was tendered by the Calgary Board of Trade last week to Mr. Peter McGonigle of Midnapore, on the occasion of his release from the Edmonton Penitentiary, where he had spent some time trying to live down a conviction for horse stealing. Quite a number of prominent citizens were present, and the songs, toasts and speeches, passed off with all the éclat possible on such short notice. Letters of regret were read from Lord Strathcona, Earl Grey, Premier Rutherford, Joseph Seagram, W. F. Maclean, Rev. John McDougall and others.

Now Sir John was Canadian correspondent for one of the big London dailies. He realized right away that such a thing as a Canadian High Commissioner sending congratulations to a convicted horse thief was news, especially in London. Sir John hurriedly wired an account of the story to his paper in London, and the fun began.

---

*Adapted from an article in the *Calgary Herald.*

135

For you see, Peter McGonigle was Bob Edwards' personal property—a purely mythical character conceived by Edwards as a butt of all the jests for which he couldn't find a living target. Peter McGonigle was well known in Alberta, indeed he was one of the famous characters of the West. The banquet on the occasion of his release from the penitentiary served to introduce Peter to the world.

For when Lord Strathcona in London casually picked up his favorite paper, this is what he saw:

> Lord Strathcona's letter was typical of the general sentiment, saying, "I regret exceedingly that I shall be unable to attend the McGonigle banquet, but my sympathies go out to your honored guest. The name of Peter McGonigle will ever stand high in the roll of eminent confiscators. Once long ago, I myself came near achieving distinction in that direction, when I performed some dexterous financing. In consequence, however, of stocks going up instead of down, I wound up in the House of Lords."

> Joseph Seagram's affecting letter of regret said: "Though unable to be with you in the flesh, my spirit is with you. Wishing McGonigle all luck in his next venture."

> It was a sumptuous banquet, and as the walnuts, prunes and wine came on, cigars were lit, and Mayor Emerson of Calgary proposed the toast to the King. His honor expressed satisfaction in his Majesty's reign, insisting indeed that he was as good a King as could be got for the money. He did not believe that the time was yet ripe for the British Empire to be ruled by a commission, as this had been tried in Calgary with poor satisfaction. He was quite agreeable that the King should remain on his throne to the end of his term.

The toast to the Army and Navy was ably responded to by Mayor Charlie Fisher, Speaker of the House. In graphic words he sketched the careers of great soldiers from Julius Caesar to Major Walker, pointing out the tactical blunders of Napoleon, and criticizing in caustic language Nelson's clumsy handling of his ships at Trafalgar. He turned merciless light on Von Moltke and wound up with a glowing tribute to the Alberta Light Horse. He resumed his seat amid thunderous applause.

R. J. Hutchings, replying to the toast to the Great West, said: "I presume this toast has special reference to the firm with which I have been connected. I am proud to say that the guest of the evening is endowed with a marvellous sense of discrimination. Even in that moment of abstraction, when he abstracted the horse, he selected one of our magnificent sets of single harness from the owner's stable and moved the animal along those lines. I earnestly trust that Mr. McGonigle whose pallid countenance shows the effect of his residence in Edmonton will soon be able to resume his chosen avocation. Before sitting down, I might perhaps mention that a company is being formed to harness the Kananaskis Falls, and our firm is hopeful of getting a little business out of it."

Mr. C. W. Rowley, manager of the Bank of Commerce, then obliged with his great song, *Ye Banks and Brays*.

Mr. Rowley spoke aptly, saying: "As you are all aware, our guest has been for some time most hospitably entertained by His Majesty in his Edmonton shooting box, where he had the honor of meeting our talented fellow townsman, Mr. Callahan, who is sought after everywhere, and our young Mr. Wilson, the Macleod chicken fancier. This district is splendidly adapted for gentlemen of Mr. McGonigle's pursuits owing to the persistent reduction of our police force." (Tremendous cheers.)

137

Mr. Matt MacAuley, the hospitable host of H
Majesty's shooting box, rendered *Abide With M*
with deep feeling. His rich staccato voice, howeve
would be none the worse for a little sandpapering
Messrs. Heibert and Robertson, the sweet warbler
then sang their favorite duet, *O That We Two Wer*
Haying, followed by the encore, *Okotoks the Gem*
the Ocean.

Mr. McGonigle's rising was the signal for vociferou
applause. It was fully ten minutes before the hono
guest, who was visibly affected, was allowed to procee
He then said he was willing to let the dead bury i
dead. The horse in question had died shortly afte
he was parted from it. Had it not been for the igno
ance of his lawyer, he might have been acquitted, fo
the horse he stole was not a horse at all, but a mar
This point was overlooked at the trial. The speake
paid high tribute to the hospitality of his Edmonto
host, Mr. MacAuley. But he lamented that in spi
of the number of bars on the premises there wa
nothing of an enlivening nature to drink. In co
clusion he asked that a silent toast be drunk to th
memory of the dead horse."

Lord Strathcona wasted no time. He uttered a how
both loud and long, grabbed his telephone and got th
London editor on the wire. What he said to the edito
makes no difference. It is enough to know that in a ve
few moments a cable was on its way to Sir John Willison

Sir John, possibly feeling proud of being on the spo
with news, was equally dismayed by the editor's cabl
For Sir John was of the East, and the East, notorious
behind the West in matters of pure humor, had nev
heard of Peter McGonigle. So Sir John sent a hot wir
to the Mayor of Calgary and learned, to his amazemen
that the whole affair was a hoax.

138

What Sir John did then is not known. What Lord Strathcona did is known and has furnished the West with many a laugh.

Having never heard of western humor, Lord Strathcona wasted no time. He got his battery of London solicitors and prepared to deal the author of this outrage a death blow. Consultation was heated and long. At length another cable was humming toward Calgary. This time the wire was for Senator Lougheed, a well known Calgary lawyer related by marriage to Strathcona. The wire said: "Begin civil and criminal actions at once!" and named the culprit and mentioned the battery of legal talent in London standing by ready to back the Senator up.

Senator Lougheed, in his turn, was amazed, for he was a Westerner and understood the humor of the West. He sent a cautious reply to London, hinting that the whole matter was a joke.

The London solicitors, however, had never heard of such a thing as a joke. "Does not the King's writ run in your territory?" they screamed. "Toss the beggar in jail!"

Lord Strathcona kept inquiring whether Edwards was yet in prison and wanted to know why, when informed that he was not.

Senator Lougheed, wise in the ways of the West, knew that if action were brought against Edwards, it would end in a downright farce. Edwards knew this, too, and in the highest glee went about saying: "Let 'em sue me. I'm ready for 'em!"

Senator Lougheed finally succeeded in persuading Lord Strathcona to call off his dogs. The legal side of the affair ended then, but the West is still laughing.

XII

❧

The Remittance Men:
"Green, But By God, Not Yellow!"

IN THE EARLY DAYS OF THE WEST MANY YOUNG ENGLISH-
men, some of them from notable families, were sent to
Canada for England's good. These young greenhorns
brought a great deal of color, and their deeds, while
perhaps not always valorous, were an unfailing source
of humor. Here are some of the stories about the remittance men that I gleaned around Calgary.

This is a yarn about the perdition-bent son of a peer,
who was sent off to Canada with a handshake and a sigh
of relief. The boy was liberally supplied with funds to
invest in a ranch near High River. This money and the
various sums that followed it were, of course, invested in
the bar of the hotel at High River. So far as is known, the
boy never owned an acre of land nor a single head of stock.
One day the remittance man received a telegram from
Calgary saying that his honorable father would arrive on
the next train to inspect the "property." Hastening to
a friend who owned a few hundred head of stock and a
ranch house, the prodigal asked assistance in bamboozling
his respected parent. The friend agreed, and when father

140

arrived, son met him in a democrat wagon with a spanking team. The friend's ranch house was quickly reached, and proclaimed as the son's, while a few hundred head of cattle were magnified into thousands by the simple expedient of visiting them time after time—cowboys driving them a few miles while the unsuspecting father was taken on a detour of eight or ten miles to see the next roundup. The father was so impressed that he gave the boy £1,000 to invest in more cattle.

A similar yarn concerns a remittance man extremely well known in the Calgary and High River bars. This good companion showed up one day in a cloud of dust at the Bar U Ranch. Following the whisky-hero of England, was a panting, bedraggled photographer. When George Lane of the Bar U saw the Englishman, he said, "What do you want this time, Henry?"

"Oh, Mr. Lane," cried the remittance man, "you've got to help me, sir. I'm in horrible trouble."

"Well, now," said Lane, "maybe you'd better tell me about it. Might be able to lend you a hand."

"You see," explained the remittance man, "several months ago my father wrote and asked how I was getting along. I wrote back, of course, and told him that I had the finest herd of—ah—gophers this side of the Rocky Mountains. Father thought that was fine and sent me an extra allowance. But now some dirty beggar told father that a gopher was a naughty little animal that lives in a hole in the ground. So father wrote me a scorcher! He's going to cut me off without a penny unless I furnish proof that I've been a success!"

"You are in a *terrible* fix," said Mr. Lane. "What do you suppose I can do for you?"

141

"Won't cost you a cent, sir," said the Englishman. "All I want to do is have this photographer fellow here take a few pictures of your biggest herds of cattle. When father sees those pictures—"

"All right," said George, "go ahead. But it's your funeral!"

The remittance man got his pictures, and apparently the Lane herds satisfied the angry parent, for the young man was frequently seen in various barrooms for a considerable period thereafter.

A green Englishman was batching with an old-timer who went off to Calgary for a week, and left the young man to cook for himself. The larder was well stocked with canned beans, bannocks, butter, eggs, tea, and canned milk. There was little chance that the Englishman would starve.

But four days later he staggered into a neighbor's house some five miles away, timing his arrival with the noon meal. Of course he was invited to join the family. After he had eaten enough for a threshing crew, he confessed that he was half starved, as he had been existing on a diet of clear tea (either so weak it was helpless or so strong it was like lye), hard bannocks, and melted butter.

He couldn't get the lids off the cans of beans or milk; he didn't know how to get the eggs out of their shells to fry, nor did he know how to boil them. The butter kept on a shelf above the stove had melted, and he didn't know that it would harden if put in a cool place.

To Bob Edwards, of course, the remittance men were a source of never-ending delight. He made up a famous remittance man character whom he called Albert Buzzard-

Cholomondeley, son of Sir John Buzzard-Cholomondeley of Skookingham Hall, Skookingham, England. Bertie as he was affectionately known, was making his way in Alberta and finding the going very tough. He was usually down, but never completely out.

From time to time in the pages of the *Eye Opener* Bertie felt it necessary to write a letter to his folks in England. This one is typical:

Dear Father:

Since you have not heard from me for some time, I thought a line might be of some interest to the family, showing at least, that I am well. I often think of dear old Skookingham Hall and the shooting. Is old John, the head gamekeeper, still with you?

I ran across a copy of *Truth* a couple of years ago and noticed that Violet, who was always my favorite sister, was married to the Earl of Pockingham. I well remember Pockingham. He was my fag at Eton and not a half-bad chap. There should be some fine shooting on his estate. How I should enjoy one of our good old grouse drives again! The only shooting I have done out here of late years, has been at craps —a different species of game from grouse or partridge.

But about things in this country. The few thousand pounds you gave me to start farming in Manitoba are duly invested in a farm. In my labors I had several assistants: Hi Walker, Joe Seagram, Johnny Walker and J. Dewar—men of great strength and fiery temperament. They soon became my masters, so it was not long before I had no farm. I then quit farming and went to tending bar for a hotelkeeper in a neighboring town. This fellow's prosperity seems to have dated from the hour of my arrival in the country.

The love of liquor, which is inherent in my blood, and which I must have inherited from you or from

143

my grandfather, made me a failure as a bartender, and I soon got the bounce. So I packed up my things in a large envelope, and hit the trail for the West, where I went cowpunching—worked all summer until the beef-gather, then lost all my earnings in one disastrous night of poker. After a long, hard winter working as cookee for a timber camp, I struck for the Peace River Country, where I am now knocking life out, to keep life in. You can get five gallons of whisky at a crack, if you have a government permit.

I am married to a half-breed and have three ornery-looking, copper-colored brats. We are all coming over to visit you at Christmas time, when you will be having the usual big party at the hall. The hall will be quite a change for my wife, from the log shacks and tepees she has been used to all her life.

If I only had a thousand pounds right now, to start afresh, I would invest it all in cattle right away, settle down to business, and forego the pleasures of a trip home and remain right here. But I do not know where to lay my hands on that amount.

With love and kisses to mother and the girls, your affectionate son,

ALBERT BUZZARD-CHOLOMONDELY.

Without doubt, Bertie got his thousand pounds.

In building up to these fictitious, but nonetheless typical letters, Bob wrote:

Many readers seem to doubt the truth of that story of a young Englishman borrowing a neighbor's ranch for a day to palm off as his own when his father and mother came out from England to pay him a visit. Perhaps we had to embellish the details a trifle, but in the main it was true and actually occurred. Old Fred Stimson, who managed the Bar U Ranch at that period, used to tell that yarn with even more details, especially when he had a snifter or two. He claimed to have had a hand in it himself.

One could go on *ad infinitum* spinning yarns about the vagaries and pleasantries of the young Englishman of the remittance period. He built Calgary. Without the money he put in circulation, Calgary might have withered away on the prairie. He was far more useful to the community than many of those who laughed amusedly at his wild pranks but who were not above benefitting by his useless expenditures. The hotels, of course, got all his money, which later radiated from the bar-till in all directions to keep the economic situation steady.

Of course the amount of each chap's monthly remittance was known to every bartender and hotel-keeper in town, but it often used to puzzle these worthies how mysterious extra remittances seemed to arrive at unexpected moments when most required. Had they seen Mr. Remittance Man sitting down in the hotel writing room, with just enough horns under his belt to stir his imagination, composing a letter to his dear parents in England, they would have understood. Here is the sort of letter which a combination of fertile imagination and financial desperation was able to create on these occasions. (While reading this letter you have to keep in mind that the writer of it had no ranch, had no cattle, had no property, had no nothing, except an ever-lengthening bar bill. His daily existence whirled round and round his damned bar bill which it was vitally important to protect. Otherwise, the world for him was liable to come to an end.)

The Raunch, (say) 1902.

Dear Dad:

Can you not use your influence, which I know to be great, with the British Government to get the embargo lifted on Canadian cattle. I simply won't export any of my steers under present conditions. My cattle are still in prime shape this fall, but by waiting a little longer and seeing what your Board of Agriculture over there propose to do, I may be able to sell the steers at an enormous profit and take a run home for a six month's holiday. I need a rest. The work here is very trying.

A neighbor of mine, Claude Fitzmaurice (a splendid fellow—one of the Epileptic Fitzes of Lushingup Manor) has just sold me a purebred Hereford bull, Rudolph III, for $750. He wanted an even "Thou" for him, but I did not feel like paying that amount, though the animal is well worth $1,250. I needed a new bull, anyhow, to infuse fresh blood into my herd of purebred cows. It does not do to inbreed.

As I am a trifle short for the moment until my bunch of steers are disposed of, kindly drop me the amount ($750) by return post. Enclosed find my I.O.U., which I merely send for form's sake, as business is business. Love to all at home.

Your affectionate son,

PERCY.

Here is another sample, written by a chap who was stoney broke and with an awful bar bill hanging over his head, and the hotelkeeper showing signs of getting peeved. We won't bore you with any more samples but read this one.

Dear Mother:

The head of the buffalo I shot last month and which I am having mounted for you, to hang in the hall at home, is nearly completed. It is said to be the finest specimen ever shot on the western plains.

Unfortunately, the injuries I received from the infuriated brute when it first charged have laid me up in the hospital and I am still far from well. An eminent surgeon came all the way from Toronto to set my *fors clavigera* and rearrange a few of my bones. There is no doubt that he saved my life. His fee is

rather steep—a thousand dollars plus expenses—
$1,250 in all, but happily I can well afford it. When
I am myself again I may take a run over to England
to convalesce. The specialist recommends an ocean
voyage. Love to everybody.

Your loving son,

BERTIE.

P.S.—By the way, mother dear, as I am too weak to
leave my bed and attend to the matter myself, would
you mind cabling me the specialist's fee at once? I
hate owing anybody. When I am allowed to get up,
will send you a cheque. May be confined to my bed
for six weeks yet. Am having a small silver plate
engraved, to place on base of the buffalo head, with
date of killing, etc.

A remittance man was very desirous of seeing the
Alberta countryside. He rented a horse and buggy and
started out from Calgary. He hadn't gone far before he
had to cross a little stream. The horse stopped, wanting
a drink. Of course, the Englishman didn't know that the
horse's head was held back by a check-rein, so he got out,
waded around behind the buggy, lifted up the hind wheels,
expecting that this would tilt the horse, buggy and all
down to the water. The horse looked around, gave a long
snort of western laughter, and started back to Calgary.

It was easy, sometimes, to part the remittance man from
his money. In the early days, just as now, when you
bought a farm, you bought land, buildings and all for a
fixed sum. Never having heard of this custom, a remittance man who had a pocket full of money wanted to buy
a homestead near Calgary. He went out to see the homesteader from whom he wanted to purchase the land and
asked him how much he wanted for it. The homesteader

147

thought a moment, then he said, "Well, I reckon three thousand would be about right."

The remittance man jerked out three thousand dollars. "Here, this is for the land. Now, how much for the barn?"

"Why," said the surprised homesteader, "I—well, I reckon about a thousand dollars."

"Here," said the remittance man, jerking out a thousand, "this is for the barn. Now, how much for the house?"

"Well—" said the homesteader, "I reckon if the barn's worth a thousand, the house is worth fifteen hundred."

"Here's the fifteen hundred," said the Englishman, "and now, I really own the place!"

"Wait a minute," said the homesteader, "You forgot the well. I'll have to have five hundred for the well."

The remittance man gave him five hundred and went to inspect his property. The homesteader lost no time getting to Calgary, where he put the story into circulation while enjoying refreshment at the Alberta Hotel.

A rancher's wife took pity on a remittance man who had had no laundry done for a long while. She washed the man's clothing, ironed it, and soon had him looking like the son of noble blood, which he might very well have been.

The day following this great clean-up, a couple of the remittance man's friends heard of his whereabouts and came out to the ranch to see him. The old friends exchanged reminiscences of the homeland, and then the time came for the remittance man to introduce his friends to the rancher's family. When the lady who had been so kind to him stepped forward, the remittance man said, "And this, boys, is my washerwoman."

The woman's son lost no time. He aimed a terrific

left hook at the remittance man's jaw, connected, and in a few moments the man's friends were bearing him sorrowfully back to Calgary.

Of course, the remittance men were not all bad. Some of them turned out remarkably well. They were an absolutely fearless crew, and they made excellent soldiers. A number of them joined the famous Mounted Police. Some of the heroic episodes in Mounted Police history are the result of action on the part of remittance men. It is a sad but unmistakable fact, however, that the popular conception of the heroism of the remittance man is that of a hero at the bar and with the bottle, rather than of a hero with gun and horse.

Illustrative of this sad bit of truth is the tale told by Dr. G. D. Stanley of Calgary, in an admirable little quarterly published by the doctors of the Calgary Associate Clinic. Dr. Stanley wrote:

> When I first arrived in High River in 1901, there was a rough and ready cowpuncher, Jack Rivett, who used to be mixed up in most of the poker games and other revelries of Jerry's old barroom. Everybody addressed Rivett as "Sir John." I inquired from my new and wonderful friend, Scotty McNeill, how this peculiar picture of culture and the uncouth came by his title. Scotty replied, "Why, don't you know? He is a great astronomer. He discovered the fourth star on Hennessey's Three Star Brandy."
>
> Jack went to the South African War, and when he returned, wandered up toward Bassano. In 1914 he enlisted for France in a British Columbia unit. My friend Scotty McNeill did likewise. I corresponded with Scotty regularly in France, and in one letter he wrote: "You'll be surprised to know who is in my unit, no less than our old friend, Jack Rivett!"

In my next letter I referred to Jack's title, and how he had earned it. Scotty's next letter bore the news of Jack's death in action, and Scotty added, "By a strange coincidence, his grave is on the Hennessey Estate!" . . . A few days later I saw an item in the *Calgary Herald* seeking the "whereabouts of Jack Rivett." Two days later the *Herald* reported the fact that Jack's uncle in England had passed away, and had left an estate exceeding one million dollars in value, and that, had Jack survived, he would have been the heir to the entire estate, and successor to the title, Sir John Rivett.

Dr. Stanley, in the same little magazine, relates another remittance man story. This time about Coyote Charlie.

Coyote Charlie was a unique character in those days. He had achieved his nickname by reason of the dirt and uncouthness of his person and home in a dugout on the side of one of the Buffalo Hills, about forty miles from town (Calgary). He had been an educated Englishman, raised in a cultured home before he went mining in Montana. All exterior indications of body and clothing suggested only too strongly that he had forsworn bathing and the use of unprofane language when he had left his beautiful English home.

Ultimately his health began to fail and he moved into town during the height of the last World War and rented a one-room shack in the middle of a small stock corral on the edge of town. The corral was in daily use by a local German live stock dealer, and cattle or hogs were constantly penned around Charlie's home. It became humanly impossible to approach Charlie's door without wading through inches of ripe manure. Grass never had time to grow. One night the hogs were more numerous than usual, likewise more inquisitive and aggressive. They had besieged the shack and Charlie's peace of mind beyond endur-

150

ance. So he arrived at the Doctor's office in the early morning and addressed his medical adviser as follows:

"Now look here, Doc, I'm a sick man. Old K—'s pigs have pestered me all night long. They've rubbed the corners off my shack and smashed open my door and eaten up my breakfast porridge. You've got to do something about it! It's a blankety-blank-blank outrage, that a German blankety-blank-blank should be allowed to corral his blankety-blank-blank dirty hogs on an *English gentleman's lawn!*"

But there were remittance men of all types. Mr. Chief Justice Ives of Calgary related to me the story of a most remarkable remittance man. This fellow lived alone in a shack in the foothills. Half of each year he spent hunting and sketching the hunting scenes and the natural life of the mountains. When he returned to his cabin after a hunting trip, he would string unbleached muslin all around the walls, then using charcoal, he would transfer his hunting trip sketches onto the muslin. The result was a marvelous set of murals, telling the story of the entire hunting trip. When he grew tired of one set of murals, he would go on another trip, come home, pull down the old murals, hang new muslin, and draw a fresh set. Everyone who viewed the murals said they were the most marvelous pictures they ever saw.

Yes, the remittance men were an interesting lot, and reports about them vary. One well-known Calgary business man told me that he agreed with Bob Edwards that the remittance men were responsible for much of Calgary's early growth and prosperity. They had money, and the enterprising tradesmen of Calgary were able to sell them tremendous amounts of material. On the other side of the picture, I have heard others say that much of the early resentment against the Britisher which undoubtedly existed in the West was because of the arrogance and bad manners of the remittance man.

The remittance men were certainly a bunch of green-horns, but as Bob Edwards said, when war was declared in 1914 and the remittance men joined up almost to a man:

"Those fellows were green, but by God, they're not *yellow!*"

XIII

❦

The Greatest Wit in the West

ONE DAY WHEN PADDY NOLAN WAS SITTING IN HIS CALGARY law office, Shorty McLaughlin from High River came to see him. Shorty was mighty sore. The C. P. R. had recently run over and killed twenty-one of his horses.

After listening to Shorty's bitter thrusts at the railroad, Paddy Nolan leaned back and asked with a smile: "Well, Shorty, what do you want me to do?"

"Do!" yelled Shorty. "Did I understand you to ask what I want you to do? Sue 'em, man! I want double, maybe triple value for every cayuse those blankety-blanks have slaughtered!"

"I'm sorry, Shorty," said Paddy Nolan, "but I can't take your case."

"You can't! Why not? Ain't my money as good—"

Paddy Nolan held up his hand. "It's nothing like that, Shorty. You see, the railroad men are right. Any horse that can't outrun the C. P. R. deserves to die."

Upon such retorts grew Paddy Nolan's reputation as a master wit and joker. He became equally famous as a criminal lawyer and humorist. When Paddy was defending a criminal case, the courtroom was apt to be packed. Juries expected wit and usually got plenty of it.

According to one of Paddy's contemporaries, he was not an especially handsome man. He was below middle height and pretty nearly as broad as he was long, with a paunch that shook and trembled as he walked. He had keen eyes and wore a black moustache. He was usually in a state of profuse perspiration and was constantly mopping his brow. Despite his bulk, however, he was very active and bounced about like a rubber ball. His extraordinary wit was one of his greatest characteristics and gave him a remarkable standing in the West.

Paddy was a great friend of Bob Edwards, and it was Paddy's steady advice which probably helps explain why Bob was so seldom bothered by libel suits. Bob, of course, poked fun at Paddy in the *Eye Opener*, just as he did at all his friends. In a letter published in the *Eye Opener*, reputedly written by Bob's fictitious remittance man, Albert Buzzard-Cholomondeley, Albert states to his father in England:

> I must have a few hundred pounds immediately to secure the services of a lawyer from Calgary. There is a famous lawyer there by the name of P. Nolan. All the best murderers go to him. On one occasion my friend the bartender told me that Mr. Nolan once defended a man who had killed another by filling him full of buckshot. His line of defense was that the deceased had come to his death through natural causes, because how could a man be expected to live with a pound of lead in his vitals? The jury took the same view, and the murderer is now living a virtuous life as a traveling man.

The yarns about Paddy are many, and give evidence that his wit was not confined to the courtroom. On one occasion Paddy was attending a dance at Medicine Hat.

154

Paddy, remember, had a really big bay window. His hostess, seeing him standing alone in a corner, approached and said: "Mr. Nolan, why aren't you dancing?"

Paddy looked at the lady for a moment, then he remarked, "Madam, I will be most happy to dance, if you will find me a partner with a concave stomach!"

One time Paddy was coming back to Calgary from a trip and when the C. P. R. train stopped briefly at High River, Paddy got off to have a bite to eat in the lunch-room. No sooner had he seated himself at a certain table than the waitress came to him and said, "You'll have to move. This table is reserved for the trainmen."

Paddy didn't say anything but laboriously got up and moved to another table. Presently the newsboy came and sat down beside him.

"You must be a stranger here," said the newsboy. "Otherwise you'd know that this table is reserved for the newsboys."

Paddy Nolan didn't say anything, but he stayed right where he was. Presently the waitress came to take the order. The newsboy ordered a piece of pie and a glass of milk.

"And what will you have?" asked the waitress turning to Paddy.

"Just bring me the same as the other newsboy," replied Paddy.

Paddy's speeches to the jury were famous; and to demonstrate how effective they were, Paddy used to tell a story about a man whom he had just got off on a charge of horse stealing.

"Honor bright now, Bill," asked Paddy, "you did steal that horse, didn't you?"

155

"Now look here, Mr. Nolan," replied the culprit, "I always did think I stole that horse, but since I heard your speech to that 'ere jury, I'll be dog-goned if I ain't got my doubts about it!"

But sometimes Paddy's smooth flow of words backfired on him. One time Paddy was addressing Magistrate Saunders. "Your Honor, my learned friend Mr. Short refers to my client as a double-dyed villain! That's what he is, your honor, that's what he is! He is only a villain by reason of the dye with which the infamously false testimony in this case has colored him. But it will come out in the wash. I look confidently to your decision in this case, your honor, to remove those spurious stains from the character of a cruelly and unjustly persecuted man and reveal him as he really is; an upright, honest citizen, white as the driven snow."

Whereupon Magistrate Saunders screwed his monocle a little further into his eye and found the prisoner guilty of stealing the ham.

A tale that is most often told about Paddy involves his cross-examination of a famous Calgary character known as Mother Fulham. Mother, who was a free-lance garbage collector in Calgary, was herself widely noted for her adroit comebacks. Paddy's cross-examination involved in some way the revealing of Mother's bare right foot to the jury. When she had slipped off her shoe, Paddy staggered back, recovered himself, and said, "That's the dirtiest foot in the West!"

"No it ain't," retorted Mother, "I'll show you a dirtier one." Whereupon she slipped off her other shoe and held out her *left* foot.

156

XIV

❦

Foothill Bad Man

ONE OF PADDY NOLAN'S MOST NOTABLE CASES, AND ONE which he lost, was the famous Cashel case, now a folktale in southern Alberta.

*Among the land seekers hurrying across the American border to the fertile Alberta plains in 1902 was a slim, unimpressive young man named Ernest Cashel. Cashel was hurrying too, and for an adequate personal reason— a battalion of American sheriffs from several states was not far behind.

By trade Cashel was a barber. By inclination he was definitely a crook and a killer. By his own word, backed by a ten-gallon hat, he was a cowhand looking for work though much preferring a deck of cards to branding iron or mowing machine.

Cashel did secure a job for a short time with John Phelan at Shepard. But the novelty of making a living by such unusual methods soon wore off.

Money being scarce, Cashel cashed a pure rubber check at the T. A. Hatfield Calgary Store one day shortly after his arrival in the country. The merchant remem-

---

*C. I. Ritchie, *The Canadian Cattlemen*, Vol. 11, No. 4.

bered Cashel. Police soon swore out a warrant for his arrest. But the young forger had disappeared.

Putting two and two together, the Mounted Police in turn, sent a constable to a farm near Red Deer where the wanted man's mother resided. Cashel was picked up, brought to the town, and turned over to Chief of Police English from Calgary. That appeared to be the close of the Cashel case. Actually it was hardly the start.

The train with Cashel and an officer aboard snorted and shunted its way toward Calgary as trains of the era were wont to do. It was a pleasant day, the law was satisfied, and the little crook busy planning.

En route he was allowed to visit the washroom. The officer sat nearby, momentarily lost in the beauty of the autumn landscape. Suddenly recalling he had a prisoner to account for he went to the door. It was locked from the inside.

Grabbing the nearest fire ax, entrance was soon forced, but an open window provided mute evidence that the resourceful young Cashel had made a neat getaway. The officer, however, retained his coat and vest as evidence of a bungled business.

The escape resulted in widespread descriptions of the barbering bandit, and at last came word of his whereabouts.

It appeared a rancher near Lacombe supplied a young man with a coat and a vest and a horse. Everything, including the man, thought to be Cashel, had vanished. The rancher decided he had been swindled. So did police as they grudgefully chalked up another success to Cashel and then tightened up the manhunt.

Weeks stretched into months and still no Cashel. He was seen here and there, momentarily. Police would arrive too late. Newspapers were making a big "play" of the elusive Cashel. Officers were irritated and getting more so. Headquarters at Regina took up the cue and, in common parlance, told the hard-worked force in Alberta to "turn on the heat."

Around Lacombe, however, there were suspicions the wanted party was not far away. He had been seen some time previous at Pleasant Valley on the Red Deer River and was presumed to be the guest of one, Rufus (I. R.) Belt. A neighbor of Belt's, by name A. N. Thomas, recalled that a young man, who gave his name as Ellsworth, had been about. And Ellsworth, as the police well knew, was one of Cashel's aliases. The logical step would be to question Belt.

This was much easier said than done, for when police arrived at the Belt holdings there was no Belt, no Cashel and very little to work on. There was, however, more mystery.

Belt had not been seen, neighbors recalled, since the visit of the young man presumed to be Cashel or Ellsworth or whatever name he might be using at the moment.

Furthermore, Belt was a quiet, orderly individual of sixty years, methodical in his habits and not one to leave with the house wide open in November. Nor was he likely to pull up stakes so suddenly as to leave a full bucket of water on the trail leading to the Red Deer River, 200 yards from his cabin.

Along with the dual disappearing act, investigation showed such sizeable items as a pony and new saddle also

159

missing. The saddle was penciled "I. R. Belt." Then there were certain items of clothing, blankets, and tools from an open box to be accounted for.

Nearby residents also recalled that Belt carried a considerable sum of money on his person, including an American fifty dollar bill. Here, they thought, were the makings of a prime murder set-up. Police were reasonably sure they were correct.

In less time than is required for the telling the police net was thrown over all Alberta. Constable J. Macleod of the Mounted Police, assigned to the case from Red Deer, soon picked up promising trails.

Two days after checking over the Belt cabin, the constable located the saddle of the horse stolen from the Lacombe farmer in nearby Pleasant Valley. Cashel had sold it there on November 1st. The buyer recalled the young man had been packing a rifle and revolver and appeared anxious to find the shortest and least traveled route to the U. S. border.

All settlers and ranchers were warned to watch for the young desperado but, as days again stretched into weeks, official circles became more irritated. Mounted Police sent out their ace sleuth, Corporal Pennycuick, to try to overtake Cashel.

By this time December had clamped an icy fist over the West, and travel, let alone investigation, was badly hampered by severe storms. Pennycuick, after prowling around the Belt place, came to Calgary feeling decidedly low.

In the interim Chief English at Calgary had been doing some work on the case. He ascertained that a party whose description was at least similar to that of Cashel had left a tired horse at Shepard but had taken the saddle along. Discussing this with Pennycuick brought to light the fact that Cashel had passed one of his famous "no account" checks at Shepard.

The chief had traced the suspect from the village to Calgary where a ticket had been purchased for the coast. The next train west carried Pennycuick, hot on the trail of someone at least like Cashel.

The records tell how the hunt went to Vancouver where inquiries showed the man, easily identified by the saddle he carried with him, had left for Seattle only a couple of hours before Mr. Pennycuick's arrival on Pacific shores. From Seattle the saddle was traced to Portland, Oregon, where a hotel register showed the party was using the name "B. Nail, Moose Jaw." And Mr. Nail had left the previous day for a place called Princeville.

In due course the sheriff at Princeville was contacted by wire. His reply looked like the end of the chase and Cashel. For Mr. Nail was in the town bastille.

His face was similar to Cashel's, his clothing tallied in a way, but age and height were definitely at a difference. Furthermore Nail was as silent as the tombs, but he nearly elevated out of his boots when the long list of charges were presented to him.

Finally he told all. He was not Cashel. He was not a murderer, nor a thief, nor a forger. He was a ranch hand of the Calgary district who had suffered some "woman trouble," as he put it, and was seeking escape from the irate female by roundabout routes.

Though it was Christmas time, Pennycuick returned to

161

Alberta far from being in the merry mood of the season.

Two weeks passed and then again Cashel sort of popped from a snowbank. A Jumping Pound rancher reported a Mr. Ellsworth had borrowed a horse to recover his own which had run away. The rancher was able to give a fairly complete description of the hunted man.

Then, Pennycuick found, none other than Nick Carter in person had appeared on the Indian reserve at Shaganappi. Mr. Carter of the dime novel fame had arrived in a two-wheeled rig more than a month before. He had a .44 revolver. More important, Mr. Carter had managed to get a half-breed to buy some ammunition and clothing in Calgary. *And he had given a fifty dollar American bill to pay for the articles.*

The chase again was warming up. Police found Cashel had changed part of his clothing here and there, stolen the horse mentioned from Jumping Pound, and taken a diamond ring from a woman living near Kananaskis. The detachment at Banff was ordered to check upon everyone in sight. The country around Canmore was scoured until finally Cashel was located, surprised, and captured. There was no struggle. He appeared quite pleased at having managed to elude the law for three months. The Mounties were still sore from the chaffing attributable to Cashel, alias Ellsworth, alias Nick Carter.

Actually it was the astuteness of W. L. McDonald, station master at the little town of Anthracite, west of Calgary, who was responsible for the capture.

The westbound train had just left when a young chap walked into the station and cashed a check. McDonald was suspicious for the visitor looked like Cashel. He made further inquiries, found out the stranger was living at a nearby boarding house, and immediately notified police at Banff.

Arraigned at Calgary on theft charges, Cashel on May 14, 1903, was sentenced to three years in jail.

He was quite composed when the term was pronounced. At the same time, Pennycuick, with true bloodhound instincts was busy—at the Rufus Belt farm and in adjacent territory.

Pennycuick, in brief, gathered sufficient evidence regarding the disappearance of Belt and the part Cashel played in it to send the latter to Hades several times over.

Neighbors, including Belt's distant relative Thomas, by photos recognized Cashel as the Ellsworth who had paid the recluse the impromptu visit months before. A rancher recalled Cashel riding Belt's pony. Another was located who had sold him the two-wheeled rig in which, as Nick Carter, he invaded the Indian reserve in the foothills. Cashel had exchanged ten dollars in cash, a new saddle and bridle, and a pair of spurs for the outfit.

The saddle had the Belt monogram on it. Pennycuick now had the saddle and all the evidence required except the mortal remains of the missing Belt. And murder is virtually impossible to prove without having some direct evidence of the victim. But Pennycuick was a determined man.

It is a matter of actual record that he, assisted by a Mountie, grubbed in every sand bar, brush pile, and tributary along the Red Deer for three weeks. The pair covered almost 400 miles in all kinds of weather—and still they could not locate the lost corpse.

June passed, snow had disappeared and still no body while in the Calgary jail house Cashel was growing increasingly confident and the persistent Pennycuick an object of some public comment.

Then came the break. On July 23rd a settler found a body washed ashore opposite the mouth of Haynes Creek emptying into the Red Deer.

It was an unusual body, in a way, for though badly decomposed it was nude except for socks and boots. There were marks of a wound in the chest and there were signs that the remains were those of Belt.

The boot on one foot had a steel clamp on it. The big toe of the left foot was twisted under the second due to an ax wound—there was ample circumstantial evidence to persuade Pennycuick that he had an air tight case.

Cashel, much of his composure evaporated, came to trial on October 19, 1903, before Hon. A. L. Sifton and Jury. He was defended, of course, by Paddy Nolan.

For more than a week Cashel listened to the evidence. He sat in the dock, pale and worried. Pennycuick had so few weak links in his chain that after thirty-five minutes the Jury returned to the trial chamber.

Cashel carefully scanned each face. In reply to the Judge's "Have you anything to say?" he observed, "Nothing except that I ain't guilty."

He was sentenced to be hanged December 15th, and the men who always 'got their man' carved another niche in their records and marked the case closed, except for the actual execution.

Cashel's day of doom was approaching when a brother, John, arrived from the U. S. He was a likeable sort of citizen.

In company with Rev. Dr. George Kerby, venerable head of Mount Royal College at Calgary, the brother was allowed to enter the cell. All the while, however, the two officers guarding Cashel kept careful watch.

Time rolled on, Cashel had a week left to live. On December 10th, the brother John paid his usual visit. Shortly after the erring Ernest walked out of jail. It was not quite as easy as that, however. The official version from police records says:

On the afternoon of December 10, John Cashel paid another of his usual visits and at the time Rev. George (now Dr.) Kerby was in the cell. From what has transpired this is what occurred:

At one end of the cell was Ernest Cashel, in the middle the clergyman and at the end, the constable who was the death watch. The provost and two constables were in the room facing the cell.

John Cashel came in, and, in direct violation of the orders governing his visits, walked to his brother's cell and stood talking to him with his hands on the bars. While this conversation was going on Rev. Mr. Kerby wished to leave and the provost decided to change the death watch. One of the constables went to the front door to open it for Mr. Kerby.

While Mr. Kerby and the death watch were leaving the cell and had their backs turned on the two brothers, the provost and relieving watch were in the corridor on each side of the cell door to let them pass out, so that for a few seconds at least, no one could see what was taking place. It was at this critical moment that John Cashel passed his brother two revolvers.

Nothing further happened until between six and six-thirty that evening, when the provost and day guard commenced to make preparations for the handing over to the night guard. Part of the preparation consisted of searching the prisoner and seeing he was safe in his cell for the night.

At that time the provost had one constable in the front part of the guard room and the death-cell watch in the cell. The latter was unarmed. The provost unloaded his revolver before entering Cashel's cell for fear it might be snatched from him by the prisoner. Thus only one guard was armed.

Entering the cell the provost directed the death watch to take Cashel into the prison dining room and, after checking over the blankets and cell itself ordered Cashel back to be searched.

The prisoner walked toward the door where the provost stood and suddenly drew two revolvers from his trousers' pocket. He covered the two unarmed constables. The armed constable hearing some noise foolishly walked up to the grating without drawing his revolver and was told to put up his hands. Cashel was now in a position to cover all three at once.

From testimony of all other prisoners who were eye witnesses to the affair, the provost made several attempts to close with Cashel and delay him. But he was to a certain extent helpless. The armed constable could have saved the situation but lacked presence of mind.

He and the provost were made to undo their belts and drop their arms to the floor. The three constables were ordered into the cell and locked up while the prisoner went to the provost's desk, got the keys and walked out. The night guard coming on duty ten minutes later gave the alarm.

With the parting word, "I don't want to shoot you but I'm in a bad way," Cashel disappeared into the December blizzard and for the next forty days the country hummed and buzzed while the greatest manhunt in the history of the West got under way.

166

The Mounted Police brought reinforcements from all their posts with a man to spare. Settlers looked to their shooting irons. Doors were barred and housewives jittery. "Nick Carter" Cashel was on the loose again.

But Mr. Cashel, despite his repose in the death cell, soon came back to form. On December 15th, the day fixed for his death, he entered a ranch home a few miles from Calgary, stole clothing and a diamond ring and left an I.O.U. for $1000 signed "Ernest Cashel".

As is always the case rumor bred rumor, with result that the elusive Mr. Cashel was reported one day in Cochrane, another in Calgary, at Ponoka 100 miles north, and at Gleichen 60 miles east. Montana borders were an armed camp.

And all the while there were developments coming to light indicating that Cashel was not far from Calgary. Some unofficial reports later had it that as police scoured far and wide, Cashel watched them from a hideout in the bush on the north bank of the Bow, well within city limits.

While all this was going on, a drab soul arrived from Ottawa—Executioner Radcliffe. He continued to hang about while Cashel continued at large.

With Christmas approaching Cashel sent a note to the Mounted Police indirectly, in which he "kidded" the scarlet riders, reminded them he would not be taken alive, mentioned he intended to remain in Calgary "for some time yet" and suggested they "just tell Mr. Radcliffe he might as well go back to Ottawa, Ontario—and take his scaffold with him".

This did not help salve the ruffled temper of officers and the hunt was pressed even harder.

167

In order to keep their movements from being public property, the police asked newspapers to refrain from detailed reports of the hunt. Then they swore in about two dozen deputies at Calgary and on a Sunday morning this posse set out to find Cashel, once and for all. Inspector Arthur Dufus was in charge.

The force crossed Nose Creek and from there on undertook a minute search of all houses and haystacks. At a ranch layout the hired hands told police that a man with whiskers was sleeping in a stack. They did not think it was Cashel, but told them to go ahead and have a look.

At first glance the stack appeared as all others—but it was different. Officers found a hole burrowed in it. In the straw they unearthed a military cloak and other clothing stolen by Cashel during his December raids. This discovery was on the Pitman ranch at 11:30 on the morning of January 24th. Near the strawpile was a ranch hands' shack apparently deserted. Two officers entered. They found the room empty.

There was a trap door leading to the cellar. A constable dropped his weapon and let himself into the gloom. Suddenly, with a flash and a roar a bullet zinged past his head. The officer came through the trap door like a jack-in-the-box, grabbed his gun and let fly. The other men surrounded the shack.

Inspector Dufus ordered Cashel to come out, with his hands up. Silence answered.

Dufus decided to burn the building and, when flames and smoke were circulating nicely, again ordered the trapped killer out.

168

Cashel growled, "I am not coming out. I am going to kill myself." Bang! There was silence except for the crackle of the fire.

Police were again on a limb. Was Cashel dead or was it another smart bluff?

Once more Dufus called to him to come out. This time there was action. Covered by a half dozen rifles, a weird looking creature crawled from the murky cellar. It was Cashel with long tangled hair and whiskers and the observation, "I am sick of the whole business."

Cashel was taken back to jail. His brother was sentenced to a year in prison. Confession of the murder of Rufus Belt was duly recorded and on February 2, 1904, he hurtled through the scaffold, his nerve still unbroken.

Paddy Nolan was possibly a bit dismayed by the whole affair. On the night of the execution, so the story goes, Paddy was engaged in a game of billiards in one of the local poolrooms. Who should walk in but Hangman Radcliffe. Paddy took one look, grabbed his cue and started to chase the hangman in and out among the tables. Friends grabbed Paddy and calmed him down, while the hangman slipped hastily out the door.

PART TWO

FOOTHILL COUNTRY

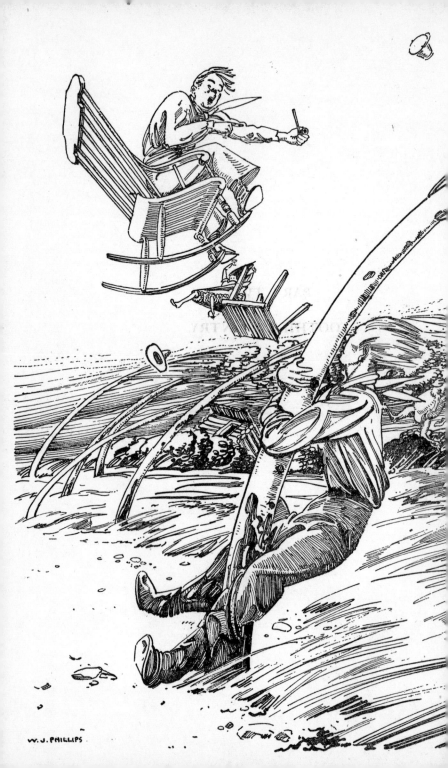

W.J. PHILLIPS.

You know how it is, Johnny. Sometimes, during the the winter, you'll see out there in the west, a wondrous sight. Looks like the whole arch o' heaven forming, low down there, just over the tops of the mountains. Chinook arch. Or in summertime the mighty shafts o' light you see slanting down, and shadows that flicker across the rolling land to blend, faster than sight, with the blue-black of the mountain shade. You know the craggy peaks, Johnny, and the rumbling thunder that's like the deep tones of a great, mysterious organ. Maybe this thunder is laughter, Johnny, or maybe it is the mutter of an angry tragic god. Foothill country, Johnny Chinook!

I

~~~~

Avalanche

THE CROW'S NEST PASS, ACCORDING TO LEGEND, RECEIVED its name as a result of a great battle between the Indians of the Blackfoot Nation and the Crows. The scene of this battle was entirely obliterated by the greatest land slide ever known in the Rocky Mountains.

On the morning of April 29, 1903, a C. P. R. westbound freight train crawled slowly through the Crow's Nest Pass, through the little mining town of Frank, and past the dim, massive shape of Turtle Mountain. The time was just after four o'clock.

To the boys on the train the trip was routine. The sounds were just the same; the dim, cold light was normal for the time of year. In the caboose Sid Choquette, the brakeman, was thinking that he'd be glad when the sun came up, for the air was cold and damp.

In Frank the bartender at the hotel had just finished cleaning up. He'd had a hard night. He was going home to bed—just as soon as he got rid of a lone drunk who was hanging around. The barkeeper sighed, put on his hat and reached out his hand for the drunk's collar.

Down the street, Sam Ennes stirred in his bed. For some

174

reason he was uneasy—couldn't sleep. He struck a match and looked at his watch. The time was seven minutes past four. He lay down again, pulled the bedclothes over his shoulders. He shut his eyes, but in a minute he flicked them open again and lay there in the darkness. He strained his ears to hear the breathing of his wife. From another room, one of his daughters coughed.

In the Frank coal mine the night shift was getting ready to lay off. The nineteen men were tired, dirty, ready to quit. They plodded toward the mine entrance. One of the men noticed that the mine horses were acting very nervous. He was too tired to care.

In the Leitch household, the baby was crying.

At ten minutes past four hell broke loose in Frank. The whole top and north side of Turtle Mountain slid with a terrifying roar directly down into the Crow's Nest.

The freight had just passed the mountain when the avalanche struck. The startled crew, looking back as the train bumped to a halt, heard a sound louder than the loudest thunder and saw what they thought was a heavy gas or fog rising from mountain and town. To their surprised eyes, the town of Frank seemed to have completely disappeared. The crew gathered at the rear of the train, huddled together silent, awed by the sudden tragedy.

It was Sid Choquette, the brakeman, who first remembered the *Spokane Flyer*. The express was shortly due to speed through the Pass on its way to the coast. The men could guess, as they looked back, that the C. P. R. tracks lay covered by stone many feet deep.

There was only one thing to do, and Sid did that thing.

He started back toward Frank, over the slide with pieces of rock still hurtling down from the mountain. The dust was so thick he couldn't see what lay ahead. Some of the stones were as large as boxcars, but Sid went right ahead. He arrived in time to flag the *Flyer*.

Sam Ennes, who couldn't sleep, suddenly found himself pinned under the jagged timbers of his home. Desperately Sam pushed at the weight that held him down. After a terrible struggle he got free. His legs were torn by the nails in the boards. His face was bleeding from many cuts.

Somewhere he could hear his children crying.

He began to frantically search in the ruins. He found the three girls first, then his wife. They had miraculously escaped serious injury.

Suddenly Mrs. Ennes began to shriek that the baby, Gladys, was missing. They searched in the dust-filled darkness, and then Mrs. Ennes found the baby buried in slime and mud. Believing that the child was dead, Mrs. Ennes stumbled toward the faint light in the Maclean house beyond the stricken area. When she arrived, she discovered that the baby was alive and not even scratched. Mrs. Ennes herself had a broken collar bone.

In the mine the workmen reached the entrance. They found it blocked up tight. Believing that it was just a small cave-in, the men turned and went west to another smaller exit. The horses remained in the mine.

When the miners finally got outside, many of them knew they would never see their homes and families again. A number of the houses were buried over 100 feet deep.

In the Leitch house three children escaped, while three

176

others and the parents were killed. One of the children, a baby, was completely unharmed. It was found on a huge rock that had been pushed quite a distance along by the slide.

The unharmed people of Frank wondered what had brought the catastrophe upon them. Some said it was a volcano, others that it was an earthquake. Many thought it was a mine explosion or a great quantity of gas suddenly released.

That the side of Turtle Mountain, which seemed so friendly and protective, had simply slid down on the little town crouching under its shoulders did not occur to many, those first few hours. Tales of a visitation for sin were heard, and to the drunk leaving the barroom this seemed likely. He started to run—no one knew where.

Help was rushed to Frank—not that there was much anyone could do. The dead were already buried. The living were in mortal terror that the rest of the mountain would come smashing down.

Many of the passengers on the westbound train held up by the slide tried to walk across to the train waiting on the other side. They found their shoes cut to pieces, their clothing ruined by the limestone dust. A *Calgary Herald* reporter on the scene wired his paper: "To traverse two miles of boulders, some bigger than a railway coach, tossed into piles and ravines, is a task that tries a strong man, well shod. For people with thin shoes, unaccustomed to mountains, the trip is almost suicide. I had a suit of clothes ruined by the white lime, my boots were cut to pieces, and my physical system is a wreck that calls for at least a week's recuperation. Editor please note."

The slide had occurred on Wednesday morning. On Saturday Frank was a deserted village. A committee, including the mine inspector, crawled up the side of Turtle and reported that they had seen large cracks, newly formed, which led them to believe that the slide would reoccur. This report, backed up by the statements of Engineer McHenry of the C. P. R. that he had kept a careful watch on Turtle Mountain for most of a day and had seen the mountain creeping, convinced the remaining citizens of Frank that they should vacate. Most of them went to Blairmore.

For nine days a careful watch was kept. At the end of nine days, when no further general slide had occurred, Premier Haultain decided the citizens of Frank could return if they so wished. Many did return to live most of the summer in terror. Finally there was a smaller slide in September. The slide, according to the *Calgary Herald,* was never really reported. The Frank citizens feared the report would "damage the town commercially."

One of the touching incidents connected with the story concerns the horses imprisoned in the mine. All but two of the men escaped fairly easily, but all the horses stayed in the mine.

When the rescue party managed to clear the main slope, some twenty-nine days later, they encountered a depressing sight. All but one of the horses had died of starvation and thirst. The animals had gnawed the mine props and the wood on the cars in search of food.

The remaining horse was fastened between a car and the side of the entrance. He was very weak—almost gone. The horse was given a few drops of water and brandy.

He lifted his head. The party left in search of blankets to keep the horse warm since they could not move him. As they went they heard the horse neigh faintly several times. When they returned ten minutes later, the horse was dead. Old-timers say the horse died of a broken heart. He thought he was being left alone in the mine.

The greatest slide in the Rocky Mountains was the result of a combination of causes. There had been a mild earthquake in the region in 1901 which may have been a factor. The fact that large chambers had been opened up in the mine was thought by some to have caused the disaster.

Turtle Mountain, however, is peculiar. It is of limestone, overthrust upon shale, sandstone, and coal beds. The whole thing is an unusually weak mass of rock. There is some reason for believing that the slide can happen again, but Frank folk, apparently, are not worrying.

Passengers on the C. P. R. are amazed at the desolation still to be seen. The railroad now runs right on top of the slide. It took 4,000 Japs a month, working twenty-four hours a day, to rebuild the railroad.

When they were clearing up the debris for the railroad, it was necessary to use quantities of dynamite. The blasting caused snow to fall in the middle of May. Newly born calves on ranches in the Frank area smothered and died as a result of the snow.

For weeks the Frank school was used as a morgue. Parts of a human body would be found, and a jury empaneled to try to make identification. This was not often possible.

Most of the eighty persons killed that terrible morning

were buried at the moment of death. Some were not, and they lie in a grave near Frank, with the following inscription on a common stone:

Here Lie the Remains of Some of
the Victims of the Frank Slide.
April 29, 1903.

The Frank slide has become a tragic legend of the Canadian Rockies.

❧ ❧

The Tale of Kootenai Brown and the Saga of the Mountain Oil

KOOTENAI BROWN, WHO WAS NAMED BY HIS PARENTS, JOHN George Brown, and was rumored to be a son of Queen Victoria's John Brown of Scotland, first saw the Waterton Lakes in the late 1860's. He was in a hurry at the time since he was being chased by a party of hostile Indians, but he paused long enough to appreciate the beauty of the spot. He made a vow that he would return to Waterton Lakes to live just as soon as he shook off the redskins. And he did return to establish a trading post at the "Dardanelles" between the middle and lower lakes. He brought with him a beautiful French half-breed girl as his wife; but not very long after they had arrived at Waterton the wife died. Later Kootenai brought to his cabin a young squaw of the Cree tribe named Chee-Nee-Pay-Tha-Quo-Ka-Soon (Flash of Blue Lightning) who was his faithful wife until his death in 1916.

There are many, many folktales about Kootenai Brown. He was said to be an Oxford graduate and subsequently became army officer, convict, jailer, sailor, prospector, dispatch rider, interpreter, storekeeper, buffalo hunter, rancher, cowpuncher, gamewarden, park superintendent, and other things. He was certainly one of the first white men to cross the Canadian plains by pack horse. He earned his name Kootenaie (afterwards changed to Kootenai) as a result of his trading activities and masterful command of the language of the Kootenaie Indians.

He was a great tale-spinner, and one of the stories he was fond of telling was the saga of the discovery of oil in the mountains. The tale has slightly different versions, but here's the way Kootenai told it in 1914 to Mr. D. E. Cameron, librarian at the University of Alberta:

It seems that in 1876, Dr. Dawson of the Geological Survey, made a trip up to the Waterton Lakes and secured Kootenai as a guide through the wilderness. When leaving, Dawson asked Kootenai whether he had ever seen any indications of crude oil. Kootenai said he wouldn't know it if he saw it. Dawson took a bottle, put a little grease and kerosene oil in it, shook it up, and told Kootenai to smell the mixture. He asked Kootenai to let him know if in his travels among the mountains he ran across anything similar. Kootenai put the bottle on a shelf where it remained for a long time.

The Stoney Indians used to visit Waterton at regular intervals. One day when the Stoneys were there preparing for a hunt, Kootenai remembered the bottle Dawson had mixed for him. He had the Indians look at the mixture, smell it, and asked them to let him know if they discovered anything similar. Kootenai left Waterton himself to guide a party through the Kootenaie District in British Columbia, and the Indians went off on their hunt.

Later one Stoney Indian hunted up Kootenai Brown

and his party in the mountains and showed Kootenai a bottle containing crude oil. He explained that he had found it not far from Waterton, up Cameron Creek, where, he said, there was a pool of the stuff. Kootenai took the bottle home, put it on a shelf, and forgot about it.

Later still, he had a man working for him named Bill Aldridge. Aldridge was out cutting hay one day and suddenly reappeared at Kootenai's cabin to say that he'd have to go to Pincher Creek for oil. He had run out and the mower was running too hot. Kootenai said that he was going to Pincher Creek himself and would bring back oil. Aldridge then asked whether there was any oil on the place to tide him over that day. Kootenai at first said "no," but then he remembered the old bottle the Indian had given him, still on the shelf. He brought the bottle out and said, "Will this stuff do?"

Aldridge took out the cork and whiffed a big whiff. He looked startled and yelled, "Where did you get that stuff?" He had, apparently, been an oil man down in Texas and knew what the bottle contained. Kootenai told him where the pool was, and Aldridge at once exclaimed, "I quit!"

Aldridge immediately moved up to the pool where he built a shack, and for some years made his living by straining the oil through a gunny sack and selling it to farmers. Finally the place was taken over by an oil company which drilled a well.

One morning, while the well was being drilled, Kootenai was having his breakfast. Suddenly he heard a horse galloping up the trail from the lakes. He went out to meet the rider—a man from the drilling rig. The man

183

was very excited but managed to say, "You have to hitch up right away. Go to Pincher! We've struck a gusher! Get hold of the stock!"

The man was so excited he didn't even want Kootenai to finish his breakfast. Kootenai did finish, however, and while he was eating he was thinking that he'd like to see the gusher with his own eyes, so he saddled up and rode over to the derrick. When he came within sight of the well, he could see the crew standing around the derrick, almost paralyzed with excitement, with their eyes "poppin' out of their heads so far as you could hang yer hat on them!" In the middle of the circle, the oil was coming out in great bursts. "Whoosh!" right up to the top of the derrick. Then there'd be another great "Whoosh!" and another!

Kootenai wasted no time. He headed for Pincher Creek and fortune. But when he was nearing his own cabin, he heard a horse coming along behind him. The rider shouted to Kootenai to stop. The gusher had ceased to gush!

I am interested in some of the amendments to the tale that Kootenai told Mr. Cameron, and since they concern Kootenai's own region they'll bear telling.

Mr. J. Y. Card, son of the founder of the Mormon town of Cardston, told me that Mountain Bill (Bill Aldridge) had heard that there was oil in the mountains (presumably he was told by Kootenai). So Bill and his son Oliver, then about thirteen years old, set off to find it. They took their bedding and the proverbial frying pan and coffee pot, and tramped through the thick timber. One noon camp, the old gentleman sent Oliver to the creek

184

for a pail of water, while Bill built the fire. The boy shouted to his father, "Ah, Dad! Come on down here and see this black water!"

Bill trudged down to the creek to see the oil seepage in the wallow where the bears had been covering themselves with oil at the edge of the creek. Oid Bill tasted it, felt it, and smelt it. Then he said, "My gosh, boy, that's *ile!*"

Bill then threw a log across the creek, catching the oil as it seeped into what is now Cameron Brook. This done, he returned with some gunny sacks, dropped them flat on the surface where the oil was floating on the water, then he wrung them out into a barrel. He boiled the oil to get the water out and to thicken the drippings. He took the oil to Cardston—some forty miles—and sold it for lubricating oil, cough medicine, sore throat cure, sure-cure for pneumonia, and antiseptic gargle.

One time when Bill was returning from a trip to Cardston, he was taken very ill and was afraid he was going to die. He said to his boy, "Oliver, go to the jockey-box and get me a bottle of *ile!* It is sure to kill or cure!" He took two swallows of straight crude and was able to drive back to Waterton Lakes!

One time when I was visiting in Calgary, Dr. McNab of the Associate Clinic told me that he had a wonderful old man in the hospital I really should see. He took me to see Mr. A. P. Patrick, in his ninety-fourth year, who was rapidly recovering from a broken hip. Mr. Patrick had a whole regiment of beautiful nurses waiting on him and standing around listening to his yarns and blarney. I managed to push into the circle, and the first thing Mr.

Patrick told me was *his* version of finding the mountain oil. Mr. Patrick's account went something like this:

Kootenai fell in with some Stoney Indians and asked them about crude oil. "What is that?" asked the Indians. So Kootenai half filled a cup with blackstrap, added kerosene, stirred the sticky mess, and held it under their noses.

"If you see anything oozing out of the ground that looks and smells like that, you hustle and tell me!" Shortly after, the Indians reported finding an oil spring, and Kootenai staked a claim; then he forgot all about it.

Sometime later, Lafayette French (the same prospector who spent so much effort looking for the Lemon Mine) got hurt in the Waterton Lakes Country, and a squaw greased his wounds with a peculiar grease. French sniffed the scent of crude oil! A little later still, French ran into Patrick who had a ranch west of Calgary. French mentioned the accident and the salve. The two men hunted up the squaw and offered her a rifle and ponies if she would lead them to the oil.

They set out in the spring of that year, and by fall the squaw was still leading them around in the mountains "holding out" for the sake of the grub!

One morning French told the Indians that they were breaking camp—were going home. The squaw watched them go but suddenly discovered that they had taken all the grub! She rode like fury and overtook the white men.

"You lied to us," said French. "We intend to go home."

The squaw then said she would really lead them to the oil. Three days later they found it—saw a thin trickle of oil coming out at the foot of a spruce tree.

Patrick finally persuaded a British geologist at Calgary to come and inspect their discovery. The geologist got to within ten miles of the find and suddenly decided there couldn't be oil in such geological formations, and refused to go the rest of the way.

Meanwhile, Bill Aldridge had discovered the oil and set up a sort of little refinery on the spot, selling the oil as lighting fluid and medicine for men and beasts.

Finally Mr. Patrick interested John Lineham and J. K. Leeson, of Calgary, in his oil find. The Rocky Mountain Development Company was organized, and land purchased outright. A drilling outfit was purchased for $700 and was taken over a specially constructed road to the oil seepage.

Drilling was started in November, 1901. After drilling for ten months and reaching a depth of 1,010 feet, the oil was struck. Patrick estimated that the well flowed 300 barrels of crude a day. A small boom developed. Oil City—as the place was called—was, for a short time, a flourishing community!

A rival company was organized: the Pincher Creek Oil and Development Company, and this organization got hold of adjoining territory. To reach its lease, however, the Pincher Creek outfit had to cross the Rocky Mountain Company's lease. "They shall not pass!" was the cry. And when the Pincher Creek outfit attempted to pass one dark night, the boys of the Rocky Company turned out with sticks, stones, and guns to stop them. Wagons were broken up and harness cut to pieces.

The boom was soon over. The discovery well petered out, just as Kootenai Brown said it did. Anyway, the whole enterprise was impractical because of the bad roads, and the distance away from refineries.

Mr. Patrick, however, is still going strong and may at any time organize a new company to open up the Waterton oil fields!

Kootenai Brown was a noted pistol shot. Senator Dan Riley told me that one time he and his partner, Lafayette French, wanted to see Kootenai's horses, so they all walked down the path toward the lake and Kootenai's corral. As they walked along, two prairie chickens jumped into the trail and ran along ahead. Kootenai pulled his six-shooter and shot the birds while they were running—first one, then the other—shooting their heads off. He was never seen without his gun, a Colt's .45.

Senator Riley also mentioned that the Brown house was spotlessly clean. Chee-Nee-Pay-Tha-Quo-Ka-Soon was apparently a fine housekeeper. The story of this good Indian woman is so closely bound up to that of Kootenai that it is impossible to tell about one without mentioning the other.

Early one spring morning—nobody knows exactly when —the Indian woman who became Mrs. Brown left her prairie home in Saskatchewan to accompany her people to the mountains. They were going to visit relatives at Babb, Montana, and trade with a white man named Kootenai Brown. When the party reached Brown's place at Waterton, he was so fascinated by the pretty Cree maiden that he offered to trade five cayuses for her on the spot. The offer was accepted.

A folktale relates that Brown also proved his shrewdness that day, for after giving the Indians some firewater, he staged a pony race and won back his five cayuses.

188

Mrs. Brown's life with Kootenai was filled with romance and adventure. She was the envy of all the other Indian girls, because Kootenai kept her dressed in bright silks. He gave her many gifts of beads and rings and always treated her with respect. His pet name for her was Nitchimouse which means my good woman. He was the only one who could call her this pet name, and he saw to it that others called her Mrs. Brown. She never attempted to speak English, for fear someone would make fun of her, but she could understand almost anything anyone said to her.

Only one time was she unhappy. That was when Kootenai brought home a white girl. Mrs. Brown would not stand for that. She waited until Kootenai and the girl had gone hunting, then she piled all the household goods into the wagon, hitched up the ponies, and trekked back to her relatives at Babb. Kootenai followed very soon. Finally, after he promised that nothing like that would ever happen again, she agreed to go home.

She bore a deep love for Kootenai. When he was dying, he told her that if he could, he would return in the form of an eagle.

Mrs. Brown waited eagerly for this to happen. Brown died in 1916, and sometime afterward the first airplane to come into that part of the mountains landed near Waterton. As Mrs. Brown saw the great bird skimming over the trees, she thought Kootenai had come back to her. She rushed over to a neighbor's place, calling, "Kootenai Kootenai! He come! He come!" Then she ran toward the machine. When she reached it, she stroked it all over, murmuring, "Kootenai—Kootenai—"

189

They say she stayed by the machine all night long.

Kootenai is buried near Chief Mountain with his two wives. It is a fitting place for the sleep of a legendary figure; for Chief Mountain itself is rich in legends. It was here that the spirit of the Great West Wind had his home, and in a fierce encounter with a hero of the East, hurled the great rocks which form a direct line for about forty miles eastward.

III

❦

The Death of a Prophet

THE REVEREND GEORGE MCDOUGALL WAS ONE OF THE pioneering missionaries of Alberta. His missionary zeal sent him on endless journeys; but sometimes he would take time off from his missionary work to make a prophecy. He prophesied that Edmonton would become a great city. He instinctively knew that the beautiful Canadian Rockies would draw a vast tourist trade, and that the West would some day come into its heritage.

Among other missions he established, or helped to establish, was the Stoney Indian Mission at Morley, under the shadow of the great peaks. The establishment of the Morley Mission was one of the Reverend's last works, and it was near Morley that he died.

His son, Dr. John McDougall, no less a zealous worker than his father, tells the story of George McDougall's death—itself one of the sagas of the foothills.

*"Early in the new year (1876) he (George McDougall) returned to Morley, bringing word that the buffalo were now moving westward, and that this was now an oppor-

---

*From *George Millwaid McDougall*, by John McDougall, Ryerson Press, Toronto. Reprinted by permission.

191

tune time for striking for meat, and as this was very much wanted by our party, arrangements were made to go out. Horses were driven in, sleighs mended, and, at the last minute, the man we expected to go with us was not forthcoming. In vain we looked for another, and then father said, 'I will go with you, for we must have meat—'

"On the third day we came to the buffalo. The condition of the prairie for running with unshod horses was very bad. The weather was extremely cold. However, we secured some animals; but Saturday morning found us with about half loads, and the weather getting colder all the while. We saw that the buffalo were slowly moving westward; we concluded to go back without teams to the first point of willows, where we could get wood, and there spend the Sabbath, hoping that the weather would moderate, and the buffalo draw nearer. We spent a quiet Sabbath in our leather lodge. Our party numbered five. An Indian and his boy, about twelve years of age, had joined us to obtain meat for themselves. Our party proper was composed of father and his nephew, a lad he had brought from Ontario on his last trip, and the writer.

"Monday morning, from a hill alongside of our camp, we could see buffalo. Father and I, taking four sleighs with us, and a little wood on one of them, and two loose horses for running, started out towards them. The Indian and his son, with one sleigh, accompanied us. We left my cousin to look after the camp and watch the horses. The weather had moderated some, but the prairie was still very bad for unshod horses.

"Coming as near as we could without starting the buffalo, father took charge of the horses and sleighs, and

I attempted to run, but so slippery was the prairie with its patches of snow and ice everywhere, that the sharper hoofed buffalo could get away from the unshod horse.

"Changing horses three times, getting one tremendous fall, which shook me up pretty well all over, I eventually succeeded in killing six buffalo. The Indian had not been successful. We gave him one and began the work of skinning and cutting up the other five. It was now late in the afternoon. We had butchered and put on to the sleighs three of the buffalo. We were at the fourth. While I was working at this one, father said, 'I think I will melt some snow, John, and boil the kettle, and we will have a cup of coffee—'

The coffee drunk, we went at the buffalo again. Just as we were finishing the fourth animal, we heard the Indian call, and answering him, he came to us with his sled loaded with the animal which had been given him. Altogether then we moved on to the fifth animal, and now, with the Indian's help we soon had this one skinned and cut up and loaded on the sleigh. This being done, I put my running pad on one of the loose horses, and gathering up the lariat attached to the halter, handed it to father, expecting him to ride. We then started for camp.

"As I walked behind the last sleigh, father would ride beside me, or, dismounting, sometimes walk.

"We came to the valley of the Nose Creek. Here there was a long incline to the creek. The Indian started off on a run before his horse, and I cracked my whip, and sent my horses after him. Father had been walking when we came to the top of the hill, and as the rest of us ran down the slope, we left him some distance behind. We crossed the creek, and were nicely strung out on the flat on the other side of it, and as fast as we could were making our way to the gently rising hill near the summit of which our camp was situated. I should judge we were about two miles from camp, when father, having mounted his horse, came up at a gallop. Instead of stopping behind, he rode alongside. I said, 'Father, are you going on?' 'Yes,' said he. 'I think I will go and get supper ready. That bright star there is right over our camp, is it not?' I looked, and answered, 'Yes.' It was impossible for me to think that he could go astray. The landmarks were extremely good; the night was not stormy. Away he rode into the darkness. Little did I think that I had spoken to my father for the last time in this world.

"We went on to our camp until we were within two hundred yards of it. When I came in sight of the spot I saw no light; my heart misgave me. I rushed the horses up to the tent, and shouted, 'Father; father; Moses; Moses.' (This was the name of my cousin we had left in the camp that morning.) But no answer came. I jumped into the lodge. There was no fire. I felt around, and found the boy buried under the buffalo robes, evidently having become frightened as night came on. I shook him up. Said I, 'Moses, did father come?' He said, 'No, I have not seen him!' I jumped out and grasped my rifle, which I had fastened on one of the sleighs, and fired several shots in rapid succession. I told the Indian to shoot off his old flint-lock, and he did so repeatedly, putting in large charges of powder. Then I said to myself, how foolish to get so excited. If father had missed the camp, he will be in before I can get these horses unharn-

194

essed; or he has ridden past to hunt up our horses we left here today; and with this thought I went to work and unharnessed the horses, and disposed of them for the night. But no father came. We did the best we could.

"The next morning, with the first peep of daylight, I found the horses, and was glad to see that the one he had ridden was not with them, for I had thought that father might have been thrown and hurt badly, and if so, the horse would come to his partners. He was not there, and again I said to myself, it is now daylight, and by the time I get these horses back to camp father will be there; but he didn't come. The Indian and myself scoured the country the whole day. We did it systematically. The Indian was a first-class moose-hunter. I was no novice in such work. Evening came without a clue; then I said, father missed the camp last night, and passing on up to the ridge west of us, Morley would appear so near to him this morning, that he concluded to go right on to the mission. Someone will come out to meet us tomorrow. This was my theory; the Indian thought so, too. Since Sunday the weather had been moderating.

"Monday night, when father left us, it was comparatively fine. Tuesday was a beautiful winter's day. Tuesday at midnight the weather was still fine. Shortly after this the wind changed, and a most terrific northwest storm set in. It was impossible to move on the plains. Sheltered as we were in the valley, we had hard work to keep the fire going. We said, 'No one will start from Morley today.' The storm continued all day, and a greater part of the following night.

"Thursday morning bright and early, we started for

home. Getting my party fairly on the way, I left them to come on, and hurried home, reaching there late Thursday night, but father was not there. Then he must have gone to Calgary. We hurried down to Calgary. There were no tidings of him. We secured help and began the search. Saturday afternoon we found the horse. Saturday night we heard from some half-breeds that they had seen a man leading a horse, the whole description corresponding to him and his horse. The time they had seen him was on Tuesday afternoon. Some continued the search, and others went for more help, and on Sunday we had all the available force we could get out on the search, but the weather became intensely cold, and Sunday night we had to fall back on Calgary for food and wood.

"We then saw the necessity of better equipment, and went home and gathered in all our available horses and sleighs, and starting out with all the men we could get, we camped on the spot, and continued the search.

"The following Sunday I was riding up a coulee, had dismounted and tied my horse, so that I might search the clump of brush I found there. Presently I heard some one shouting; running out, and getting on to my horse and moving up the hill, I found it was the man next to me in the line of search.

"Said he to me, 'They are making signs to me over yonder.'

" 'Ah,' I thought, 'father is alive.' I had not yet given him up. When I reached the now rapidly congregating party, my poor broken down brother said, 'Oh, John, father is dead; they have found his frozen body.' A half-breed, one who was not with us on the search, but was out hunting, had killed a buffalo, and going back to his camp, had taken his horse and sleigh and was making a bee line as much as possible to where his buffalo lay, and in so doing drove right on to father's lifeless body. He put him on the sleigh, and took him back to his camp, and sent us word. Soon we stood beside the lifeless form. A kind native woman had spread her shawl over it. I lifted the shawl, and as I saw the position in which he had frozen, I said, 'Just like him; he was thoughtful of others, even at the last moment.' As I looked at him and beheld his features, I said, 'Whatever may have happened to father, toward the last he was conscious, and feeling that death was upon him; he had picked a post as level as he could, and laid himself out straight upon it, and crossing his hands, had thus prepared to die.' His face was perfectly natural. There seemed to me to be the expression upon it of conscious satisfaction. Reverently we lifted him and laid him on the sleigh, and solemnly we started on that Sunday afternoon on our homeward journey . . .

"It was a sorrowful company that bore his remains to the grave. With trembling utterance we laid him in, in sure and certain hope of a glorious resurrection. His work is finished but not forgotten, nor yet will it be."

The old church still stands at Morley, and the wind has a lonely sound as it whistles past the tall, thin steeple. On the hillside above the church, George McDougall lies in his grave, and many who pass on the busy Calgary-Banff highway have scarcely heard of him at all. But George McDougall is doubtless watching the traffic flowing into the mountains. Perhaps he is smiling; for his prophecy has come true.

IV

❦

Tales of Foothill and Mountain

JOHNNY CHINOOK IS A FAMOUS YARN SPINNER. HIS TALES
are accepted as gospel truth over the length and breadth
of Alberta, and have, of course, taken their rightful place
as part of the permanent folk history of the Province.*

Like most good yarn spinners, Johnny borrows the
sources of many of his tales from other regions, or from
the classics of the tall tale. This doesn't make his yarns
any less indigenous to Alberta, however, since Johnny
gives the tales his own particular twists in keeping with
the geography and the climate.

The best known tall story in Alberta is the one Johnny
tells about the chinook. There had been a big snowfall
—one of the biggest in history. The snow was so deep
that it covered all of Morley church except the tip of the
steeple. The Indians would come to church, tie their
horses to the steeple, go down through a snow tunnel to
the door of the church, and so inside.

One day during the big snow, Johnny had to go to
Calgary. He harnessed the horse, hitched him to the

---

*Johnny's tales are variously attributed to Fred Stimson, Dave McDougall,
Jack Symonds, an Irishman named Conley, and others.

sleigh, and set out. When he was about half way to Calgary, he heard a rustling noise. He knew what that was. It was a chinook stealing up behind him. He whipped up the horse, but the harder he whipped, the harder blew the chinook wind. The snow melted like magic!

"Boys," says Johnny, " 'Twas all I could do to keep the front runners on the snow! Those back runners was raisin' a hell of a dust storm!"

And the Indians in Morley church had a terrible shock when they came outside. The snow was all gone, and there were their horses dangling down from the steeple like Christmas bells!

Of course that wasn't the only experience Johnny had with the chinooks. Another time he was going from Morley to Calgary, and a chinook slipped up behind him. "I was sittin' in the front o' my wagon," says Johnny, "and by drivin' like blazes I was able to keep ahead o' that chinook and got my feet frozen. But I had a squaw ridin' in the back o' the wagon, and she got a sun stroke!"

One time Johnny was camping in the foothills. He was completely out of provisions. He'd had nothing at all to eat for several days and had only one bullet left for his gun. He hunted day after day and found no game. Toward evening one day, when he was very weak from starvation, he came to a tree on which a flock of partridges were perched, all on one limb. He took careful aim but missed the birds. The bullet, however, split the limb on which the birds were roosting. As the two parts of the limb came together, they caught all the birds by their feet.

The tree was beside the river bank, and as Johnny was wringing the necks of the birds, he slipped and fell into the stream. There was a large school of fish swimming in the water below the tree. Johnny's clothes were somewhat loose, and a great many fish lodged between his stomach and trousers.

When he was climbing out of the stream, a button snapped off his trousers and hit a moose in the eye. This so startled the moose that Johnny was able to kill it with an ax.

Johnny says the moral of this tale is: *You never know when your luck'll change!*

Johnny's experiences are truly remarkable. In the old days when he wanted fish, he merely took off his red wool socks and dangled them in the water. When the fish struck at the socks, Johnny would flip them out onto the bank.

One time Johnny was crossing the Bow River on the ice which was leathery and quite thin. It was a wonder how he got across at all! When he was about half way over, he heard a queer thumping noise under the ice.

"I stopped," says Johnny, "to look into the matter, and what do you suppose it was? 'Twas a big bull trout, jumpin' at the red in my moccasins! Do you know, I told that to a man the other day, and he said I was a liar. The ignorance of some people is shockin'!"

"And 'tis not generally known," Johnny continues, "that a cyclone passed through the Morley reservation some twenty years ago. 'Twas a corker! A squaw was standin' right in the path o' the cyclone, and the swirl o' the blast swept under her blanket and carried her 10,000 feet into the sky. There she spun like a top until she reached the outer rim o' the cyclone where I reckon the pressure wasn't so great. She descended gently and easily to the ground just like a parachute! I was standin' close by at the time and saw the occurrence which, you'll admit, was a mighty strange one."

One of the biggest fish Johnny ever caught was a pike that weighed forty-seven pounds. When he was cleaning the pike, Johnny found seven whitefish inside it, and *each whitefish weighed six pounds!*

One time Johnny was driving his heavy wagon up a hill on which there were a lot of trees. Suddenly his mules played out. The wagon started to roll back, but the quick thinking mules grabbed hold of the trees with their teeth and saved the day!

Johnny says that when the C. P. R. was building, the railroad men simply followed the tracks of his old Red River Cart across the prairie.

One of Johnny's best yarns is the one he tells about the *hot winter.*

"I'd just come to Calgary from Renfrew County," relates Johnny, "and was just fixin' to get me a homestead. It was about August then and I got a job harvestin', no binders nor nothin'—all hand cradled. Got a bit of a grubstake to tide me over the winter and a shack by the Elbow.

"Well, the fall was mighty warm, just like summer. It cooled off a little early in October, though we was mostly workin' in shirt sleeves when we worked. Middle of December came and no snow. In fact it was warmer 'n ever. Some of the boys began to plant a few potatoes just to see what happened. When they started to sprout, a lot of the homesteaders caught on and put in wheat and some garden stuff.

"Crops come up all right and by February were doin' fine. We got rain 'stead of snow, not unusual considerin' the weather was like one long chinook. Biggest trouble we had was with mosquitoes. The danged things was as big as sparrows by now, not havin' died off in the fall like they usually do. It got so we carried baseball bats to fight 'em off. They was too fat to fly much, just buzzed around slow like.

"Come spring the boys decided not to do no spring sowin' 'cause the winter-sown stuff was doin' so well. Began to get purty risky by midsummer, though. Potatoes up to your shoulder and wheat with stems like small willers. It come mighty hot in August, and, fearin' fires, we had to cut the grain with bucksaws. The straw made fine drainpipes once it dried out.

"We decided to take up the spuds by September, and that was a job. The little ones we could lift, but the big ones we just heaved up with a crowbar and let 'em lay. Carrots we drawed with a block and tackle. Feller south of me covered over a coulee to make a root house. Had to use a well sweep for a flail to thresh the grain.

" 'Twas mighty lucky we had such a good crop 'cause next year there wasn't any summer at all."

\Animals figure in a lot of the tales. Johnny once had a pet beaver. The beaver was such a fast woodcutter and so neat a stacker that Johnny was able to hire him out to the neighbors. One day Johnny went away on a short visit and left the beaver locked in the cabin. The beaver cooked and ate his supper, but somehow he had never been trained to shut off the water. When Johnny returned, the beaver was dead. He had drowned.

But when Johnny was living at Rocky Mountain House, he encountered what was probably the most industrious beaver in history. This beaver worked so hard and so long that Johnny feared the beaver would cut down every last tree on his homestead. So with true western ingenuity Johnny solved the whole problem. He simply lighted a lantern and hung it out on a tree—thinking that this would frighten Mr. Beaver away. But when Johnny went out next morning he got a terrible shock. The lantern light was just what the beaver needed. With the added illumination, he had cut twice as many trees!

As a mountaineer Johnny has a neat way of catching grizzly bears. He first bores a hole in a tree trunk, fills the hole with honey, and from a limb sticking out above the hole, he ties a stout rope. To the rope he ties a large rock so that the rock is hanging close to the honey-filled hole. After a while a grizzly will come along. He is hungry and smells the honey. He gives the rock a little push with his paw, and it swings back and hits him a little tap. This annoys the bear, and he gives it a harder push. He receives a harder tap. He is really annoyed now and gives the rock a still harder push. He receives a severe smack. The bear is fighting mad. He gives the rock a terrific push, and it swings back and bats his brains out. Johnny then hurries over and carries away the bear.

In much the same manner Johnny secures rabbits. A bare spot is found with a big, round rock in the center. Over this rock he spills a lot of black pepper. Then he puts a shiny object on top of the rock and retires to await results. Along comes bunny. He spots the shiny object. Up go his long ears. Presently his curiosity is too much for him and he hops over to the rock to investigate. He leans down to look at the object and gets a strong whiff of pepper. His head goes back. He lets out a terrific sneeze and knocks his head against the rock. Johnny then goes over and carries bunny home.

But some of the mountain creatures display remarkable intelligence. One very cold day Johnny was strolling through the timber. Suddenly ahead of him on a rock, he saw what he thought was an insane woodpecker. The bird would stand on the rock, do a kind of Charleston shuffle, and then he would peck the rock very hard. As Johnny came closer he saw that the bird was far from crazy. When he pecked the rock, a lot of sparks would fly, warming the stone. The woodpecker then shuffled his feet around, absorbing all the heat.

Another example of animal intellect was displayed by a deer that used to hang around Johnny's house when he lived in Banff. Banff is, of course, in the park, and the animals are protected. But this deer became so friendly and Johnny so hungry for venison that a dastardly scheme was evolved. Each day when the deer appeared Johnny would go out with a hammer, hold it under the deer's nose, swing it around, and in general accustom the deer to the hammer. Finally the day arrived when the deer would let Johnny do whatever he wanted to with the hammer—swing it in any way he wished. The time had thus arrived when venison would grace Johnny's table. On the appointed morning, the deer appeared as usual. Johnny went out with his hammer. He lifted it and swung down a terrific blow. Wisely, but very gracefully, the deer turned his head; the hammer landed against

Johnny's leg. In the hospital with a badly broken bone Johnny swore never to molest a deer again.

Continuing the animal theme, Johnny tells how in 1873 he was traveling through the mountains. One night he unpacked his four horses and his saddle mare and hobbled them in a meadow. He enjoyed a good supper of trout and turned in. In the middle of the night he was awakened by a bloodcurdling roar. He jumped out of his blankets and saw two fierce eyes staring at him. Of course Johnny wasn't afraid. He knew the eyes belonged to a big grizzly. He merely got his lasso and roped her. She dragged him fifty miles up and down the mountains before he got her broke to ride. When he rode the bear back to camp, he found that another grizzly and her cubs had eaten all his grub except some prunes. His saddle was still there and also his rifle.

It was getting light by that time, so he went out after his horses. The bears had eaten all the horses, so he saddled up the grizzly he had roped and started on his way. That afternoon he saw several elk grazing on a meadow. He needed meat, but on looking for his bullets Johnny found that they had disappeared. With amazing intelligence he chewed a prune and rammed the seed into his muzzle-loader. He took careful aim and hit a bull elk in the neck, killing him on the spot.

That night Johnny and his trained grizzly had a delicious feast. The elk meat was flavored with prunes!

Johnny loves to relate yarns about the high winds. "One day when we were on the roundup," begins Johnny, "a heck of a wind started to blow. I knew it was going to be a humdinger, so I picked out the biggest beef I could find and slung it back of my saddle to hold down the horse and keep us from being blowed away. The other boys saw what I was doing and they did the same. The wind blew so cold, and so hard, and so long, that all of us got pneumonia, and all them other fellers kicked off till I was left alone.

"The wind blew for days, but me and the horse and that beef stuck together. Barns, houses, chickens, fences, and all kinds of things kept blowing past us; but the funniest thing of all was an old feller asettin' in a rockin' chair, sailing along through the air. As he came nigh me, he yelled for a match to light his pipe. By the time I'd dug through three inches of dirt in my jeans, he was out of sight. Pretty soon a telephone came blowing by, so I grabbed it and told the operator in the next township that an old feller in a rocking chair was heading that way and would she see to it that somebody had a light ready for his pipe.

"The storm finally blew itself out, so I dumped off the steer and rounded up the 10,000 head of cattle that had drifted for more 'n a 100 miles! When I got 'em home to the ranch, I saw a big hat lying on the ground, so I picked it up. Under it was my old friend still in his rocking chair and puffing away at his pipe. 'Ah,' I said, 'so you got a match!'

" 'Oh, no,' he said, 'but I got her going just the same. They gave me one of them new-fangled cigarette lighters. It lights my pipe fine, but it ain't so good for pickin' my teeth!' "

If you don't care for high wind stories, you may prefer Johnny's yarns about the plenitude of buffalo, insects, and frogs.

"Buffalo?" says Johnny, "Why, there was more buffalo in the old days 'n you ever dreamt of. I once seen 100,000,000 buffalo all at one time. Yes, sir, me and forty-two other men was caught in that stampedin' herd for eight days. Had to keep firin' our rifles all that time to keep from bein' tramped under. Well, we finally got away to the top o' a high hill. 'Twas a good thing we did, for when we got up there we could see the *main herd comin'*!"

Yes, the buffalo were plentiful in the early days, but they weren't so plentiful as the mosquitoes. Johnny tells me that the pests were so thick that when he built a smudge fire he'd have to take a long stick and twirl it through the dense cloud of insects so the smoke could ascend!

But if the buffalo and the mosquitoes were plentiful, so were the frogs. Johnny relates how, one year, his crops were drowned out. His fields were completely flooded. To make matters worse, a plague of frogs arrived to inhabit the pools around his farm. Then suddenly winter came—as it does in Alberta—and just as the frost hardened the surface of the sloughs the frogs leaped into the water and were frozen solid with their hind feet in the air. Johnny merely took out his lawn mower, cut himself ten bushels of frog legs to the acre, and lived lusciously until spring!*

If you don't care for the Johnny Chinook wonders already related, you may at least admire Johnny's tale of the famous Jasper high jump. Johnny was calmly walking

---

*This tale is also told about Keuka Lake in Central New York. The lake is shallow and is supposed to freeze very rapidly.

along a mountain trail when he was suddenly confronted by a huge grizzly. Thinking of nothing better to do, Johnny let out a whoop and began to run—*the other way.* The bear ran, too—*in the same direction.* Johnny thought he was done for, but away down ahead of him he saw a lone tree with a branch sticking out. The branch was over thirty feet from the ground. The bear was gaining at every jump but Johnny put on a final desperate burst of speed and jumped for that limb.

"Did you catch it?" asked his friends.

"Sure did," Johnny replied, "caught 'er *on the way down!*"

Anyone who knows the mountains will hear, along with the humorous tales, many Indian legends. There is a very beautiful legend about Castle Mountain, twenty miles from Banff, where the chinook wind is said to have her home. The chinook is the little blind daughter of the great southwind. Sometimes in the dead of winter, the little chinook steals out of her hiding place in the Castle and blows through the mountain passes down onto the frozen flatlands, bringing with her a temporary springtime.

The Stoney Indians also have a beautiful legend about Lake Louise. When the world was very young, giants peopled the earth. A certain giant chief, a very famous hunter, was never satisfied with the number of animal monsters killed by his arrows or caught in his snares.

One day he saw a rainbow in the sky. The more he watched it, the more he wanted it, because he believed it would make him a magic bow. Climbing the tallest tree on earth, he tore the rainbow from its place, but when he grasped it, the colors melted. In exasperated anger, the giant dashed the rainbow against the nearest rocky peak, and it fell shattered to the bottom of the nearest lake. The gods of the elements then made another arch to hold up the sky when it rained, but the colors of the shattered rainbow are still seen spreading through the waters of Lake Louise.

One other mountain story might be mentioned. It concerns an interesting ghost town near Castle Mountain. Very few persons passing the mountain station on the C. P. R. know that the once flourishing boom town of Silver City stood nearby; there is nothing to show where it was except a faint trace of the main street, filled-in cellars, old wells, and bits of rubble. But the old-timers in Banff will tell you that in 1883-84 Silver City hoped to be one of the really great towns of the West.

In 1881 a prospector named Joe Healey saw a Stoney Indian with a specimen of ore and induced him to show him where it had been found. Healey spread the news around, and when the railroad came through in 1883, the great trek to Silver City began.

Actually, not much silver was found. Some copper was located, and thousands of dollars spent in different wild-cat developments, none of which came to anything. The romance of Silver City is not a romance of wealth but of golden dreams and high hopes. Some of the mines had names like Queen o' the Hill and Home Stake. It is said that the Queen o' the Hill was a salted mine. One of the principal shareholders of this mine was offered $20,000 for his share, but he refused, hoping for a larger profit. A month later his share wasn't worth a cent.

When Silver City was abandoned, the boards and logs of the houses were scattered far and wide. Some of them went to Banff; some were used by the railroad for section shacks; the prairies got some of them for homesteaders' houses. And of the 1,000 men and women who once inhabited Silver City, no one is left. Until recently, Joe Smith, one of the original prospectors, lived there all alone; but now Joe is gone, too. The wind, the gophers, and Castle Mountain watch over Silver City.

V

Rocky Mountain House

THERE IS NO DOUBT IN MY OWN MIND: ROCKY MOUNTAIN House leads Alberta in the export of curious news items, friendliness to strangers, and that special atmosphere that breeds adventure. Perhaps David Thompson, the explorer, touched that region with a magic wand when he wintered at the Fort on his way to the Pacific. Possibly the old Indians endowed the place with their magic; or perhaps the spell goes farther back, to the time when the Rocky Mountains were forming. Draw your own conclusions but take it from me, there's witchery at Rocky Mountain House.

I had heard so much about this fabulous spot that I almost hesitated about visiting it. Perhaps I had a fear that a mysterious portal would open, and like the fabled traveler of old, I would find myself shut within some mystic cavern.

I must confess that this romantic nonsense was mostly shaken out of me by the C. P. R. when I rode their thrice-weekly train from Red Deer to Rocky.

The spell came back, though, when I arrived. I was met at the train by the young school inspector, Finlay

Barnes, who carried me off to a typical Rocky Mountain House dinner, and delicious fare it was—baked moose meat with dumplings and mountain blueberry pie. In the evening I made a little talk in the Legion Hall and was not at all surprised when a large dog, named Skipper, came gravely in and seated himself on the platform. The townsfolk also took Skipper's presence as a matter of course and I was informed that the dog was *especially* fond of music—Bach and Beethoven were his favorite composers—but that he attended every meeting of more than two persons and seemed to know beforehand when meetings and concerts were going to take place.

I was much impressed by Skipper, especially when he arose and offered to shake hands just before I began to speak. I told the audience, "When the dog walks out, it will be time for me to stop speaking." I had spoken perhaps six words when Skipper gravely stalked off the platform and walked toward the door. I hurriedly said something about the excellence of a dog's standards of judgment and brought Skipper to a halt half way down the aisle. He thought the matter over, finally decided to stick it out, and even offered to shake hands again when the talk was over. *Some* dog! But not unusual for Rocky. They accept Skipper just as they accept the Ogopogo.

For my less well-informed reader perhaps I should explain that the Ogopogo is a horrible monster which lives beneath the waters of the North Saskatchewan River and has special headquarters at Rocky Mountain House. He or she—they've never been able to determine which—in much larger than the *Okanagan Lake* Ogopogo in British Columbia and much more fierce and terrifying than those rather meek Ogopogos occasionally seen in Ontario.

A hint as to the great serpent's sex I found in one account which tells of the Ogopogo having been seen shortly before freeze-up last fall, swimming toward Edmonton with six little Ogopogos happily trailing along in the wake. This, I would suppose, seems to imply that the Ogopogo is a female. I mentioned this tale to a citizen of Rocky who immediately began to suspect the presence of a second Ogopogo—a male.

The Rocky Ogopogo was, apparently, first viewed by an Indian named Chief Walking Eagle who, staggering into town one day in 1939, gasped that a "fish fifty feet long, and as big around as an elephant" had pursued him across the river!

When asked where he got the "fire water," Walking Eagle became most indignant and recited numerous of his Christian virtues, which settled the matter as far as Rocky was concerned. Folks knew that Chief Walking Eagle was telling the truth.

Unfortunately, the river was frozen over when I visited Rocky, and I was not able to catch a glimpse of the monster. I have promised, however, to return during the month of May when the Rocky folks have promised to have a special showing of the Ogopogo for my benefit. I haven't a doubt in the world that they'll really produce a monster. They do such things at Rocky.

One time—back in 1927 to be exact—the gods of the plain and mountain became angry with Rocky. Why this should be so I have not been able to discover. Possibly it was because the region hadn't furnished its usual tribute of mystic events that year. Whatever it was, it was enough to cause the gods to loose a terrific cyclone on the village. Cyclones were usual in Kansas where I grew up, but at Rocky a cyclone seems to me to be the deliberate act of an outraged deity.

The cyclone struck in July after a long spell of oppressive hot weather. The storm swooped down about three o'clock in the afternoon and caught the town entirely unprepared. Folks simply didn't know what was happening. One fellow ran into the open vault of the bank, while another hopped into a big icebox and slammed it shut. Another man grabbed at the nearest object, the knob of a door. The wind blew the door away and left him holding the knob. A schoolboy was out in the woodshed when the storm hit. The cyclone blew the building away, leaving the boy standing there with his arms full of kindling wood. The wooden sidewalks along the main street actually changed sides! Down at Ross's garage, an envelope blew right into a plank—so far they had to dig it out with a jackknife. They didn't dig it out right away, of course. As a matter of fact, it stayed there quite a while and became one of the local wonders.

One lady, who knew about cyclones from living in South Dakota, was out in the yard. She took one look at the approaching storm, knew what to expect, grabbed her baby and dove for the cellar. She heard the storm hit, knew the house was shaking. Presently when it was over she climbed the cellar steps, only to find that the trapdoor was no longer there. The house had moved six feet! Her husband had to cut a hole in the floor to get her out.

The children at Rocky were especially delighted to find

the storm had carried away the curfew bell. The bell hasn't been found to this day, but the kids didn't know when they had a good thing, for now a whistle is blown for curfew.

One whole side of Main Street was demolished—with a single exception. One store was left undamaged. The Indians were so impressed by this obvious sign of the Great Spirit's favor that they took their trade to that store for years.

But the unusual applies to *individuals* as well as to Ogopogos and cyclones.

At Rocky I encountered what I believe to be the only "tree man" in Canada. His name is John Eagle. He doesn't live in the tree anymore, but he did until it blew down. You see, John Eagle used to be a sailor. He traveled around the world more than a dozen times, saw just about everything there is to see in the world, and came to settle down in a tree at Rocky Mountain House. He was tired of the ocean and the cities. He explained:

"You see too many strangers in the cities, and too much of too few strangers on a ship. The noise and crowds are worse than the wolves and bears."

He wanted solitude. At first he lived in a tent, but one night a high wind arose and blew the tent down on him. At the same time he fancied he heard the howling of wolves. He climbed a tree and spent the night there. The swaying of the tree reminded him of the swaying of the ocean. He got a wonderful idea! He would build a house in the tree.

He began the house the next day. First he built a platform, and on the platform he set a tidy little cabin.

215

He insulated it with shavings from the planing mill, and finally, he had a warm, comfortable dwelling. Fuel was the biggest problem, but he solved it by leaning poles up against the platform, pulling them up, and sawing them on his own doorstep!

Sawing wood makes me remember the tale about a former inhabitant of Rocky who bore the impressive name, Silas K. Vandermark. Silas came from Oklahoma where he was said to have extensive oil holdings. This was evidenced by the rolls of money he occasionally had in his possession but not by his appearance; for Silas was a man who had a horror of washing. So great was his affinity for earth, in fact, that he lived in a dugout some little distance from Rocky. When that dugout fell in, Silas simply dug another and crawled into it.

It is generally thought that Vandermark's family wanted to get rid of him, so when buying him a railroad ticket, they just touched a spot on the map. To my mind, their selection of Rocky was not chance; it was simply magic. The fuel problem was easily solved by Silas K. Vandermark. He would merely draw a pole up to the entrance of his dugout, stick it through the door and into the opening of his stove. Whenever the log burned off, he would just shove it in a little farther. This absolutely eliminated any wood cutting. His kitchen economy also showed ingenuity. Silas would kill a pig and hang it up in a tree. He never bothered to dress the pig at all; he'd merely walk out and cut off his morning bacon, ham, or whatever he was after, and let the rest hang. He never built any sort of shelter for his pigs and horses. He simply took the pigs into his cave with him and would have done the same thing for the horses had there been space.

216

In spite of his many eccentricities Silas was most kind-hearted and always insisted on offering a visitor something to eat. Not many cared to partake, but they appreciated the gesture just the same.

He would have certain Rocky businessmen write letters for him, but he never let the man who wrote a letter read the answer received; that he took to someone else.

Whenever Silas got a shipment of money from his Oklahoma oil fields, he would attend local auction sales. He bought large quantities of junk; though what he ever did with it, nobody knew!

One time his money was late in arriving, so Silas was forced to look for a job. He went to a lumber boss and applied, but the boss was not impressed with Silas' appearance. He handed Silas a bar of soap and said, "Here. Scrub. Shave. Get a haircut. Come back and I'll give you clean underwear, overalls, and maybe a job." Of course, Silas refused. He stated indignantly that no job was worth that much. He went back to his cave; soon afterward more money arrived from Oklahoma. Nevermore was Silas forced to humble himself in that manner.

When he finally died from pneumonia brought on by the general atmosphere and condition of his dugout, he had no money. What did he do with the sums which he received from Oklahoma? He certainly didn't spend them. It's a fact that he neither drank nor smoked. His only expense was auction goods, and all he bought was junk. Did he bury his money? Well, a lot of Rocky Mountain House citizens think he did. In fact, looking for Silas' money is a favorite summer sport!

Rocky Mountain House has two railroads. When I

remarked that this was an interesting if not an astounding fact, I was told about the famous "Battle of Horburg" which once furnished excitement, not to mention comedy, on a battlefield sixteen miles long—from Rocky westward to Horburg.

The Canadian National Railway was on the job first and had some twenty miles of grade completed west of Red Deer before the Alberta Central awoke to the fact that a competitor was seriously threatening its territory. The Alberta Central at once began a railway of its own.

The old settlers were amazed! For a long time they had been dreaming of a railroad, but here, in the wink of an eye, were *two* railroads working day and night to beat the other out! The citizens lapsed into happy anticipation of two payrolls, two bridges across the Saskatchewan, two gangs of laborers to feed—in fact, double of everything! They didn't mind that the two railways would be easily within whistling distance of each other!

In 1911 the C. N. R. was far in the lead. They had, in fact, laid tracks to within a mile of Rocky Mountain House. Here, however, they encountered their first serious obstacle in the form of a new piece of grade that cut right across the C. N. R. location. To the C. N. R. boys the solution was simple and direct. At night they tore the barricade away. By day the Alberta Central boys built it up again.

All this was done with good humor. As T. C. Hargrave, writing in the *Calgary Herald,* says: "On the one side were Swedes, Norwegians, Austrians, Italians; on the other side were Italians, Austrians, Norwegians, and Swedes. The battle was on, according to our old-timers, until the ties

218

had been turned four ways and were plumb wore out!"

The river, of course, had to be crossed before any train could run on to Horburg, but the Alberta Central didn't wait to build a bridge just then. They sent gangs across and built a couple more barricades on the other side of the river at right angles to the C. N. R. right-of-way.

This didn't stop the C. N. R. boys. They jumped the river, too; and both outfits began playing leapfrog with stretches of track clear on to Horburg.

The Alberta Central, however, was first to attempt bridging the river. This was an expensive undertaking, since their own rails did not yet run even to Rocky Mountain House. They'd been too busy checkmating the C. N. R.!

So the citizens of Rocky saw their pastures turn even greener. Cement must be hauled from Red Deer, Lacombe, Innisfail, and Bowden for the new bridge; and it must be hauled by teams, since nothing could be hauled on the C. N. R. rails.

The cement was hauled, but it was not easy; the roads were nothing but bogs. The mules died off under the strain. Oxen were the only animals which could stand up under the heavy loads of cement. As Mr. Hargrave says: "Skinners left the Calgary and Edmonton Railway with sacks of cement and a fresh shave, and arrived in Rocky with long beards!"

However, they received $1.25 per sack for hauling, and the job looked like a long one; for as soon as the Alberta Central bridge was completed, the C. N. R. would certainly begin their own bridge. However, this dream of fortune was not to come true. The Railway Commission decided in 1912 that only one bridge was needed across the Saskatchewan; they also stated that the Alberta Central (now taken over by the C. P. R.) would stop at Rocky Mountain House, while the C. N. R. would continue on to Horburg and Nordegg.

So if you are interested in knowing—should you ride from Red Deer to Nordegg on the C. N. R.—why the train runs for three or four miles on C. P. R. track, and why it crosses the C. P. R. bridge, remember the "Battle of Horburg," possibly the longest battle in Canadian history—and maybe not yet entirely finished!

I think a great deal of the magic which I attach to Rocky Mountain House lies in its romantic name. It was explained to me that the name was given to the old fort by John MacDonald of Garth when in 1802 the Union Jack, together with the flag of the North West Trading Company, was raised above the main building. He named the place Rocky because of the rocky formation of the river bed, Mountain for the beautiful view of the Rocky Mountains from the point, House, of course, was the usual designation of a fur-trading post. Rocky Mountain House! a lengthy name but a good one, a name that one remembers. A much, much better name than the one the railroad wanted to change it to (but I shall tell more about that presently).

Only the chimneys of the old fort are standing now, and these are partial restorations made a few years ago by the Historic Sites and Monuments Board.

Romance hangs heavy over the spot, however, and it is not hard to recall that the first white man to reach the site was Peter Pangman, one of Mackenzie's partners, and that Pangman inscribed his name on a great pine tree near the river edge which for years was known as Pangman's Pine. Nor is it hard to recall that David Thompson wintered at the fort before his trip to the Pacific.

Stan Hooker, manager of the bank at Rocky, who drove me out to the Chimneys, told me that often a square nail or other relic of the past is picked up on the spot. A few years ago Mr. E. C. Brierly, who now owns the land on which the old fort was situated, was digging a well, and down about four feet he came onto a two-foot thick layer of ashes, which seems to imply that the ground level was once much lower.

Mrs. Grace Schierholtz, Rocky Mountain House correspondent for a number of western newspapers, gave me other interesting sidelights on the Chimneys. I had heard that a treasure of some sort had once been buried near the fort, and I asked Mrs. Schierholtz to tell me about the treasure.

"Oh," replied Mrs. Schierholtz, "that's a long story. Well, you asked for it, so here it is! You see, the country around here was known for years as Blackfoot country. The Blackfeet didn't seem to get along with the other tribes or with the white men. In the winter of 1819 the Indians decided they had some kind of grievance against the traders. They held a council of war and made plans to sneak over to the fort in the night, burn it down, and scalp the whites.

"Most fortunately for the traders, there was an Indian, half Cree and half Blackfoot, who had been doctored by the Factor, and chose this time to display the gratitude that is sometimes lacking in both white men and red. He had been one of a party at the fort with furs the year before; and after the dipper had been passed a few times, this young brave became so jovial that he danced too close to the steep river bank and tumbled over. The bank goes straight down for almost 100 feet, and the fall might easily have killed the foolish young Indian. He got off with a broken leg. The Factor and his men, perhaps feeling a trifle guilty when they remembered the whisky barrel and the dipper, took the victim and set his leg. They cared for him until he was able to rejoin his tribe.

"When this young brave heard the murderous plan of his chief, he slipped away and warned the Factor. There had been peace for a number of years, and the white men had begun to think their troubles with the Indians were over.

"The fort was understaffed, without enough guns, and almost no ammunition. The only thing to do was to flee; but before going, the traders buried as much of the supplies and furnishings as they could, including three cannon and a keg of rum.

"The Hudson's Bay Company had a map showing the location of the three buried cannon, and a few years ago they sent a man out here to locate them. He hired a crew and they worked here for weeks, but they didn't find a trace. The Company reluctantly decided the measurements shown on the map must be inaccurate."

"What did the Rocky Mountain House people think about this digging?" I asked.

"Oh," said Mrs. Schierholtz, "they watched with great interest. But perhaps they were really more concerned about the keg of rum—rum aged for 100 years! And would you believe it? The location of the rum is not shown on the map!

"After the trading post closed in 1875," continued Mrs. Schierholtz, "there were very few white men in the district until 1904 when the homesteaders began to trek in. Red Deer was well started by then. There were rumors that the railway was going west, and the pioneers were in a hurry to get in on the ground floor. By 1907 there was a fair-sized settlement of Ontario and Old Country homesteaders.

"These pioneers were over sixty miles from the railroad until the 'Battle of Horburg' brought the railroad scurrying through to Nordegg, sixty miles west, to tap the rich Brazeau coal fields.

"Some years ago, one of the railroads decided the name Rocky Mountain House was far too cumbersome to print in timetables or on tickets, so they quietly undertook to change it to Lochearn.

"The howl that went up must have been heard as far as Ottawa; for every old-timer was justly indignant. Rocky Mountain House means something, but what is there to an insipid name like Lochearn? They admitted that the three words made considerable writing, but they liked them. The name links the modern town with the days of the fur-traders and explorers. It makes readers remember that this place, though it looks like a new town, is really over 200 years old!

"One of the few residents in favor of the change pointed out that the name is *odd,* to put it mildly. He cited an instance. His brother in New York went down one day to send him a telegram, and when the girl in the office read the address, she flatly refused to believe there was such a place. The customer insisted in vain that he had a brother living there; furthermore, he had many letters postmarked Rocky Mountain House.

"The clerk repeated that there simply couldn't be a town with such a name, and she stuck to her guns. The man had to call an official before he could have the wire dispatched.

"Our citizens retorted that they didn't care whether New Yorkers believed there could be such a place or not! They insisted on keeping their name which had a history. They protested so loud and so long that the railway company finally pretended that it was all good, clean fun, and they had never intended to make such a drastic change. But for some years the place was listed as Lochearn in the timetables—until that issue was out of print!"

Lumbering is Rocky's leading industry. At one time the place was one of the leading lumber centers on the continent. Lumber from the mountain slopes built homes and schools and churches the whole length and breadth of western Canada. Lumber went from Rocky as far as Chicago, Detroit, and New York. Rocky shipped out ties to build the railroads, corral posts for the ranchers, pit-props for the coal mines, telephone poles to string across the endless prairies. That was in the boom days. Today Rocky has settled down to steadier times, shipping out millions of feet every year, going farther and farther back into the woods to get it.

Some of the camps are far out. Nobody calls in, and lumberjacks are inclined to lose track of time. According to one story, a traveler showed up at one of the camps

224

in the middle of January. The camp cook greeted him with great joy and asked him to stay for dinner. The traveler replied that he was sorry but he couldn't stay. "Please stay!" urged the cook. "It's mighty cheerful to have a visitor for Christmas dinner!"

Every Wednesday at Rocky is Pig Day. Pig raising is one of the thriving businesses of the region. Pigs have always done well there. On Wednesday long lines of pigs converge on the town. Some come by truck and wagon, but many are simply driven. It is a common sight to see a pig-drive down Main Street, with the animals behaving just as contrary in town as they do on the farm.

One old farmer came to town one day and brought a few pigs to sell. He sold his pigs, bought half a dozen others, and started driving them right up Main Street to where he had his wagon. It was a boiling hot day in mid-summer, and he was dressed in just a shirt and bib overalls. He used nails—like all bachelors—in place of buttons, and this day because of his strenuous exercise the nails worked a little loose. He was racing down the middle of Main after his pigs when a couple of the essential nails gave way. He lost his overalls. Nobody knows where they went, but one thing is certain: their owner didn't show up in Rocky again for a long, long time!

Travelers leaving Rocky don't care to go on the train leaving Wednesday morning. All the trains are mixed, freight and passenger, but the pig-train on Wednesday is more mixed than usual. The odors are not entirely pleasant, and the train stops at every siding to pick up pigs and more pigs!

Furs are still shipped from Rocky, too. Not so many,

of course, as in the old days, but this year at least, the trappers are doing well. When I was there I was told about two trappers who had come in a day or so before with over three thousand dollars worth of fur. This was only half through the fur season, at that.

There is coal, natural gas, and oil in the country around Rocky; and wild berries come out of the region in crates and carloads. The Indians gather lots of Seneca root which goes, or did go, to China to be made into cough medicine. One Indian lady—so they say—brought in enough Seneca root to get herself a permanent wave!

And there's gold, too. There has always been gold in the North Saskatchewan, not in large quantities, but an industrious man can still make four or five dollars a day panning if he chooses. Stan Hooker drove me down to the river bank to look at a curious boat built by a man named Frank James who had the idea that there must be lots of gold in the deep potholes of the river. He built the boat with a special pump to hoist out the deep river sand. His scheme has never been tried; the boat is standing idle on the river bank, but old-timers tell me that there *might*, there just *might*, mind you, be something in the James scheme.

You will find a variety of types of people at Rocky, and among them all the spirit of independence is strong. Some of the settlers have done well; anyone can do well just now if he chooses, there's such a shortage of help. Nature is kind to Rocky folk and provides meat and fruit, plenty of wood for building and fuel; one doesn't need much actual cash.

I am told that many a family around Rocky seldom sees

more than fifty dollars in cash the year round. I was told the story of one settler who came to the municipal council for aid. He wanted enough road work to do him till spring. "How much money will you need?" asked the council. "It's three months till spring, how much money will you need each month?"

"Well," replied the settler, "I could get along fine on a dollar and a half!"

They tell me of a woman who once worked in one of Europe's royal households. She came out with her husband, farmed with oxen, cleared brush, and pumped water by hand for eighty-five head of cattle. She's now one of the district's honored pioneers.

I heard also of a former officer of the Russian Imperial Army who fled his country at the time of the Revolution. When he came to Rocky he didn't have a nickel in the world. Today he and his wife own a 160 acre farm and are doing well.

One man came to Rocky only a few years ago with nothing except two dollars worth of groceries. He made a deal to cut cordwood that first winter in return for a team, some traps, and a gun. He got the equipment, but when spring came he needed a dollar's worth of garden seed, so he walked twelve miles in to Rocky and persuaded the Chinese laundryman to give him a dollar's worth of work. For a year or two he went on like that. Now he makes a fair living and has relied only on himself.

The Indians at Rocky also maintain their independent spirit. One of the very few remaining bands of Non-treaty Indians lives about thirty miles from Rocky Mountain House. Last summer the government tried once more to persuade them to accept treaty, but this proposal was flatly turned down by a vote of 177 to 23. In refusing the offer the Indians argued that this was their country and had been theirs long before the white men arrived. Since they had never taken treaty they had never given up their right to the land. They said that the white man was the intruder and should leave them in peace on the land that had been theirs since the world began.

An interesting legend exists among this little band of Nontreaty Chippewas. The legend concerns Chief Jim O'Chase, a famous Chippewa who died in 1932. When Chief O'Chase was a lad of seven, his band was camped in the hills along the Red Deer River. A scout suddenly reported that a larger band of hostile Indians was spying on the camp. Under cover of darkness the Chippewas moved out to safety, and in the early morning hours resumed their journey. It was not until the forenoon that they discovered Jim O'Chase was missing.

The boy had become separated from the band in the darkness, and later when he wakened under a clump of bushes, he was being nosed about by a big bull buffalo. This was in early spring, and the boy followed the buffalo herd about all summer, snuggling up to their shaggy bodies for warmth during the night, and eating—nobody knows what!

Late the next fall his uncle, still searching for some trace of the missing nephew, heard him whimpering in a dense, scrubby coulee and there found the lad alive and well. The boy said that his buffalo friends had deserted him that morning—when human help was within reach.

Asked what he lived on, he replied that his God had fed him.

Most of the people at Rocky are convinced that their region is the best in the world and wouldn't want to live anywhere else. They hope that sometime a road will be put through from Nordegg, sixty miles west, to connect with the Banff-Jasper highway. They believe this will make Rocky one of the important tourist centers of Western Canada.

Two or thre years ago some of the enterprising citizens of Rocky decided that they would take a car from Rocky to the Banff-Jasper road, just to show doubters that the idea was practical. They chopped down trees, forded rivers, and succeeded! A remarkable feat when one remembers that they went right through the mountains.

The foresters at Rocky told me that this road would almost certainly be put through, and when it is I hope Rocky has the boom the citizens anticipate; for I have a real fondness for this place of so much good humor and so much that is laughably mysterious.

I like Rocky just as I like High River. High River is the capital of the ranching tradition. Rocky Mountain House is a capital, too—a capital of courage, good humor, and independence. Long may they both live!

PART THREE

PARK BELT COUNTRY

W. J. PHILLIPS

"Listen," said Johnny, "hear 'em? Hear the people talking? They're telling you about Edmonton and the North Saskatchewan River. About the Barr Colonists and Father Lacombe and the Frog Lake Massacre. They're telling you about Park Belt Country, rich country, Johnny Chinook country. Listen!"

I

Front Door to the North

IN 1928 THE *Edmonton Journal* CARRIED AN EDITORIAL that began: "Away back about 1807, Edmonton was destroyed by the Blood Indians, which was the liveliest bit of scalping seen in these parts until the real estate salesmen got busy about 1910. The town lot fellows chased the Edmonton settlement until they ran five miles out of town from where the post office now stands. There they left it trembling and panting for breath, with a city council panting for ways and means to collect taxes. The result of the mad chase that went on in 1910-12 was to give Edmonton a far-flung border line with plenty of great open spaces within. When the speculator got out or gave up after an ambitious programme of street-opening, paving and sidewalk building had been put into operation, the city was left holding the bag. . . ."

Yes, one may wander for miles inside the city, and only the occasional sign post nailed to a poplar tree or a telephone pole reading: "165th Street"—or some such—destroys the illusion of taking a long walk in the country. Not that Edmonton isn't fast growing into its britches, it is. I'm in a position to say since I spent most of a year

234

looking for a house to live in. So perhaps the real estate boys did the city a good turn after all.

Just as Calgary has a background of cattle, oil, and wheat, Edmonton has a background of the fur trade; and a pretentious background it is, stretching way back to 1795 when the Hudson's Bay Company and the North West Company erected forts near the site of the present city. It is not my purpose to add any combustible material to the ever-smoldering fire of sometimes-friendly rivalry between the two main cities of Alberta, but I might mention two or three of the sources of long standing contention.

Edmonton received one of its early influxes of settlers when it was believed that the main line of the C. P. R. was coming north instead of south. The C. P. R., however, did go south—right through Calgary!—leaving Edmonton some 200 miles off the track. This did nothing to lay the foundation for friendship and tolerance between the two towns.

Edmonton got its railroad in 1891, a branch line from Calgary, and thereafter Edmonton received other coveted prizes. It became the Provincial capital. It obtained after a great hue and cry, the Provincial University, and apparently it was Edmonton influence which prevented a newly formed Calgary College from attaining University standing; for in 1912 Bob Edwards wrote in the *Eye Opener*:

Those green-eyed sumphs up at Edmonton killed the Calgary University bill by a vote of 17 to 15. Well, this makes things so much easier for us Conservatives down here at the next political election. We know where we are at now.

It will have to be Calgary College now instead of Calgary University, but once affiliated with the famous McGill University, students will be able to pass the regular McGill examinations and receive McGill degrees. This should place Calgary College on a higher level in the popular imagination than the Strathcona (Edmonton) institution, where the papers for degrees will probably consist of "Why is a hen?" "Who killed Cock Robin?" and kindred posers.

Strathcona degrees will soon become a joke. It is too near Ponoka (the Provincial Mental Hospital).

And Bob goes on to give some examples of a Strathcona University examination paper for the B. S. degree:

ENGLISH COMPOSITION

1. Write a 300 word eulogy on Principal Tory, and explain why he is.
2. Is what?
3. Parse sentence: "Good grammar teached here".
4. Is the word punk a predicate, superlative, or past participle?

HISTORY

1. Give brief history of Principal Tory.
2. When did Principal Tory draw up the Magna Carta?
3. Give date of Johnson-Jeffries fight.
4. How long did the Seven Years' War last?
5. Write what you know about Adam and Eve and their antecedents.
6. Give dates of Battle between Edmonton and South Edmonton for possession of Land Titles Office.

GEOGRAPHY

1. Where was Principal Tory born?
2. Name the principal rivers in Principal Tory's bailiwick.
3. Is Calgary on the map?
4. Name the capital of Alberta.

236

And of course (continues Bob) the above are only a few samples, but they will give you a line on the outfit up north. Calgary College will now go ahead and erect a splendid institution on the heights over-looking the city and the valley of the Bow. The right men are behind it and will be more zealous than ever in furthering the interests of Calgary's seat of learning. They are now on their mettle.

After all, it's only the matter of a couple of years when there will be a change of government, and then Calgary will come into her own as far as the University is concerned. So cheer up!

But despite Bob's valiant championship of Calgary University, the scheme came to nothing. The site that Calgarians chose for their institution is now a fox farm; while in Edmonton, Alberta University is scratching madly about trying to find space to house its growing departments.

There are good traditions at Edmonton. Edmonton people were not sufficiently conscious of their traditions to prevent the wanton tearing down of the Hudson's Bay fort, but in other ways they have demonstrated that they like Edmonton, are proud of its history, and want it to have the best possible chance.

They are willing to fight for their city. In 1891 the railway came to South Edmonton, and South Edmonton folk thought they saw a fine chance to have the entire city built on the south side of the river. Possibly the railway thought so, too; for if the city were on the south side, then the building of a bridge across the river might be put off for a considerable time. In those days of real estate development the Land Office was the central agency of the town, and the Land Office was on the *north* side of

237

the river. The south side folk knew that they must have the Land Office, so a team and wagon was sent over on the ferry to bring the office records across. Everyone knew that if the Land Office went, then Edmonton would grow up on the *south* side.

This was an abhorrent thought. The fort was on the north side—had been for almost 100 years. To Edmonton settlers, Edmonton *was* the north side of the river; so when the rumor of the dastardly scheme reached the citizens, things began to happen.

Thomas Anderson, the Land Office Agent, had arrived with his wagon to load up the records, when suddenly he was confronted by the Edmonton Home Guard, a truly valiant body of citizenry who had been organized during the Rebellion of 1885. The guard had been called out by Mayor McCauley and was under the command of Major Osborne, the Edmonton Postmaster.

Under the Major's direction the wheels were taken off the wagon, and according to one story, the wagon was pushed right into the river. Another wagon was sent over from the south side, but the drayman was met at the ferry by a determined group of men who told him to go home or he'd regret it.

Signs of general rebellion were in the air. The Mounted Police were summoned from Fort Saskatchewan a few miles down the river, but when the police got as far as Rat Creek near Edmonton they were met by the stalwart Home Guard. The Guard defied the police to enter the city. Meanwhile offers of assistance were coming from Calgary, Macleod, Medicine Hat, and from other Alberta towns.

In the face of such determination, it is needless to say, the center of Edmonton stayed right where it was—on the north side. No blood was shed, but poor Major Osborne paid the price of independence by losing his job as Postmaster. This was on the grounds that he had taken up arms against the government! He paid a price that patriots have often had to pay.

The famous tale of the Edmonton brass cannon also demonstrates the Edmontonian's willingness to fight for his town; and though this tale has a laughable ending no glory is thereby detracted from the fellows who would have become heroes if they'd had a chance.

It was 1885, and there was great unrest among the Indians of Alberta in sympathy with the Riel uprising elsewhere. After the fight at Duck Lake on March 26th, the Indians showed signs of hostility, and rumor of wide bloodshed spread among the settlers. Along the Saskatchewan at Red Deer, Beaver Lake, Battle River, and other points in central Alberta, the Indians were pillaging and plundering. On April 2nd at Frog Lake, Big Bear's band murdered a number of settlers and carried off the rest.

News that Riel had called on all the Indian tribes to rebel and that Poundmaker's men had arisen hastened the defense of Fort Edmonton, and all arms and ammunition in the district were collected. Inspector Griesbach, who was in command of the Mounted Police at Fort Saskatchewan, took command of the Edmonton district. From Edmonton the detachments of soldiers and Mounted Police spread out to Frog Lake, Fort Pitt, Frenchman's Butte, and Loon Lake. Eventually the mutinous Indians were quelled and Big Bear was captured.

At this time rumors, tales of scalping and other atrocities spread like wildfire among the Edmonton people. Word came in that there was a huge Indian encampment on Miner's Flat and that Indians, besmeared with war paint, were engaged in war dances.

The Mounties were sent out to investigate and found not a single Indian. Nonetheless, the rumors persisted. Fort Edmonton was the site of feverish activity. All guns and ammunition were collected, and it was decided to load the two heavy brass cannon which stood outside the palisade facing south across the ford in the river.

It had been some time since the cannon had been loaded, and no one around the fort could remember how they should be primed. Malcolm Groat, who had been an old whaler, was called in to superintend the job. His memory, too, was dim, and he could not remember whether it should be one pound of powder and five pounds of shot; five pounds of powder and one pound of shot; or five pounds of powder and five pounds of shot. After much discussion it was decided that the larger the amount of each, the more effective would be the charge. Consequently the cannon was loaded with five pounds of powder and five pounds of shot.

It is history now, of course, that during the '85 Rebellion the Indians never attacked Fort Edmonton, and gradually the normal activities of the settlement were resumed. The Mounties eventually went out to the nearest encampment in the Edmonton district, smoked the pipe of peace, and buried the hatchet.

The Factor of the fort decided that all danger was past and that the loaded cannon were a menace. The question was: could the cannon be unloaded or would it be simpler to fire them? Whether there was any question as to whether the charge was correctly proportioned has never been told. However, it was decided it would be a greater celebration if the cannon were fired.

A crowd gathered around, the light was applied, and those in the gathering swear that for some time they thought the whole world had exploded! The cannon blew back and lodged in the palisade of the fort. Everything for many yards behind the cannon was flattened to the ground. What happened to the shot? Those present on the occasion swear that it is still traveling around the world; for, though they searched high and low on the south side of the river, none of the shot was ever recovered.

No less a heroic gesture—and similar in results—was the great fireworks celebration worthy of their town. It was decided to stage a spectacular fair featuring fireworks, which had not been presented in Edmonton up to that time. Consequently the display was advertised far and wide, and the Indians as well as white settlers came from points as far distant as Athabaska Landing, 100 miles away. Gaily painted Indian tepees were erected all around the fairgrounds.

One thousand dollars worth of fireworks had been imported in two enormous cases approximately six feet square. Two local residents who professed to know the art of handling fireworks were appointed to officiate. They piled all the roman candles, skyrockets, and pinwheels from one box to the top of the other, making an enormous mound of explosives. The other packing case was upended beside it.

The great event was announced with much heraldry. One of the officials took his place on the empty case and applied a light to the skyrocket which he held in his hand. Instead of rising skyward and bursting into a myriad of colored balls, it shot backwards into the mound of fireworks; immediately the whole world seemed to be alive with colored balls, and the very air vibrated with explosions. Skyrockets exploded in every direction, some shot directly through the Indian tepees, while others entered and exploded inside.

The white spectators took refuge behind any available shelter, but the Indians, thinking that all the devils in hell had been unleashed on them, had but one idea: to put distance between them and Edmonton. The terrified natives gave not a thought to their possessions.

One pony was seen heading north with three full-grown Indian braves on its back, another had children hanging from mane and tail. So many crowded into a buckboard that the horses couldn't move it, and the Indians wasted much time cursing and whipping the animals. Finally they took to their own heels.

One of the official starters grabbed an armful of fireworks and started to run, but the fire had got to them and they went off in his arms. People scattered from him in every direction.

This celebration meant real work for the Mounties. The Indians were convinced that the white people had brought them to Edmonton to destroy them, and it was felt that such conviction in the mind of all the Indians in this territory could have serious consequences. Accordingly, the Mounties were sent out to bring them back, to

242

restore to them their possessions, and to convince them that no real harm had been done. Some of the Redcoats went almost as far as Athabaska before they rounded up one large group of Indians.

Even in the early 1880's, Edmonton had a Vigilance Committee to guard the town property rights. There were only five white families at Edmonton, but other people were beginning to arrive. The country was unsurveyed, and the original settlers had no right to the land. The newcomers, therefore, attempted to squat and build shacks wherever they chose.

Something had to be done, so a Vigilance Committee was formed with Matt McCauley, a sturdy pioneer, as captain. Whenever a new settler attempted to squat on land already claimed, he was promptly warned. If he persisted in maintaining his squatters rights, the Committee usually tossed shack, squatter, and all over the river bank. The river was called the Vigilantes depository.

⁄ 1.—THE RIVER

But if Edmonton people are proud of their city, they are no less proud of the North Saskatchewan River. It's a friendly river, as John Collins Mathias could testify. Mathias was a dwarf who spent much of his forty years at Edmonton just watching the river flow. People who knew him say that he used to talk to the river, and the river answered him back.

There is gold in the North Saskatchewan. Not very much, but during the depression men panned gold along the river, and it kept them alive.

The great days on the river are now only a memory.

The York boats have vanished, and very few persons recognize such words as tracking or tump line—words that had a very real meaning in the days when heavy boats were bodily dragged upstream.

Many a newcomer to Edmonton in the old days found employment on the river. One such newcomer was William Spindler, now of Breton, who told me:

On my arrival in this town of Edmonton like many another Old Country boy, I looked around the river bank. There wasn't much to be seen as it was Christmas and the whole country was snowbound from the mountains to Winnipeg.

When I was a boy, I wanted to be on the water, but after ten years at sea I wanted to view a big piece of land and get as far away from the sea as I could. That's why I chose Edmonton.

However, when I got out here I found that the water still called me, so when the ice went out I went to see Jock Walter who ran the saw mill and the ferry.

Jock had installed this ferry just in time to carry the troops across in the '85 Rebellion. He was very proud of the scow because the cable on which it ran he had fetched from Winnipeg. How did he fetch it? Well, he hooked a yoke of oxen onto it and dragged it. Yes, sir, two thousand miles round trip, and Jock used to say that it took him all of six months!

I ran Jock's ferry for a while, but I kept watching the two old steamers on the river; they were the *City of Edmonton* and the *City of Strathcona*. The *Edmonton* was a sort of pleasure boat, hauling on "moonlight trips" down to Clover Bar or up to Big Island. The *Strathcona* was used for taking supplies upriver to the logging camps.

Well, I could see that the old *Strathcona* was getting ready for a trip upriver and I wanted to be along. Finally, away we went with a lot o' hissing and snorting and grunting. It wasn't all beer and skittles, for after we got under way I went up to the bridge where Captain Pearce was in command. He spit through the window a couple of times and hollered that it seemed like lunch time. "Can ye cook?" says he. "No," says I, "only for myself."

"Ye'll cook," says he. So I did, and we made out all right for supper with bread, spuds, eggs, and sow belly, with a can of jam for dessert.

We tied up late that night after making about twenty-five miles or so; and about noon next day it was all hands and the cook digging coal from the river bank. Next day, it was digging coal, too. Or if no coal showed up, we went ashore with axes and saws and cut cord wood.

At one spot, we found it hard to dig coal, so one of the hands suggested dynamite. None of us knew anything about the stuff, and this hand knew less, because he didn't get away in time and we spent half an hour digging him out from under lumps of dirt and coal. He was mighty sick and only did light duty for the rest of the trip. This pleased me since he relieved me of the cook job.

When we reached the narrower parts of the river where there are sometimes two or even three channels, we reached the bend two or three times, and as many times, we drifted down again. I saw the great Jock Walter standing beside the escape valve, and in order to help the old tank over the rapids, he stood outside on a narrow ledge of boards with one foot holding down the valve so as to conserve every ounce of steam. Even if the whole shebang should blow to Kingdom Come, he intended that we should climb that rapid! And we did.

In about five or six days, we reached our point and unloaded our supplies for the river boys who were still a few miles farther upstream.

We were looking for a cozy spot to tie up for the night, when my eyes spotted what looked like a bundle of blankets just awash on a gravel bar the other side. I drew Captain Pearce's attention to it, but he said, "Nope, just a deadhead" (meaning a water-soaked log).

However, I was curious enough to launch the boat— an old flat-bottomed tub almost square. No one else was interested so I pulled over alone, and before I'd got very near to what I'd seen, I wished I'd minded my own business; for what I saw was the body of a big man floating face down, his hands and feet digging the gravel.

With the painter I tied him fast and dragged him across. It was a job nobody wanted, but we went over him for identification. All we could find was a small purse containing some U. S. silver pieces, some U. S. stamps, a notebook, a jackknife, and a rifle shell. He also had the letters M. V. D. tattooed in India ink on his left hand. That's all we knew about the poor fellow, and all we ever did know.

The interment wasn't easy. Solid gravel is not easy digging with only a pick and coal scoop. We made a rough and very big box out of slabs we rustled on the boat. This was July, and the body had been in the water for probably a month. We had to run windward several times to revive ourselves but we got the job done. I made a little cross and on it put the date and the identification marks. We got all this done in time to get ready for a new day's work.

They were long days on river steamers, those times. Four o'clock turn out, and if you're lucky, turn in by eleven. But we didn't care.

We anchored our lonely traveler in the Port of Forgotten Men, and the bar where we planted him was dubbed Dead Man's Bar and probably will stay that way. I learned later that that summer was the worst in several years, for three other men were drowned within thirty miles of that stretch of river.

I left the boat before we started back to Edmonton—thinking I'd go logging. I hired out to a skidding gang on the flats below Rock Rapids. I'd bought me an old 30-30 rifle just in case I should run out of a meal sometime; but it was always in the wrong place at the right time! For instance: once during the raspberry season—a very hot day in July—I had picked a can of raspberries from among the billions of mosquitoes and had gone out to the river bar to escape some of these pests.

I ate my berries and intended to have a little snooze. I picked me out a big Balm of Gilead that had washed down with the flood and was just about asleep alongside it when the gravel seemed to be moving. I got up and looked over the tree just at the same moment that a bear decided to look across and find out what was on *my* side. He literally grunted right into my face. I could smell his breath for the next several years.

I dropped, and the bear dropped. After a couple of hours—or maybe a minute—I got up courage to look again. There was the bear a quarter of a mile away heading for the Rocky Mountains. I guess the bear was as scared as I. Anyway I never told any of the crew, for they were the bravest men I ever saw—together in a tent. A Belgian working with us at the time (very brave) volunteered to go to another camp about ten miles away for something the cook needed. He apparently got there all right and started back with his pack in a gunny sack. Just before dark we heard some wild yelling and brush-breaking, and Le Belgique, minus coat and gunny sack, fell right into the tent.

He seldom mentioned the incident except to announce that a bear had chased him; but that fall, I accidentally came across the same gunny sack and its contents scattered through the brush *quite near the other camp!* Le Belgique had run for nearly ten miles!

Life on the river in the early days was full of hazards. It was a tremendous job to get the boats through from York Factory on Hudson Bay to Edmonton. Much of this upstream travel was tracking. Half the crew would land and, attaching themselves to the heavy line fastened abaft the bow, would commence to march upstream along the beach or in the water inshore. The steersman, occasionally assisted by the bowsman, guided the boat. The watch off duty immediately rolled themselves in their blankets—head and feet—to keep off the mosquitoes and went to sleep.

Where the beach was good, the men went quite rapidly. However, there was often no beach to track on, and then the men had to plunge into water anywhere from ankle to waist deep—quite a trick when pulling at a heavy line.

248

Sometimes, too, the water would be too deep along the banks to wade, and then the men had to tear their way up the bank through brush and forest where the line often fouled. At times the banks would be very steep and of slick clay; at these spots, the men would be forced to cling to anything they could grasp—still tugging the boat ahead.

After passing the portage over the Grand Rapids and other rapids near Lake Winnipeg, the Saskatchewan was more or less free of interruption to Edmonton. The lower river was ascended under oars unless a favorable wind lent an aid to navigation. When the high and dry banks above The Pas were reached, the men went out ahead on the track line and pulled fairly steadily to Edmonton.

There was a new danger now, however, from wandering parties of Blackfeet. Many attempts to capture the boats were made by the Indians, but the vigilant boatmen usually shoved off just in time.

Nearing Fort Edmonton, the boatmen might put on their best shirts of red wool or tie fresh handkerchiefs about their heads. The tracking was always easier when they could finally see the fort on the river bank with the Hudson's Bay flag, bearing the letters H. B. C. (sometimes interpreted, Here Before Christ), flying in the wind. Perhaps the great Chief Factor Rowand would be standing on the shore to greet the boatmen.

Rowand was known for a number of things. First of all, perhaps, for his fiery temper. He was said to be master of several Indian dialects and a good enough master to terrorize an Indian in any of them.

He was also known as the builder of Rowand's Folly. The house of the Chief Factor at every Hudson's Bay post was known as the Big House, and Rowand's Folly was the biggest of them all. In its early days, the house was spoken of as the most palatial building ever constructed between Norway House and the Pacific Ocean.

Gay events took place at the Big House. In 1848 the artist, Paul Kane, visited Edmonton under the courtesy of the Hudson's Bay Company. He had traveled across the continent from Toronto and stopped at Edmonton on his return journey. It was near Christmas, and the 130 people living within the palisades of the fort were anticipating a great feast.

On Christmas day the flag was raised, and everyone appeared in his best clothes. The feast was held in a large room used as a reception hall for the Indian chiefs when they paid Fort Edmonton a visit. Kane described this particular Christmas: "No table cloth shed its snowy whiteness over the board; no silver candelabra or gaudy china interfered with its simple magnificence. The bright tin plates and dishes reflected jolly faces, and burnished gold can give no truer zest to a feast.

"At the head . . . was a large dish of boiled buffalo hump; at the foot smoked a boiled buffalo calf (whole) . . . My pleasing duty was to help a dish of mouffle, or dried moose nose; the gentleman on my left distributed, with graceful impartiality, the whitefish delicately browned in buffalo marrow. The worthy priest helped the buffalo tongue, whilst Mr. Rundle (the Protestant Missionary) cut up the beavers' tails. Nor was the other gentleman left unemployed, as all his spare time was occupied in dissecting a roasted wild goose. The centre of the table was graced with piles of potatoes, turnips, and bread, conveniently placed so that each could help himself without interrupting the labors of his companions. Such was our jolly Christmas dinner at Edmonton, and long will it remain in my memory, although no pies, or pudding, or blanc manges, shed their fragrance over the scene."

In the evening a great dance was held to which all the inmates of the fort were invited. Indians, *voyageurs*, half-breeds—all decorated with countless trinkets—were present, as well as Paul Kane and the fort officials. Kane led to the dance floor a young Cree squaw and danced a mad reel; the Indian lady gravely jumped up and down.

Chief Factor Rowand is a truly legendary Edmonton figure. Before his death in 1861, he directed that his bones be shipped to his old home in Quebec for burial. His request was taken literally. A Cree Indian was given the job of boiling Rowand's remains and cleaning the flesh off the bones. The story goes that the Indian took the liberty of slicing off a piece of Rowand's heart and eating it so that he might become brave like the great man.

I have also heard that Rowand was shipped East in a barrel of rum. I leave you to judge the preferable method. Whichever means was employed, however, Rowand had a long journey before he finally came to rest. It was feared that the river boatmen would revolt were it known they were transporting a dead man; so poor Rowand was actually shipped as cargo to Europe and then back to his final resting place.

2.—THE BRIDGE

One of the Edmonton traditions is the famous high level bridge which spans the whole Saskatchewan River valley. The bridge can hardly be called a thing of beauty, but perhaps its very stark ugliness has endeared it to the Edmonton heart. Edmonton would simply not be Edmonton without that bridge.

It was built as a joint enterprise by the city and the C. P. R. after there was no longer any doubt about Edmonton growing up on the north side of the river. The street cars crawl their way across on tracks laid at the very outer edges, and a first trip across on the cars turns more than one usually hardy passenger a pallid green.

A mammoth celebration had been planned for the opening of the bridge in 1912, but the actual opening was anticipated by an event which threatened to disrupt the civic life. Here is the real story of the opening of the high level bridge.

The year the bridge was completed was the first year that graduates from the Calgary and Edmonton high schools were admitted to the University. These lads anticipated their college education with boisterous glee and were really rarin' to go.

In consequence of this distinct nonacademic spirit, the older fellows who had already enjoyed a year or two at the new institution, felt that something should be done to steady down the Freshmen, especially the ones from Calgary.

The older students waited for several days seeking a favorable opportunity; at last the fatal hour struck. As the Freshmen entered Athabaska Hall—then the only building on the campus proper—they were seized one by one.

A terrific battle was fought on every floor and in every room and corridor. For a while, it was nip and tuck. It looked, indeed, as though the hardy Freshmen might turn the tables and teach the upper classmen a few tricks; for there were more Freshmen than all the other students put together. To the everlasting shame of the Sophomores, they had to call in the aid of the Seniors; at length the Freshmen were all hog-tied and put on trial.

The Calgary boys were put on the block first. They were charged with three crimes. The first crime was that they were from Calgary. "Guilty or not guilty?" asked the judge.

"Guilty! And proud of it!" yelled the Freshmen.

The second charge was that they had conspired to form a so-called University in their "cow town" of Calgary.

"And we'll do it yet!" bellowed the Freshmen.

The third charge was that the Freshmen had broken all academic tradition by making up a most materialistic yell for their embryo institution. The land boom was on in full blast in Calgary, and the yell which the upper classmen accused the Freshmen of creating was:

Rah! Rah! Rah!
Buy a lot in Crescent Heights!
Rah! Rah! Rah!

When accused that this was a crime against tradition, the Freshmen boldly told the judge he was a liar. This was the signal for the mayhem that followed.

The boys were pasted with pea meal and led to the second story of Athabaska Hall where a greased slide had

253

been prepared. They were shot out of the window down the slide and into a trough filled with water. This preliminary ordeal completed, they were tied by the ankles to a large logging chain and marched to the neighboring Theological College.

The procession was headed by a donkey which absolutely refused to co-operate when the steps at the north end of the College were reached. After much difficulty the donkey was bodily lifted up the steps and led along the corridor. When they reached the rotunda, the donkey lay down and refused to budge; he was bodily pushed along the new and beautifully polished floor and down the front steps where the procession formed again and started—nobody knew where.

At that time the grounds around the University were a forest of trees, broken here and there by a few new streets. The curb was being laid on one of these, and into the fresh cement some of the freshest of the Freshmen were pushed, head first.

Edmonton was having its own real estate boom at this time, and signs advertising property were nailed to trees on every side. The boys pulled off these signs and, holding them aloft, marched on.

Their march carried them to the south end of the high level bridge. It was blocked at both ends. It seems that the city had not paid its one-third of the cost, and the C. P. R. refused to allow any traffic until it received its pound of flesh.

The boys began to yell that the C. P. R. had long enough dominated the country and that there "came a time in the affairs of men," etc. So the barricade at the south end was tramped down, and the entire procession poured over.

254

The whole city was terrified. Word had reached downtown Jasper Avenue that hell had broken loose at the University. Screaming shopkeepers took every moveable thing inside and double locked the doors. They were just in time; for down Jasper Avenue came the serpentine dance.

The street cars were boarded, the motormen shoved into the street, and one of the most hectic traffic snarls ever known in Edmonton materialized. The police were powerless. The Mayor tore out all his hair. One alderman is said to have committed suicide but, of course, I can't vouch for that.

A message was sent to the Alberta government for aid. "We want the Home Guard! We want the Mounted Police!" screamed the citizens.

The government, however, knew a more direct method. Dr. Tory, the University President, was called and told that if the students weren't quelled, the government grant to the University would be withheld. Can you think of a better way to terrify a university president? I can't.

The direct method worked. President Tory appealed to the students who were having a wonderful time taking Edmonton apart piece by piece. The students thought Tory was a pretty good sort, so they disbanded. But the scars of the battle remained on the face of the city for a long time. And the bridge, at least, had been opened.

Many persons wonder as they cross the bridge why the southbound cars cross on the east side, and the northbound cars cross on the west—just the opposite from what one would expect. The explanation is very simple. Soon after the bridge was completed and the cars began to cross,

255

people awoke to the horrifying fact that the street car doors opened directly out over the river. Should anything happen to the car, and should the passengers have to suddenly disembark, they would step out to a drop of some 150 feet! Edmonton people weren't willing to tempt fate quite so far. They put sudden and constant pressure on the street car company. The company changed its tracks, and now the doors open toward the center of the bridge. Of course, anyone suddenly stepping onto the center of the bridge might be run over by a C. P. R. train, but to the ordinary Edmontonian a death under the wheels seems less terrifying than a single, final plunge into the river.

3.—TALES, TRADITIONS, AND INCIDENTS

The Edmonton story embraces many separate tales. The city has its famous jests—like the story the old-timers tell about Archie Boag. Archie was spending a cheerful evening at the Queen's Hotel, a cherished Edmonton hostelry, which had a back door opening directly out onto the steep river bank. Below the door, there was a sheer drop of perhaps twenty feet.

Forgetting where he was, Archie pulled open the door and stepped out into space. A long, wild yell followed his descent to the river bank, and the sudden silence after he hit, made his friends in the hotel believe that Archie had met an untimely and undeserved end. His friends rushed out to pick up the pieces, but to their surprise they found Archie unhurt and staring up at the door in the utmost amazement.

"Boys," said Archie, "that's the highest step I ever took!"

256

They like to tell around Edmonton, too, the tale about Jim McKernan. Jim was the first telegraph operator in the district and during the Indian troubles Jim was afraid that the half-breed leader, Takoots, was going on the warpath.

Jim had some reason to be afraid since his telegraph office was entirely unprotected against attack; so he sent a wire to Sir John A. MacDonald, then in charge of Indian Affairs in Ottawa.

"Indians threatening," wired Jim, "what shall I do?"

He received no answer from Sir John so he wired again: "Indians more threatening. What shall I do?"

Sir John refused to answer, and Jim was sure Takoots was coming after him. He wired a desperate third time: "Takoots is going to scalp me. What shall I do?"

This time Sir John answered. His wire was short and to the point. It merely said: "Shave your head, Jim."

The Edmonton story would almost certainly mention the beloved Presbyterian pastor, David McQueen.

Children, dogs, and cats followed McQueen when he walked on the Edmonton streets. Indians flocked to his house seeking his advice and friendship. His faithful horse, John, took excellent care of his master. If the service at Fort Saskatchewan, or some other country point, seemed a bit too long, John would whinny—to remind the good Doctor that the sermon was getting out of hand and that it was time to start home. McQueen never failed to heed John's signal.

The McQueen legend in Edmonton is aptly summed up by one old resident who told me, "I seen aplenty of preachers come to Edmonton, yes, and go, too. I heard plenty *agin* most of 'em, but, son, I never heard a word said agin Dave McQueen. He was a straight shooter, square as they come. Knew aplenty about human weakness and never set himself up as God A'mighty. McQueen's a tradition around these parts."

The Red River Cart was also an Edmonton tradition in the early days. Often as I travel the countryside, I fancy I can hear in the wailing wind a hint of the sound these ox-drawn, all wooden carts made as they slowly crossed the prairie. No grease was used on the wooden axles—this would rot the wood and weaken the wheels. As a result, the carts moved with a fearful screeching, and old-timers tell me that you could hear the carts before you could see them.

The Red River Carts carried many settlers into the West, and carried some whose names are household words in Edmonton. Foremost among these is the name of Frank Oliver who came from Winnipeg in 1880 to establish the first newspaper in Alberta, *The Edmonton Bulletin,* itself a Western tradition.

Frank was working for the *Manitoba Free Press* in Winnipeg when he saw an ad in a Philadelphia paper stating that a hand press and two cases of nonpareil type were for sale. Frank answered the ad, and when the press arrived he loaded the whole thing onto a Red River Cart, hitched up his oxen and set off for Edmonton, 1200 miles away. Arriving in Edmonton, Frank set up his newspaper office in a smokehouse belonging to Donald Ross, Edmonton's first hotelkeeper.

Frank had had plenty of experience in the printing business, in Ontario, Toronto, and Winnipeg; but all his experience didn't make up for a shortage of type. This shortage was overcome, however, by the traditional ingenuity of the early West. Frank and his helper, Mr. Taylor, carved the caption for the new publication from a piece of dry birch wood.

On December 6, 1880, the first *Bulletin* appeared. It was a tiny thing—four pages, about five by seven inches —yet it contained general news, local news, advertisements, and editorials. Nor was the social column neglected. One of Frank's society notes states:

> The ball at Mr. Fraser's on New Year's Eve was a grand success, being crowded to the door. The room was decorated with festoons of olive branches—done up in moss bags.

Frank became one of the West's greatest men, and finally was appointed Minister of the Interior. Frank learned about this job the hard way. Jim Brewster, of Banff, told me that one day Frank Oliver came to Banff and wanted to take a trip over some of the mountain roads. Jim was willing so they set out.

It seemed to Frank that the edges of the roads weren't very well protected; and on two or three particularly bad curves, where the edge of the road fell off to a drop of several thousand feet, Frank demonstrated his nervousness by aiming a number of colorful expletives at the fellow who permitted such roads to exist. "And by the way," asked Frank after he had used all the expressions in his wonderful command of language, "who is *responsible* for these roads?"

"Well, Mr. Oliver," said Jim, "I suppose it's the Minister of the Interior."

Yes, the Red River Cart was well known in Edmonton. It was known to George McDougall, pioneer missionary at Edmonton, who built the first church.

The cart was well known to Donald Ross who was very proud of the hotel he built in Edmonton. If a guest didn't like Donald Ross's place, he might be told to go on to the next hotel—at Winnipeg, a distance of some 1200 miles.

But if people remember the Red River Cart, they are apt to forget that the thing which gave Edmonton its first real start was the rush to the Klondike in 1897-98. During this period the city's population increased in size from a few hundred to several thousand.

Edmonton was the jumping off place for the gold seekers who were so unfortunate as to choose the overland route to the Klondike. They came from every part of the world and many, unused to the travel of the north, brought with them fantastic devices for making the long trip in quick time.

One of the most ingenious arrangements was that of Texas Smith. He arranged three barrels tricycle-wise, fixed shafts to the barrels, and hitched up a horse. Inside the barrels he carried all his supplies. Texas got about seven miles before the hoops came off the barrels and he traced his way back to Edmonton by following the track of beans, rice, and flour.

In a shed near the river bank, Brenneau Fabian was preparing for the journey. Noah's Ark, the people called his invention. It was a large vessel, large enough to hold

260

score of men. Made entirely of galvanized iron, the ship was hinged in the middle so that the stern could be folded over the bow and the whole pulled along on either wheels or runners—a streamlined version of the covered wagon. A team of oxen was to be the motive power on land, and sails on the water. *The Juggernaut* did not leave its place on the river bank. For many years, Fabian's Folly was an outstanding float in all parades in Edmonton.

Another party spent a long while constructing an ice boat. Since the group expected to do a little profiteering when they reached the gold fields, space had to be allowed for cargo. Gingerly the heavy contraption was tugged out onto the ice. The towering mast was hoisted and the expanse of sails set. The boat bade fair to become part of the ice. It would have taken a hurricane to move it. The grinning citizens rounded up fourteen teams of horses to haul the monstrosity back up the grade to the shed from which it emerged with such éclat.

The prime folly was that of the I Will Steam Sleigh Company, of Chicago. This firm manufactured a single piece of equipment. This was a steam sleigh to haul a train of four cabooses on runners. Powered with a boiler and a marine engine, traction was provided by studding the cylindrical wheels of the engine with spikes or teeth. The first car behind the engine carried fuel, the second was the living quarters of the crew, and the third carried provisions. The date for the start arrived. The crew strode about oiling and wiping and testing gauges. "Let her go!" cried the leader. With the blast of a four-funnel liner, the sleigh lurched forward. The wheels churned, showering the spectators with clods of earth. The tractor

261

wallowed and settled in the mire. All the frantic efforts to extricate her failed. The "I Will" wilted. Years later, an enterprising sawmill man bought the machinery for his mill.

But the story of the rush to the Klondike was not all humor. Rather it is essentially a tragic tale, for only one in five hundred, who set out from Edmonton with such high hopes, ever arrived at his destination. Their belongings were scattered to the four winds; the Beaver Indians, the Crees, and the Dog Ribs had fat pickings for a long time after the seekers had passed.

Men with an eye to business advertised the Edmonton route far and wide, describing it as the best, quickest, and easiest road to the Klondike. Hundreds believed this golden hokum, and hundreds died of scurvy, of starvation, of heartbreak, somewhere in the North.

II

〰

The Barr Colony

ON THE MORNING OF APRIL 17, 1903, THE LITTLE TOWN OF
Saskatoon, Saskatchewan awoke to find its population in-
creased by some 2,000 Englishmen.

Under the amazed eyes of the Saskatoon natives, a tent
city was springing up which threatened to eclipse Saskatoon in size; and on the streets and over the prairies
wandered men, women, and children from Devonshire,
Yorkshire, London—from almost every part of England.
Many of the men were armed to the teeth with long knives,
revolvers, rifles, and shot-guns; and the air was filled with
powder smoke and the whine of bullets. Any available
target was perforated, for to the new settlers Saskatoon
was the threshold of the wild and woolly West. Fingers
must be made steady on the trigger, and eyes must be
readied to spot the lurking redskins.

But Saskatoon was only the jumping off place. The
real destination was the all-British colony to be established
on the open prairie some 200 miles farther west.

In 1902, the Reverend I. M. Barr conceived the idea of
establishing a British colony; and to secure land, he came
to Western Canada. The Government reserved his land.

263

and Barr returned to England in the belief that possibly a few families might be induced to come west to settle. However, when Barr announced his plans in London, he was almost immediately flooded with applications. The scheme was enlarged until fully 2,000 people—two-thirds of whom were women and children—were signed up to make the journey.

The colony was to come well equipped for settling down on the bare prairie. Barr secured quantities of tents, stores, and articles recently used in the African War. Special trains were arranged to carry the colonists to Liverpool and a special steamer, the *Lake Manitoba*, was readied to sail with the settlers and their belongings.

A large percent of the colonists knew absolutely nothing about farming. An even larger percent had not the vaguest idea of the country to which they were going. To most of the settlers, Western Canada was the far outpost of civilization where the chief dangers were Indians and wild beasts. They armed themselves accordingly.

Under such circumstances it is one of the wonders of the West that 1800 of the colonists actually arrived at their settlement. It is perhaps an even greater wonder that most of these seemed somehow to survive, and that at least a few prospered.

Among the colonists were Alice and William Rendell, their two children, Doris and Leslie, and a man named Barnes whom Rendell brought along as a helper. Rendell was one of the settlers who knew how to farm. In his own words: "As far as my qualifications are concerned for my starting farming in Canada, I may say I have farmed in the Old Country all my life, the estate I rented in

264

Devonshire having been farmed by my forefathers for over 200 years. I was paying rent at the rate of over ten dollars per acre in addition to rates, tithes, taxes, and wages. A crisis having come, and failing to get my landlord to do anything either in reduction of rent or repairs, I determined to throw up the life of slavery for others and strike for independence in Canada for good or ill."

The Rendells came from Liverpool on the *Lake Simcoe*, having arrived too late to leave with the main Barr party on the *Lake Manitoba*. This later turned out to be a blessing since the *Simcoe* had much better accomodations than the *Lake Manitoba* where the settlers were forced to sleep in any nook they could find. Many, in fact, were bunked in the holds. Even on the *Simcoe* the trip had its perils. Mrs. Rendell wrote to her friends in England: "Monday proved a terribly rough day, the waves breaking right over the ship. The climate by this time had undergone a great change and was bitterly cold. The captain had to proceed very cautiously owing to fog and icebergs. Tuesday we were surprised to see snow on the decks. It was so slippery it was impossible to keep your footing, and everyone had to take shelter in the saloons. It seemed a long day, but it was an eventful one on board; a gentleman slipped over the stairs leading to the cabin and broke his leg. There was a birth on board, and a foreigner in the steerage cut his throat and is not expected to live. In addition to all this, they have discovered no less than twenty stowaways."

Mrs. Rendell is eighty-seven years old. She lives in Edmonton now, and when I went to see her, she was all ready to climb aboard a street car—just going to town to do a little shopping. She assured me that she had been through so much that almost anything that happened to her these days seemed tame.

"A year or two ago," said Mrs. Rendell, "I got a combination of 'flu, bronchitis, pneumonia, and heaven knows what all. I guess I was pretty sick. Anyway they thought I was so sick I'd never pull out of it so they called in all the children. I asked 'em what they were doing there; for you see I knew how tough I was, and they didn't. Well, I pulled out of it, just like we pulled out of so many hard times and scrapes in the Barr Colony days."

Mrs. Rendell showed me the letters she wrote home during the first few months of their experience as Barr Colonists. They tell a story of high courage:

"We landed at St. Johns, April 15 (1903) and were just rushed off the *Lake Simcoe* like a pack of hounds in a most disgraceful way quite late in the day. We had had the usual twelve o'clock meal, and by this time, the poor children were famished and all tired out with waiting to land. We were one and all faint, cold, and weary. Mr. Barr and his party had landed a few days before on the *Manitoba,* and the customs had not been able to get clear of all the baggage and were not at all prepared to receive any more. We were driven off the boat into the bitter sleet and snow with no possibility of getting on our prospective journey for hours. . . . We never got away from St. Johns until long after midnight on Thursday, owing to the dilatory way in which the baggage was discharged from the *Lake Simcoe*. It was simply scandalous. My husband could not find a single piece of all our baggage, and they telephoned from the ship that everything was out

266

of the hold. . . . After causing us and many others hours of anxiety and great suffering and privation, they found that any amount of baggage had been left in the hold.

"At last our lost property was duly checked and on board the train en route for Saskatoon. I can only say that the third class carriages on the English railways are a king to the filthy cars we were huddled into. No sleeping accommodation, and as to the lavatory arrangements they were simply a disgrace to civilization! In this misery we were boxed up to spend just on a week. With so many little children to care for, it was a wonder there was not a serious outbreak of illness. . . . It was almost impossible to get at our provisions, and many a time we felt faint and famished with hunger, to say nothing of being starved with the cold. I took a chill at St. Johns from exposure, and a dreadful abscess formed in my face, causing me terrible suffering for three days until it finally broke. I cannot give much description of the country we passed through as pain almost blinded me; but skirting some of the Great Lakes, there were some grand bits of scenery but not a sign of life—no birds, no cattle. The vastness of it all just strikes one with awe."

Arriving in Saskatoon, the Rendells, now several days behind the main Barr party, found a huge tent city, and circulating around, they saw many humorous things.

One fellow was chopping down a tree and he was so afraid of cutting himself that he was standing in a big wash tub while he chopped.

Another was seen using a large rock for a chopping-block. When asked why, he said that he had split all the wooden chopping-blocks and had decided to solve the whole matter by using a stone.

267

Still another settler drove his team down to the river to water them but he didn't understand that their heads were held up by a check-rein. He just went around behind the wagon and lifted up the hind end, thinking that this would tip the horses down to the water.

One colonist was heard to ask a bystander how to dig a well, and the bystander said, "I think it would be best to begin at the top!" The colonist gravely thanked the stranger and walked away.

The baggage was in a terrible mix-up, and it was several days before the colonists could begin their trek west. They were all eager to set out. Many spent their time practicing driving their horses and oxen. One settler, not understanding the use of hobbles, thought they were made to check the downhill progress of the team. Accordingly, he hobbled his oxen at the brow of a steep hill, and the tale of his ludicrous descent is one of the humorous epics of the Barr Colony.

Saskatoon was literally cleaned out of all available merchandise, and large sums of money were left with the Saskatoon merchants who were enjoying an unheard of boom. All the oxen and horses on the continent seemed to have mysteriously gravitated to Saskatoon; and sad-eyed hoss traders shed tears in public and celebrated in private at having to part with their merchandise at fabulous prices.

Many of the settlers seemed to favor the ox to the horse, and, being asked why, one colonist replied, "Why, when you're not working the oxen, you can milk 'em!"

During the waiting period, the Rendells had a hard time. There was no milk for the children. Finally, after a desperate search for milk, Mrs. Rendell saw a settler milking a cow. She hastened toward him but just as she arrived, the cow kicked man, bucket, and all. They landed several yards away, and the milk was spilt. Mrs. Rendell burst into tears. In the morning, however, Mr. Rendell went to the settler and offered to milk the cow if he could have a little milk. The settler said, "Take all you want."

At last the trek began. Like the whole of the enterprise, it was badly conducted. The trail was in terrible condition. The first wagon had gone only forty rods before it was firmly mired down in a muskeg. Barr was supposed to have tents and provisions placed about a day's journey apart between Saskatoon and the new settlement. He got the tents set up finally, but there were few provisions. All, except those who were well provisioned before setting out, suffered great hardship.

Barr was falling more and more into disgrace. It had been bad enough when, on the *Lake Manitoba,* he had bought up all the flour on the ship, had it baked into bread, and sold the loaves to the colonists for ten cents a loaf—five cents more than they would have had to pay on their arrival at St. Johns. But his slick manipulation of funds became really apparent when the colonists arrived at their destination.

So disgusted had the settlers become over the criminal mismanagement of the trip, that they asked Dr. Lloyd, who had come as clergyman, to be director of the colony. A great mass meeting was held. Barr refused to attend, but was at last persuaded by Lloyd to do so. Barr spoke to the crowd, accused them of not fulfilling their agreements, and was finally quieted when a big Englishman at the back of the gathering waved a letter and shouted, "Is this your signature?" Barr replied that he couldn't tell at that distance, and asked the man to pass the letter up. Instead, however, the Englishman read the letter aloud to everybody. It was a letter addressed to all the Saskatoon merchants demanding that a commission on all sales to Barr colonists be remitted to Barr. The signature was undoubtedly Barr's.

A terrific uproar followed. Threats were made against Barr's life, but before definite action was taken, Barr had slipped quietly away. Soon, however, it became necessary to hunt him out. £350 had been raised by the colonists for medical instruments and supplies. These were badly needed, so Lloyd and a committee called on Barr and demanded to know where the supplies were being kept. Barr finally told the committee that the box containing the supplies was in a tent on "the north side of town."

The committee went immediately to fetch them. They found the tent, and in the tent was a box marked with a big red cross. When the box was opened, however, it was found to contain an old bed with a broken leg, a mattress, and one pillow. These were the sole "medical supplies" for the colony. The committee rushed back to find Barr, but he had departed. The story goes that he sold the colony's belongings for all he could get and made his escape across the American border.

He left an extremely bad odor behind him. First came the "potato scandal." Barr had ordered two thousand dollars worth of potatoes sent from Edmonton by scow. The potatoes arrived at Hewitt's Landing—the nearest point to the colony—but there was no one to receive them. The scow floated on down to Battleford. The merchant, Mr. Secord of Edmonton, demanded his money. Barr was gone. So was the money. Lloyd, therefore, believing that honesty was the best policy, went to the nearest bank and persuaded the banker to give the colony a credit of three thousand dollars. The potatoes were paid for; a few of them finally arrived at the colony, but most of them rotted. The whole transaction was a total loss.

There was the matter, too, of Barr's scheme for a trading company. He sold stock to the settlers for the purpose of "opening and running a general store for the purpose of supplying settlers with groceries, provisions, clothing, drapery, furniture, implements, horses, and cattle." The unfortunates who had invested lost their money.

Even the stoves Barr supplied to the colonists wouldn't draw. It was impossible to boil water on them. Of course, the fact that a few of the settlers, having no experience with stoves of that type, built the fires in the ovens didn't help the matter at all!

Lloyd, however, was an organizer and a real leader. In a little while, the colony took the name "Lloydminster," settled down, and the colonists went to work.

On August 6, 1903, Alice Rendell wrote a letter home. "Time flies even in camp life which, thank goodness, terminates today. This afternoon we contemplate moving up to 'Doris Court' and sleeping tonight, for the first time in four months, within shelter of four walls.

"July is the rainy month here, and when the rain does come down, it is like a deluge. Imagine the delight of being aroused night after night from your slumbers by rain trickling down on you and, as a rule, it has the habit of drifting just the very side of the tent you happen to be lying. I can assure you we have found it awfully trying."

And it was six days later that Mrs. Rendell took time to finish her letter: "Since writing the above, we have moved to our own domicile and right proud to look around, even though it be on bare boards, and feel it is indeed our *home*. All the weary treking at an end. We look from one window and see the lovely oats and barley looking splendid. From another window I look across and see the 'master of Doris Court' ploughing away for dear life with his fine pair of horses; each acre ploughed, means the better prospect for the coming year. The said team are just as fat as butter, having taken themselves off some seven weeks ago across the prairie, and having baffled all efforts to find them. Four days ago, we had some tidings of their whereabouts, and Barnes and another young fellow rode after them and, to our delight, returned the same evening with the delinquents. Their long absence was getting serious, as time is growing short and every available hour must be devoted to ploughing before winter sets in.

"Well, you will be wondering what sort of shanty 'Doris Court' is, so I will try to paint it as vividly as possible in your mind's eye. It is in bungalow form, measuring thirty feet by thirty, and contains five rooms. One is a large attic which runs the full length of the house, and is quite fit to be used for a bedroom, as we have had it all nicely boarded round and floored. We have two very large cellars in which we can store all necessary provisions for the winter. Everyone that sees it is of the same opinion: that it is the best house in the colony. There will be a veranda, four or five feet wide, around three sides of the house, which will be lovely in summer. We hope in the spring to get some fruit and other trees from the experimental farm to plant. There is certainly a great charm and fascination in planning it all out, knowing that it is our own property. I often say it compensates one largely for all the hardships we have been through."

This letter reflects a tone of growing optimism, but there is a sinister note in Alice Rendell's letter of October 21st: "Yesterday was a day never to be forgotten by the inmates of 'Doris Court' and the inhabitants of Lloydminister. For days past, we have been anxiously watching seven huge prairie fires raging in the distance, fearing that a wind might bring heavy disaster to our own homestead and town. The night of October 20th was an anxious one with the terrible circle of fire closing around us. The general opinion was that we were safe for the night, but I couldn't sleep.

"The next morning, our worst fears were realized, and we knew that a few hours would decide our fate. The only safeguard against prairie fires is a broad belt of ploughing all around your homestead. This my husband had done with the exception of one side which, alas, was the very side toward which the fire was sweeping with awful rapidity. Needless to say, the plough was soon at work and it was ploughing for dear life. Every available tub was filled with water, every sack collected together to beat out the flames when the time should come.

273

"Mr. Rendell, Barnes, and another man who is working for us were all on the alert, watching with intense eagerness at all the different points. Meanwhile, within the house, I together with Mrs. Falmank (the wife of our postmaster who is boarding with us for the winter) and Mrs. Bunyan, who nursed me when our little girl was born, stood gazing out the window horror-stricken at the awful sight that met our eyes.

"We each of us had three little children and each, one in arms. We mustered nine little ones all under six years. Our little flock, fortunately, were too young to realize the deadly peril we were in, and we had to keep on 'rounding them up,' preparatory to hasty flight. I collected a few valuables and looked around with a heavy heart, wondering whatever would become of us if in a few moments we should be left homeless.

"At last we could stand still no longer and we three women rushed out and, filling buckets with clay and soil dug up from the foundation, we scattered it all over the ground immediately around the house. The wind was blowing a hurricane, bringing—rather driving—the fire straight on us.

"Willie continued ploughing until absolutely compelled to stop by the heat and smoke. Our two men meanwhile drenched our roof with water and, arming themselves with wet sacks, hurried to the weakest points in the fireguard, only about 150 yards off the house.

"We could do nothing more than wait with bated breath. At last came the joyful sound: 'safe!' from the western side, but the danger was not yet over; for we were threatened again from the northwestern side.

"After the horses had been placed in safety, the men had to rush around to meet the enemy at the fresh point of attack. We waited in terrible suspense, and you can guess our joy when my husband came back to us with the welcome assurance: 'All danger over. *Safe* for another year.'

"We were all too overjoyed for words, and, after the dreadful strain of so many hours, you may pretty well know what the reaction was like. We lost four tons of hay, but many lost all their hay ricks. The fire started by the Vermillion River and was raging for days before it reached us; then swept on down toward Battleford. There is no doubt whatever that our fireguard in a great measure saved the town life.

"Apart from the horror of it, the fire was a wonderful sight. Of course, on the prairie you can see for an enormous distance, and for twenty or thirty miles there was nothing but flames. As it grew dusk, the effect was more weird. How thankful we were that the fire reached us in the daytime and not in the night!"

After the fire, things seemed to go well. Social life was organized. Preparations were made for a gathering of the whole colony on Christmas day. Mr. Lloyd organized a choir and held weekly meetings at his own house. There were concerts and debates, and it was decided that the community put up a building which would serve as a school, church, and recreation hall. Everyone in the colony was to donate a log, and the name of the donor was to be carved on it. They planned a "bee" to erect the building. After Christmas was over, Mrs. Rendell wrote home in a new spirit of optimism:

"There can be no doubt whatever that the colony will succeed and that Lloydminster, in a few years time, will be a very large and prosperous centre. But I hope I have, ere this, dispelled all unfavorable ideas as to our fortune. Probably many who have been commiserating our lot have far greater need of pity than we; for while they are still plodding and 'hibernating,' we are on the progressive . . . probably making greater headway in twelve months than they in as many years. This is nothing if not a 'Go-ahead Country'."

And the country did go ahead! In 1911, the community raised oats which were judged best in the United States and Canada. This performance was repeated in 1913 and 1914. By 1922, the colonists had taken sixty-five international and provincial prizes for grain and stock.

I think that many of the colonists found the freedom they sought, and possibly, in the light of such a blessing, Barr should be credited with what was at least on paper a good idea. I asked Mrs. Rendell what finally became of Barr.

She said, "I don't know where he went after he left Lloydminister, but I know where he is now. He's in a very hot place!"

276

III

The Terror at Frog Lake

FIFTY MILES NORTHWEST OF LLOYDMINSTER LIES FROG Lake; and at the Frog Lake settlement on the morning of April 2, 1885, the certainty of death was in the air. The suspense of terror hung above the kneeling half-breeds, Indians, and whites in the tiny Frog Lake Mission.

Thomas Quinn, 6 feet 6 inches tall, broad shouldered, frontiersman, American Civil War soldier, and, at present Indian Agent, knew that death was only minutes away. He looked at the few white men and women huddled together. He heard the two priests, Fathers Fafard and Marchand, chanting the Mass. He wondered if any of them guessed how desperate the situation really was.

For days Quinn had seen the rebellion growing. Riel's angry half-breeds had whipped the police at Duck Lake. Thirteen men lay dead, and the Indians were jubilant— and dangerous. Well, Quinn had urged the whites to leave Frog Lake but he'd been voted down. Now on this April morning, Wandering Spirit, war chief of the Plain Crees, had herded all the whites into the church. This was the day, Quinn knew, for murder.

Now the service was over. What was it the priest had

said? "Peace . . . calm . . . confidence in the Indians . . ." something like that. Well, Quinn knew Indians. Himself part Sioux and their interpreter, he feared the worst for himself and the others. The others: Gowanlock, the millwright, and his wife; John Delaney, the farming instructor, his wife; Dill, the trader; Gilchrist, the clerk; old Williscraft, the mechanic; Gouin, a half-breed, but probably marked for death, too; the two priests—kindly men—good men; Cameron, the Hudson's Bay storekeeper, who got along well with the Indians. If anybody squeaked out of it, Cameron stood the best chance. A slim chance, but a chance.

And here was Wandering Spirit entering the church— war bonnet and rifle across his arm. He motioned for the whites to go outside.

Quinn led the little band out into the morning sunlight. Now Wandering Spirit stopped them.

"You will go to our camp," he said.

This was the end. No safety in the settlement, none even in the church. Certainly none in the Indian camp. Why prolong the torture?

Quinn stepped toward Wandering Spirit. "I will not go."

When Thomas Quinn refused to go another step toward the Cree camp, Wandering Spirit lifted his rifle and shot him through the heart. Thereafter the massacre was rapid and absolute. As Quinn fell, the priest, Father Fafard, rushed toward him to give absolution. Wandering Spirit shot him through the neck. The other priest, Father Marchand, ran toward his brother and was instantly killed.

Father Fafard, lying terribly wounded, heard a friendly

278

Catholic Indian whisper, "Lie still. Pretend to be dead." Despite the warning, the priest raised himself and crawled slowly toward Father Marchand. As he crawled, he was shot through the heart by an Indian whom he had raised.

Charlie Gouin had fallen near Quinn. Writhing with his wounds, he was trying to get to his feet when the Indian, Miserable Man, ran out of the Hudson's Bay store, placed his rifle against Gouin's chest, and shot him again.

Mrs. Gowanlock was walking beside her husband when suddenly he slumped to the ground. She threw herself on his body, put her face on his, and waited for the ball that would kill her.

Delaney and his wife were walking a little way ahead of the Gowanlocks. In front of them, they saw old Williscraft fall to the ground; and at almost the same instant, Mrs. Delaney saw an Indian aiming at her husband. With the shot, Delaney reached out his arms to his wife. She caught him, and they fell together. She lay for just an instant with her face against his before she was carried away by an Indian.

Gilchrist, the clerk, and Dill, the trader, started to run. Indians on horseback chased them both down within a hundred yards and killed them.

Cameron, the Hudson's Bay man, with the help of his Indian friends, escaped injury. Since that terrible morning, he has often told his own story.

*I was in the Hudson's Bay shop filling an order given by Quinn to an Indian named Kittamageeyan (Miserable Man) when the first two shots were fired. The Indian

*From the *Edmonton Journal*.

snatched his parcel from the counter in front of me and raced out of the shop. I followed him. He ran to the ridge, 125 paces away, where poor Quinn lay already dead, and pressing his rifle against the chest of Charlie Gouin, the second victim lying wounded on the ground, finished him with a second bullet.

A friendly Indian, Osawask, already with me and greatly alarmed, told me to go to the Indian camp half a mile away, but fearful for his own safety, refused to accompany me. I started, although with no expectation that I should ever reach it.

After one glance at the horror across the little depression on the opposite ridge, I turned away and walked on looking neither to right nor left, anticipating momentarily my own turn would come and determined not to see when or from whence. A little later I met several armed Indians, but they neither hindered nor threatened me. A bright sun rode in a cloudless sky overhead. It was a beautiful warm spring day.

When I reached the camp, I was taken to the lodge of the Wood Cree chief, Ooneepohayo, and there, a half dozen of his leading followers in council swore to protect me. They brought in Wandering Spirit who agreed to their demands and promised I should be left alone. Not that his promise counted for much, for he would have shot me later at a council meeting but for the intervention of my red friends. I had abundant evidence that morning that whatever was to happen, I could look for no different treatment from that to which the other whites had been subjected.

. . . had I been with the other white men at the moment

of the massacre instead of a short distance away, I am certain I should not have escaped their fate. I sat with Wandering Spirit in his cell at the Mounted Police Guardroom at Battleford the night before he was hanged and asked him the question. His answer was evasive, but it showed he had no intention of sparing me when he determined on his bloody enterprise. I stood next morning before the scaffold in the barrack yard and saw him die with five more of his conspirators, including Miserable Man who had left me in the shop when the shooting began.

There is a little cemetery at Onion Lake where all but two of the victims of the massacre lie buried. After the shooting, so the story goes, an old Indian squaw washed the faces of the missionaries as they lay in death; other Indians carried the bodies back to the chapel. A folktale relates how a picture of the Sacred Heart suddenly assumed a threatening attitude, and with a gesture of its hand, signified the retribution to fall upon those who had committed the murders. In terror, the Indians threw the bodies of the priests into the cellar and set the church on fire.

It certainly is true that the buildings at Frog Lake were burned and that the bodies of the victims were later found by the Mounted Police in the cellar. The police took up the bodies and carried them to Onion Lake.

The bodies of the two martyr priests, however, no longer lie with the others. In 1928 their bodies were moved to the Oblate Missionary plot at St. Albert where their stones are a reminder of the martyrdom and terror of the Frog Lake massacre.

IV

The Man of the Good Heart

"If I were an artist," said Father Simard as we stood on the steps of the Cathedral at St. Albert, "if I were an artist, I should like to paint all that."

He meant the soft, green countryside, the old buildings, the poplar trees, and the solitary elm shading a corner of the yard. He meant more, too. He was thinking of the past and all that St. Albert had meant in the making of the Canadian West. Possibly more than anything he was thinking about Father Lacombe.

Father Lacombe built the first church at St. Albert, and even today the whole place seems dominated by the spirit of this great peacemaker of the plains. Everywhere at St. Albert the spirit of charity and interest in mankind is evident—at the Indian school, the old folk's home, in the long service of the priests and the Grey Nuns.

Even Father Lacombe's old church has its place; for it is a museum now, carrying on the heroic traditions of its builder. In this museum which contains so many relics of the past, Father Simard showed me the hand-forged ploughshare with which—despite many discouraging remarks—an early St. Albert priest grew wheat taller than a man.

282

The blacksmith who forged the ploughshare was noted for his strength. He was not a very large man and when asked, "Where does the blacksmith live?" he picked up the anvil and pointed with it to his own house some distance away and said, "He lives over there."

Father Simard showed me a belt and a few other tokens: all that remained of a priest who was eaten by the wolves.

At the altar he showed me the figures carved by the priests from poplar wood; and in one of the cases we found bits of the skulls of Fathers Fafard and Marchand who died at Frog Lake.

On the slope below the Cathedral, looking out over the broad lands where he worked so long and so well, stands the bronze statue of Father Lacombe himself—the priest who was known to the Indians as the Man of the Good Heart.

St. Albert was named after Father Lacombe's patron, and when the good priest established the mission at St. Albert in 1861, he had already performed many deeds of charity in the West. He had ministered at Fort Edmonton where he became a close friend of John Rowand, the Factor.

Rowand loved the priest, but even this love was not as great as Rowand's interest in the welfare of the Hudson's Bay Company. At one time, Father Lacombe found a couple of muskrat skins which had been caught out of season and were, therefore, worthless. The priest took the skins to an Indian woman and had her sew them onto the cuffs of his coat. He did not at that time fully realize that no one connected with the company should secure furs in any way except in the company's interest. When

Rowand saw Father Lacombe's fur cuffs, he shouted, "Where did you get that fur? Who gave you the right to wear it?" For a moment Father Lacombe was stunned, then he tore off the fur and threw it in Rowand's face.

The incident, of course, later became a humorous anecdote, and in later years Father Lacombe was fond of telling about the generosity and courage of John Rowand.

But most of Father Lacombe's time was spent among the Indians. He constantly traveled a huge territory, baptizing, and nursing the Indians through epidemics. He also learned the Cree tongue and became so proficient that he expanded his knowledge into a Cree dictionary.

When he finally established the St. Albert Mission in 1861, he straightway proved that he was a builder as well as a missionary. The nearby Sturgeon River was a serious obstacle in high water, and Father Lacombe decided to build the first bridge west of the Great Lakes. He finally won the help of the Indians and the few white men by telling them that only those who helped build should use the bridge. When the bridge was completed, it seemed like a miracle. The Indians crossed it time after time, just for the thrill. They sometimes even camped on the bridge, and the story goes that one brave built a fire right in the middle. After that the Indians had to camp on the shore.

It was as peacemaker that Father Lacombe was best known, and at one time his desire for peace nearly cost him his life.

In 1865 Father Lacombe received a mission dear to his heart: following the Indian tribes wherever they should go, helping them and converting them when he could. His quest took him into the camp of Chief Natous of the Blackfeet. The Blackfeet, while slow to embrace the Christian faith, had a deep affection for Father Lacombe. He had once nursed them through a terrible epidemic of the typhoid.

It was a dark December night, and the priest was resting in the chiefs tent when suddenly an Indian somewhere in the darkness shouted, "Assinaw! Assinaw! The Crees! The Crees!" Once again the age-old battle between the Crees and the Blackfeet had broken out.

The small camp, with which Father Lacombe was sojourning, was one of three Blackfeet camps. The other two camps, however, were a long way off, and help could not be expected for at least a few hours. The bullets were whizzing everywhere, piercing all the tepees, especially the largest one where the priest was staying.

The old chief rushed out to exhort the Blackfeet to sell their lives as dearly as possible. In the darkness his voice was lost in the gunfire, the barking of dogs, the whoops of the Crees, and the wailing of the women.

Father Lacombe calmly got up, put on his cassock, kissed his Oblate crucifix, took his holy oils, and went out into the battle. He called to the Crees to withdraw, but his voice was unheard in the terrific noise. He finally gave up and devoted his attention to baptizing any of the dying who wanted his ministration.

The first victim was a young Blackfoot woman who had been shot in the head. She asked Father Lacombe to baptize her before she died. Father Lacombe baptized her, and a few minutes later she was scalped by a Cree, and her baby, whom the priest had overlooked in the darkness, was killed.

All night the battle went on, and toward dawn the braves of the distant Blackfeet camps, attracted by the firing, arrived to re-enforce their people. One of the new parties of warriors was led by a young brave destined to become the greatest chief among the Blackfeet. In the darkness he was stopped by Father Lacombe.

"Who are you?" asked the priest.

"Crowfoot," replied the Indian.

Father Lacombe had heard of this young man already known for his wisdom and bravery. He urged him to do what he could to save his people.

When dawn broke, twenty-five lodges had been destroyed by the Crees. In the cold December light, Father Lacombe took his crucifix in one hand, his Red Cross flag in the other, and told his Blackfoot friends to cease firing. Then, holding his crucifix above his head and waving his flag, he calmly walked toward the enemy. As he walked, he called to the Crees, but they did not hear, and a heavy mist prevented them from seeing him. The Crees kept firing. As Father Lacombe walked toward them, a bullet glanced from the frozen ground, struck him on the shoulder, and glanced off only to strike him again in the forehead. Father Lacombe fell to the snow.

When they saw him fall, a fresh wave of anger and courage swept over the Blackfeet. Thinking that the Crees had killed their friend, they began to drive the enemy back. Despite their new courage, the battle continued until, during a lull in the fighting a Blackfoot warrior called out to the Crees, "You have wounded the priest!"

When the Crees heard that they had injured Father Lacombe, they hastily withdrew.*

In the early 1880's, the C. P. R. was rapidly being built across the plains from Winnipeg. When the railroad reached the Blackfoot reserve, it began to be feared that the Indians would prevent the steel from going through. They had heard rumors that the coming of the railroad was but the first step in a final taking away of their reserve and such rights as they still maintained. They had heard, too, that the railroad meant the arrival of thousands of settlers who would make it impossible for the Indians to live.

The foremen of the construction crews knew that Father Lacombe wielded a tremendous influence with the Indians. They asked him to come and save the situation if he could.

The priest lost no time. He came prepared to talk in the only language the Indian really understood—food and plenty of it. Father Lacombe brought to Crowfoot's camp 200 pounds of tea, plenty of sugar, flour, and tobacco.

After the Indians had feasted, Father Lacombe made a speech. He urged that they let the railroad go through and told them that their property rights would be respected. There was considerable grumbling among the Indians, but through the friendship of Crowfoot who asked that they respect the word of a man who had never lied to them, they let the construction go on.

There is an interesting aftermath to this story of Father Lacombe as peacemaker for the C. P. R. In 1883 when

*You may read a complete account of this episode in *Father Lacombe, The Blackrobe Voyageur,* by Catherine Hughes; McClelland Stewart, Toronto.

the main line of the C. P. R. had reached Calgary, George Stephen, first president of the road, made a trip out with a distinguished party. Father Lacombe was invited to lunch aboard the president's car. During the luncheon Stephen remarked that it was pleasant to get away from the hurry and scurry of work, out to the foothills. "In fact, gentlemen, I am going to resign as president—for one hour, and be plain everyday George Stephen."

R. B. Angus, another of his guests, said, "Well, we can't let the road be without a president, even for one hour. I move that Father Lacombe take over in recognition of his service to us at Blackfoot Crossing."

Father Lacombe accepted the offer in the same spirit as it was made. A board meeting was held then and there. Stephen tendered his resignation, and Father Lacombe was elected. The priest, always full of good humor, then nominated Stephen to fulfill certain religious duties. When the hour was up, another meeting was held, and Stephen again shouldered the burdens of his office.

Father Lacombe performed in 1885 an even greater service than that which he did the railroad.

It was on March 27th that rumor began to spread through the small settlement of Calgary. The rumors told a grim story of the uprising among the Saskatchewan Crees and Metis, of murder and pillage. Calgary was far away from the scene of such events, but the people were worried. It was known that agitators from the Cree and Metis camps had been working among the Blackfeet, and it was feared that if the Blackfoot Nation should join Riel they might easily wipe out all white settlements in the region. It was an exciting day in the history of Calgary. A Home Guard was organized. A wire was sent to Ottawa and Regina for arms. A watch was set. Men gathered on the streets and spoke gravely of a Blackfoot attack on the town. Father Lacombe was sent for, and though he expressed faith in his friend, Crowfoot, he could not quiet the fears of the Calgary people.

One morning, Father Lacombe borrowed an engine from the C. P. R. and headed for Blackfoot Crossing to see Crowfoot. Crowfoot was surprised to see the priest, and Father Lacombe pretended that his was only a casual visit.

Crowfoot said that he had heard the Metis and the Crees were killing all the whites, and Father Lacombe convinced him that this was entirely false.

The Blackfoot camp was assembled, and the priest told the Indians that the white men were too strong; it would be foolish to take up arms. Crowfoot, too, spoke to his people, and at length told Father Lacombe that the Blackfeet, at least, would remain at peace.

But it was an uneasy time and, according to tales told me by old-timers who well remember the '85 Rebellion, Crowfoot himself was not too sure he would hold his Indians. The Calgary old-timer, A. P. Patrick, who was a close friend of the great Blackfoot chief, told me that Crowfoot said to him one day, "Pack up a horse and get to the mountains. I don't know how long I can hold them. I'm not sure I can hold them at all."

However, he did hold them, and the Blackfeet caused no trouble despite the fact that they were the most warlike of all the Western Indians.

In 1886 Sir John A. McDonald invited Father Lacombe

to come East with Crowfoot and other chiefs who had remained loyal during the Rebellion. This was partly a gesture of appreciation, and partly a wish to impress these Indians with the might of the white man.

Whatever the motive, the tour was a triumph. The Indian chiefs were everywhere fêted and entertained. They were not comfortable, however, and were most unwilling to let their great protector, Father Lacombe, out of their sight. Magnificent suites of rooms were provided for the chiefs at the hotels, but they refused to use them. They preferred to sleep in a single room and insisted that the priest sleep there, too.

Crowfoot especially made a profound impression upon the Canadian public. Not only was he heroic in appearance but his public utterances were also magnificent. At one time the chiefs were offered a huge pile of guns and ammunition to take back West. Crowfoot replied that the gift would not be accepted. The Indians had come in peace—they had not even a small knife for protection. They would accept no guns.

It would be impossible to tell all of Father Lacombe's good deeds, because no man knows all the good he did. He went wherever he was needed, no matter how cold the weather or how weak his own physical condition. During the terrible smallpox epidemic of 1870-71 he bore winged feet. He was heard from at Edmonton, then Pitt, then Carleton. He was everywhere, tending the sick, baptizing the dying. His services to the Indians were rewarded as a missionary priest would like to be rewarded. Convinced that a man who could live among them in sickness and hard times for over twenty years must have a message of real power, Chief Sweetgrass and 2,000 of his Cree Indians were baptized.

Father Lacombe was a man of great faith and great courage. He faced fearful hardships, yet he lightened his own hardships with a delightful sense of humor. On one hard, cold trip, he ran out of food. Telling about the experience afterwards, he said, "If we had had a pinch or two of salt, the moccasins wouldn't have made a bad meal at all!"

Father Lacombe is a sacred tradition in Alberta. There are two living shrines to his memory: St. Albert and the Lacombe Home at Midnapore near Calgary. St. Albert represents the work of his younger years, while the Lacombe Home for the Aged represents the charitable ambition of his last years. He raised the money for the Home almost single handed.

As long as there is faith in God, human courage, and interest in mankind, Father Lacombe will be remembered in Alberta.

PART FOUR

PEACE RIVER COUNTRY

"Peace River," said Johnny Chinook, "Peace River! There she lies! Look at 'er glisten in the morning sun! Look how the land rolls, soft and graceful. That's good land—rich, growin' land!

"There's a railroad train clankin' along. Hasn't been so long since it was wagon and boat into the Peace River Country.

"Women here, too. Kind o' strange, lots of women bein' here. Was a far-off, grim sort o' land. Land for men!

"Smilin' now, though. Laughin', too. Way-down-deep kind o' laughter. Good country. Rightly named. Peace!"

I

❦

Peace River Humor

STANDING IN FRONT OF THE ASSEMBLED STUDENTS, MR. Lloyd Garrison, Principal of the Berwyn High School, gave a delightful rendition of a Peace River tall story. This was in answer to a couple of tales I had told, and I was fast learning that in the Peace River Country the telling of a yarn is taken as a challenge to spin a better one.

"You all know Griffin Creek," the Principal began, "and you all know about the Indians there. (Griffin Creek used to be an Indian reservation.) Well, it was 1918, and the big 'flu epidemic was in full blast. The Indians were dying so fast it was impossible to keep 'em buried. In fact, there were only a couple of fellows who had any strength; and these two were busy day and night burying folks. They were getting mighty weak themselves, I tell you. Well, cold weather came on, as it does up here, and naturally, everything froze up solid, including all the deceased Indians. It was a real task trying to dig graves in that frozen ground, so the two fellows who were left just stacked the Indians up like cord-wood, expecting that they'd wait for spring to come and thaw out the ground. But the piles rose so quick and so fast that they saw this wasn't going to do at all. Besides, several of the Indians were in mighty funny positions when they passed out, and one 'specially mean old codger froze in such a twisted up position that the two men who were left couldn't get him out of his cabin door. Finally they saw that something had to be done, and done fast, or else the dead Indians would fill up all the world. So the men hit on the scheme of scraping the top off a muskeg. They figured that when they got the frozen top scraped off, the soft mud would be just the place to bury all the dead Indians. Well, they did this and started to put the frozen men away. They just put 'em in the mud like fence posts. They were pretty weak, too, remember, and they soon found that the only way they could bury the Indians fast enough was to get a big sledge hammer and just drive 'em down. This worked fine on all the Indians but one. This fellow had frozen with his arm and hand right straight up in the air. They drove all of him into the muskeg except this one arm. Try as they might they simply couldn't get that arm under! Now the old-timer who told me this story—and this should prove to you that it's gospel truth—said that for years afterwards, whenever he rode out Griffin Creek way, he used to tie his horse to that Indian's arm!"

There is laughter in the air in the Peace River Country. It is laughter that comes from the land, from the lakes and the rivers, from the courage of the Peace River folk! It is a hearty laughter, without malice, and one may hear it in the whistle of the Peace River wind, in the chug of the Northern Alberta Railways Muskeg Limited, in the songs of the birds, or issuing joyfully from the throats of the honest-to-God tale-spinnin'est folks in the West.

297

The Crees love to relate the tales of their mighty hunters. Perhaps three old men are sitting around the fire at night. After a period of silence the first old man says, "I got a moose today. I was so close to it I could have touched it when I shot. It happened like this. I was out on the shore of the lake which was covered with a sheet of clear ice. Far away, on the other side of the lake, I saw this great bull moose. I was much too far away to shoot, so I had to think fast. I had my ax with me and in an instant I had chopped down a small spruce tree. This I tied to my body with cord. I then placed the ax, edge down, on the ice, stood on the ax handle and spreading my capeau like a sail I fairly flew across the lake straight toward the moose. I went so fast the moose never saw me coming at all and I was able to come within a foot of him and shoot him dead."

There is a period of silence, then the second old man begins: "Yes, you came close to that moose, but I have been even closer than that, and to a bull much larger than yours. Today I was out hunting and was following the track of the largest moose I have ever seen. I followed nearly all day, and toward evening I could see by the track that the moose was going to turn off and bed down for the night. You know how a moose will do—double right back on his own track and lie down beside his own trail so he can hear and smell anybody following him. Well, when I saw that this bull was going to turn I came around the other way with the wind and spotted him lying by the trail. I crept up and made a large X on his hoof with my knife. I then went and fetched my young son.

298

"I said to him: 'Son, I have spotted a great bull moose and have put my own mark on him. I will now take you to the spot so you can shoot this moose and see for yourself that I am not lying.' My son came with me, shot the moose, and found my X on his hoof. He was very much surprised."

There is another long silence then the third old man starts his tale. "Yes, you both did well but I had even a more remarkable experience. I was out hunting today and had only one bullet. Suddenly I saw two great bull moose standing some distance apart. Which one was I to shoot? I couldn't make up my mind, so I settled the whole matter by determining to get them both. Right between the two moose I spied a saskatoon bush. I knew how hard a saskatoon will freeze in the wintertime, and this bush was just right for my purpose. I crept up to it and with my knife sharpened the side of the bush toward me. I then crept back a little way, took steady aim at the bush and pulled the trigger. Of course the frost-hardened bush split my bullet and half flew right and killed the right-hand moose, and the other half flew left and killed the left-hand moose. I think that is very good hunting."

There is laughter, too, in the stories old La Boutaille used to tell. He was a trapper of the Lesser Slave Lake region, and he had an eternal struggle to provide for his large family.

"Many years ago," La Boutaille used to say, "I needed food for my family, though I had but little ammunition for my gun, when I started off on what seemed to be a very hopeless chase. At length, I had expended all but one bullet and was prepared to give up in despair. Just then I heard the unmistakeable sound of ducks feeding. Looking around some willows, I found I was on the banks of a small creek, the location of which was strange to me. It was a peculiar stream winding in a series of regular curves across a wooded plain. Examining it, I saw a fat drake feeding just around the first bend. Going farther, I found a still fatter duck in the next bend. The sight encouraged me, and exploring, I discovered that nine ducks in all were feeding, one in each bend! I had but one bullet left as I have already told you, and it was a big problem how to use it to the best advantage. Suddenly I saw the way to feed the hungry family waiting for me far away!

"Quietly dropping to the ground, I carefully surveyed the first bend in the stream, then placing my gun across my knee, I bent it to correspond to its angle. Examining the other bends, I bent the gun-barrel this way and that, until at last it was an exact representation of the convolutions of the stream. Then quietly descending to the level of the water, I took steady aim at the first duck. The bullet passed through it and traveling on, its course determined by the kinks in the gun-barrel, it penetrated neatly one after the other, the remaining eight ducks. Turning homeward laden with nine heavy ducks, I reflected that the old proverb about killing two birds was greatly out of date!"

Another La Boutaille tale was one he used to tell about the year of starvation, the year when game had departed from the country around the Slave Lake. "The squaws foraged for berries in vain," related La Boutaille, "and the children, too weak to play, cried themselves into what was perhaps to be their last sleep. I was preparing to join my forefathers beyond the sky's horizon.

"While thinking I was looking on its placid waters for the last time, I saw far away, but approaching me, many birds. They came nearer and I realized I was looking at thousands of geese! But alas, they did not attempt to approach the shore but alighted far out on the waters and commenced to feed. The sight of them kindled a great idea and stirred me into activity. I rushed back to my camp and shouted to everyone to prepare many cords of *babiche*, each with a running noose at one end. While this was being done, I procured a whiplike sapling. The cords were many but light in weight, and I fastened them as well as the stick to my body, rushed toward the lake, and diving in, swam with all my might toward the flock of feeding geese. As I neared them, I sank beneath the unsuspecting birds. I unfastened the cords and with deft fingers slipped a noose around each pair of legs within reach. Moving this way and that, I secured many more until at last, my supply of *babiche* exhausted, I had captured as many geese as would form a feast for half the Indian people of the North.

"Then up I popped in the midst of the still feeding birds yelling like one possessed and with my club stirred the startled geese into wildest activity. With a thunderous whirring of wings, they rose clear of the water, each one in doing so, tightening the noose around its legs. Up and still up they went, drawing me behind them clear out of the water and far into the air.

"With cunning born of many weeks of hunger, I steered the flying birds toward my camp many miles distant. As

301

we approached I gradually hauled in on my lines and as goose after goose came within reach, I would deal it a great whack with my stick, at which it would fall inert to the extent of its cord, thereby acting as a brake on the progress of the remainder. Then, as my lodge surrounded by astonished upturned faces loomed into view, I pulled in desperately on the cords securing the remainder of my winged steeds and smote right and left with my cudgel. Each blow lessened the speed of my flight, and as the supporting geese decreased in number, I gradually descended until with the last few struggling birds, I gently landed on the earth before my tepee."

The Peace River folk are invariably proud of their land and climate. This justifiable pride is imaged in the tales they tell. Campbell Young, a remarkable old-timer who now resides in Edmonton, told me how he once explained the Peace River climate to an Ontario man.

I used to live in Peace River town and before I tell you this story you must remember that the men who pioneered this country had a terrific belief in the land. They also had the flare for impressing strangers with the local wonders. Sometimes our tales were tall, but this was all the better for usually the strangers took the stories in good spirit and went back East to relate the wonders of the West.

One time some members of Boards of Trade in the East were visiting Peace River. I met one of these immaculately dressed individuals on the street. The fellow wore plus-fours, a bowler hat, a monocle, and a mustache. He stopped me and said, "How do you do, sir. Have you lived here long?"

"Several years," I said.

"Then you can surely tell me," said the stranger, "whether or not this is a healthy climate."

I thought a bit, then I said, "I'll tell you a circumstance. This will illustrate to you how healthy this climate really is. When the first settlers came up here they were very lonely. They had nothing—didn't even have a cemetery. They got to figuring that one of the things they would need was a cemetery. They, therefore, got together and fixed up a plot, then sat around and waited for somebody to die. Nobody died."

"Remarkable," said the stranger.

"Yes," I said. "So after a while they got discouraged and sent for all their oldest relatives and friends to come up—knowing that surely one of these old folks would pass away soon."

"And did they?" asked the stranger.

"Not a single one," I replied. "Not a one of 'em died. In fact, they all began to get younger. *Nobody* died. Not even a dog."

"What a dreadful situation," breathed the Easterner.

"Yes, and it was even more dreadful because, you see, we'd hired an undertaker to come up, too—told him what a fine business he'd have; and that poor fellow was slowly starving. In fact, he got so weak he crawled over to Saskatchewan where he passed away."

"How did all this turn out?" asked the stranger.

"Why," I replied, "the situation got so desperate that we finally had to shoot a man to start the cemetery—*and that's when all the trouble broke out!*"

"Sir, your conversation has a decided Western flavor!"

Even the young folk love to relate the tall ones. I was

talking one day to the students of the Fairview High School. After I had finished I asked whether any of them knew any Peace River stories. One bright young man got up and said he knew about a remarkable event which concerned Spike Drew. I asked who Spike Drew was, and after being told that he was a man to whom anything in the world could happen, I sat back and let the yarn take its course.

According to the student, Spike was going across country quite late at night. He was walking along when suddenly he heard a noise behind him. He looked back and saw several pairs of ferocious eyes. He knew they were the eyes of timber wolves, and he began to walk a little faster. The wolves kept right behind him. Spike tried all the old tricks of dropping his gloves, and other articles of apparel and food which he had with him. This didn't do any good, and the wolves began to close in on him. Finally Spike saw a lone tree standing away down ahead, and he made a break for it.

Just as he was shinning up, one of the wolves made a leap for him and snapped the heel of his boot. For a time, however, Spike was safe. He climbed to the top of the tree while the wolves gathered around the trunk in a circle and looked up at him.

Spike sat and waited. So did the wolves. Finally some of the wolves began to get discouraged and drifted away. Eventually they all left except two. These two wolves just kept sitting, looking up at Spike. Soon these two sniffed noses a bit, then went away. Spike thought he was saved. He waited a suitable time then started to crawl down. He'd come about half way down the tree when he saw a terrible sight. The two wolves who had waited so long were coming back, and to his horror Spike saw that they were carrying a beaver between them! Alas, Spike knew he was lost!

I have heard this story in different forms in many places. It's always a good story and if Spike Drew said it happened to him, I'm willing to agree that it did.

II

Colorful Names and Colorful Characters

As my friend, Mr. Norman Soars, of Peace River says, "Nicknames are a Northern habit. Witness our celebrated bootlegger, Baldy Red—which is a sort of double-barrelled nickname; and I assure you that I once heard two fur-buyers talking: one said, 'One-eyed Pete's in town.' The other replied, 'Not One-eyed Pete from Deadman's Creek!'"

Yes, the names in the Peace River Country are certainly interesting and colorful. I heard names like Baldy Red, Society Red, Sad Sam, Gyp the Blood, Buckskin Annie, attached to persons of somewhat doubtful reputation, but who in their own line were beings of enormous stature, especially Buckskin Annie.

And then, too, you run onto towns with names like North Star, Bluesky, High Prairie, Grande Prairie, Drift-pile, Beaverlodge, and Pouce Coupe.

Considering the characters I am convinced that Baldy Red is at least *one* of the best known names throughout the Peace River Country. Baldy's real name was George Yeoman, but very few people remember that. They do remember that he came from Eastern Canada, was of

English stock, and some who knew him claim that Baldy was the son of a wealthy Montreal banker. They remember, too, that Baldy got his nickname from the fact that he was bald on top with a fringe of red hair and that as Baldy Red he was known from Calgary and the foothills north to Peace River.

In police court, when asked his business, he invariably described himself as a bootlegger. Bootlegging, however, he regarded more as a sport than a profession, since it appealed more to his sense of humor and sport than to his acquisitiveness.

He enjoyed his wide reputation and loved to tell stories about himself. He used to tell how he got over to England during the First World War in charge of a shipload of horses. "And when I walked down Picadilly, every second man I met said, 'Hi ya, Baldy! How the hell did you get over here?'"

Among the innumerable yarns regarding Baldy are a few favorite tales that even the kids know in the Peace River Country.

The episode of Baldy and the foxes, for instance, took place at Grouard in the early days of the fox-farming boom. Grouard was then the metropolis of the North, and the country was full of buyers trying to pick up live silver foxes which were fetching fancy prices. Baldy got into conversation with a fur buyer in the hotel one night and casually let out that he knew where there were quite a bunch of foxes to he had.

"About three hundred or more," said Baldy, "a nice bunch, mostly reds with a few crosses and some good silvers amongst 'em."

After considerable haggling, Baldy finally named a price at which he told the buyer he could have them. A very reasonable price it was. "But at that price," said Baldy, "you will have to take 'em as they run, reds, crosses, and silvers."

The buyer by that time was thoroughly "sold" and when Baldy told him that to bind the bargain he must have twenty dollars, he promptly got it.

Next morning, bright and early, the buyer was waiting and suggested to Baldy that they go and look the foxes over.

"Me, I'm not going," said Baldy, "I'm too busy. You go and look 'em over."

"Where are they?" asked the buyer.

Baldy waved his arm around the landscape. "Out in the bush. You agreed to take 'em as they run, and by God, they're running!"

A popular story of Baldy concerns the time he was being taken out to the Fort Saskatchewan jail by a Mounted Policeman. An unfeeling judge had sentenced Baldy for stealing a cow, when all he had done was to pick up a piece of rope with a cow at the other end of it! Another prisoner was being taken to jail at the same time, convicted of stealing a watch.

Baldy, to pass the time, would every few minutes ask the other prisoner: "What's the time? Have you the time on you?"

Finally the other man, completely exasperated, snapped back: "It's *milking* time, you son-of-a—!"

Baldy's best known exploit occurred when he drove the Grey Nuns on their collecting trip along the construction line of the Grand Trunk Railway.

308

The Nuns maintained hospitals in the construction camps and made trips collecting funds. Baldy went to them and explained that he was a poor man and couldn't afford to give them money, but that he would like to drive them and put a wagon at their disposal. The Nuns made the trip, never suspecting that they were sitting on a cache of booze, and while they preached and collected, Baldy peddled his moonshine without interference from the police.

He pulled the same stunt at Peace River town when he drove in two Anglican missionary ladies. He parked his wagon in front of the Mounted Police barracks and asked Sergeant Anderson, who was a devout Anglican, to keep an eye on the ladies and the belongings. The liquor on which they sat got through!

Baldy's outstanding trait was his sense of humor. He loved to tell of finding a cache of liquor at Crooked Bridge, and of how he washed off the labels and sold it in Peace River to the bootlegger who had cached it at the Bridge.

He died at Grande Prairie, and in the Peace River Country they tell me that undoubtedly his sense of humor got him safely through the Pearly Gates.

Society Red was almost as famous as Baldy. I frankly don't know how Society got his name, but he was a clever man. One time Society had a big wagon load of hootch he wanted to get into Grande Prairie. The Mounted Police were on the job as usual and had a particular eye out for Society Red. Red knew his chances of getting by were mighty slim. It must have been fate that sent the Reverend Dr. Forbes along the same road.

Reverend Forbes was exceedingly well known in the Peace River Country and rightly so, for he had pioneered the first hospital at Grande Prairie and had done other deeds of public service. On this particular occasion he was driving a nervous pair of young horses, and as he passed Society Red's rig, the Doctor's horses shied.

"That's a skittish pair you're drivin', Reverend," said Society.

This remark did nothing to bolster the Doctor's courage, and when Red continued, "Tell you what I'll do. I'll drive those colts into town for you. You drive my wagon." The Doctor accepted gratefully.

Red drove the Doctor's rig into town, while the Reverend Doctor Forbes calmly drove Society Red's load of bottled-in-bond right into Grande Prairie. Needless to say, he wasn't molested by the police.

While we're on the subject of moonshine, it would be a mistake to pass by Sad Sam. He did a little farming, but his real job was bootlegging. Sam spent many an hour moaning about his lost reputation as an honest citizen. One day when Dr. O'Brien of Grande Prairie made a call at the Sad Sam homestead, Sam told him, "Doctor, when a feller gets a name, it *sticks*. People thinks I make a lot of money bootleggin'. That's a lie. When my kids gets into trouble I have to pay their fines. That eats up a hell of a lot. Then maybe the old woman gets sick. I tell you, if I get a crop this year, I'm quittin'."

Sam never quite managed to get a crop, so he had to continue his bootlegging to make ends meet. It's a fact, though, that he suffered much philosophical torment over his community standing.

310

One time a large ditch had been freshly dug at Grande Prairie, and Sad Sam was unfortunate enough to run his car smack into it. It was, of course, incidental that the car was loaded to the windows with booze. One of Sam's sympathizers commented that it was a shame to lose so much good stuff as well as an automobile. Sam replied mournfully, "I don't care so much about the car or the moonshine, but I sure do hate to lose my reputation!"

One of the real masters of philosophical comment in the Peace Country was John McCauley. John was a fur buyer and had a reputation among the Indians as a man whose word meant something.

One summer a great quarrel broke out among the Indians. A brave had discovered his wife in the company of another Indian, and the ensuing fracas broke the tribe up into two factions. They weren't able to settle the quarrel short of actual war and finally agreed to arbitrate the matter with John McCauley as mediator.

John heard the facts of both sides, thought for a while, expectorated a little tobacco juice, then said, "B'ys, in hot weather like this, it don't make a damn bit of difference!" Apparently these words of self-evident truth were enough, and the Indians went away happy.

While we're on the subject of colorful characters, the folks around Hythe would be upset if we skipped the Daughtery murder case. Any old-timer can tell the story. I have discovered several different versions of the affair, and possibly the best version I heard may have gained some color in the telling; but here's the way I heard it.

The Daughterys were early settlers around Hythe. They had managed to prove up on a homestead, but

311

Daughtery, especially, wasn't happy. He kept telling everyone he met that he was going to leave the country. He did, but not, perhaps, in the way he would have chosen. Certain people had often noticed that Mrs. Daughtery was a high-tempered woman, and that she had a habit of reviling her husband.

Apparently the woman's dislike for Daughtery finally became too great, and the poor fellow was one day laid low by a dose of poison slipped into his food. His passing, however, was slow, and Mrs. Daughtery was so impatient to become a widow that she opened the trap door into the cellar, shoved him down, and as he lay helpless on the earthen floor, she carefully and thoroughly shot him through the head with a rifle. She buried Daughtery where he died.

Her plans for the murder were complete. She had carefully written several letters to herself and signed them with her husband's name. These letters she had sent to a school teacher at Spirit River with the request that they be mailed. The first of these letters arrived on the day she murdered Daughtery.

Things were quiet for a month or so, and then a few people began to be conscious that Daughtery was missing. Possibly the domestic silence around the Daughtery homestead emphasized his disappearance. Curiosity grew into suspicion, and at length the police were called in to investigate. Mrs. Daughtery was duly called on, asked where her husband was, and when she showed the letters from Spirit River, the police were satisfied that Daughtery was "away" and dropped the case.

There were many who weren't satisfied, but things

drifted along until one day Provincial Police Constable Sullivan was shifted to the area. Among the things that Sullivan heard upon his arrival was the story of the missing Daughtery. He made up his mind to investigate.

Sullivan was a big man and considered handsome. He had a reputation among the ladies, and this reputation he soon put to good use. The method of investigation he adopted was somewhat unique. He took off his uniform and adopted the clothing of a traveler looking for a good piece of land. News soon spread that he was in the market for a homestead already proved up; and this news reached Mrs. Daughtery who was most eager to sell.

It had better be known at this point that Mrs. Daughtery had once been one of Edmonton's fancy women and this may partially account for Sullivan's easy access into her graces—at any rate, Sullivan, after his first call at the Daughtery place, moved in with Mrs. Daughtery. She fell, according to folktale, violently in love with him.

The widow was eager to sell Sullivan her homestead, but the cautious policeman pretended that her price was too steep for him, and invented a deal with some outside land buyer, who, he said would pay more money.

"There was one catch," explained Sullivan, "the land buyer won't consider taking the place until we can get your husband's signature on the deed—or, at least, a release so the place can be sold."

This stumped Mrs. Daughtery for a few hours, then she began to urge Sullivan to help her forge her husband's name. Sullivan refused. He built her up, too, by telling her of the fine places he was going to take her, just as soon as the land was sold.

At length she said, "If I were to tell you that Daughtery would never again be seen, would you help me forge his signature?"

Sullivan said he would.

"Very well, then," replied the widow, raising up the cellar door, "Daughtery's down there. Buried three feet under."

The following afternoon and evening must have seemed long to Sullivan. Sometime during the course of the afternoon they fixed up the papers for the sale of the land, and Sullivan said that in the morning he would take the papers to Grande Prairie to get them legalized. During the evening, however, he mentioned something about the police that aroused the woman's suspicions. On his part, Sullivan was growing afraid of Mrs. Daughtery, and when he retired, he feigned sleep.

According to the tale, this "Lady Macbeth of the North" crept to the side of his bed, lighted a candle and placed it on the table. Then she took the rifle which the disturbed Sullivan could see was under her arm, pointed it directly at his head; and Sullivan heard her mutter, "Shall I kill him now? I love him, but I can't afford to trust him."

At that point, the narrator said Sullivan heard the gun's hammer click back, and thought that the next second would find a bullet crashing through his head. But for some reason, after a long, nervous pause she lowered the gun, took the candle, and went out.

Early the next morning Sullivan was on his way to town. He secured two policemen for protection and went back to arrest Mrs. Daughtery for murder. When she

314

came to the cabin door in answer to his knock, Sullivan seized her, and the other men grabbed her from the side. She put up a stiff struggle and almost floored all three of them, but they finally subdued her. When it was over she looked at Sullivan and said, "Well, Sullivan, in spite of everything, I love you."

Sullivan seems to have been curiously unmoved by this sentiment. They tied up the woman, and then all three men began digging in the cellar floor. Presently they unearthed Mr. Daughtery who was in a remarkably good state of preservation. They brought Mrs. Daughtery down to identify her husband, and when she saw the corpse she said, "Now isn't Daughtery an ornery devil? Been buried for three months and I've poured hot water over him every day! He doesn't have any right to look so spruce!"

It is, perhaps, a comment on the exigencies of the law that Mrs. Daughtery was not convicted of murder. She was released on a plea of self defense. She was later jailed, so the tale goes, on a narcotics charge. In prison she tried very hard to slip arsenic in the prison soup. Luckily the matron discovered the poison in time.

III

❦

Selby's Cross

AT FAIRVIEW, ONCE KNOWN AS WATERHOLE, ELWYN KELSEY, the young editor of the *Fairview Post,* told me about John Selby and his famous cross. Before he told me the story, however, Mr. Kelsey explained that he hadn't got around to starting the *Post* until 1941, and when he printed an old-timer's edition the same year, he had to pretend that he was publishing the paper in 1916—really old times in Waterhole.

Mr. Kelsey explained, too, that he had received the tale of Selby's Cross from Spike Drew, one of Fairview's foremost old-timers, who came in with a survey party in 1911 and helped lay out all the section lines. The party also found stakes of the old Hudson's Bay survey made about 1881.

According to Spike's story, Selby was a surveyor who was called mad and was held for a time in an asylum, but who effected a stroke of engineering genius near Fairview about 1881 that no expert can explain to this day.

John Selby surveyed parts of the area before he turned queer and (nobody knows why) retreated into the swamps north of Fairview to make an independent survey of a

316

block three miles each way from a central stake. An X called Selby's Cross appears on old maps.

In 1910 a survey party which included Spike Drew came into the country, and this party located Selby's stakes. To the utter amazement of the engineers it was found that Selby's first peg was located to the fraction of an inch at the exact northeast corner of Section 83, Rge. 2, W 6, three miles north of Fairview.

Selby located that spot in an uncharted swamp, mind, with no section lines to guide him. How did he find the correct line north and south? How did he chance to strike the true section corner east and west? His original stake was sent to Ottawa to be kept in the archives.

Except that his calculations must have been from the stars and marvelously complicated, the miracle of John Selby's Cross has never yet been explained and remains a mystery which engineers admit none of them could duplicate.

Spike Drew recalls that Selby returned to government employ after his release from the asylum, and was finally killed when a bank on the edge of the Athabaska River caved in on him.

IV

Bard o' the North

"THERE'LL ALWAYS BE AN IRELAND," SAID JOHN SWEENEY, "and there'll always be a poet Burns. Those are two of the things that'll keep this old ball of mud rolling—if anything will."

We sat in Sweeney's neat little cabin about seven miles from Fairview. To Sweeney, who is eighty years old, writing poetry has always been easy. So easy, in fact, that he has been known for a long time as Bard o' the North. It is not my purpose to be biographical, but Sweeney once wrote me a letter sketching his life. He titled this sketch: *Outline of Sweeney's Life—So Far*. This is what he wrote:

> I was born of Irish parents near Dalesville, Province of Quebec, on April 14, 1864. Youngest of family of six. Left my home for first and last time on July 5, 1886. Came to Michigan and joined an older brother there who had been west before. Came to Butte, Montana in 1886, and farther west to Missoula, Montana in 1890. Stayed there until Klondike gold rush in 1898. Left my brother in U.S.A. and came to Quesnell Forks, Cariboo District, B. C. in June, 1898. Reasons for not going to Klondike: short on cash. Came back to United States in 1900 and found my brother working in lumber woods near Missoula.

My brother and I came north again in 1908 on a trapping and prospecting trip to the Peace River Country. Left Edmonton in July, and arrived at Dunvegan on Peace River, middle of August. Waited there for last trip of Hudson's Bay boat up-river. Paid fifteen dollars fare on steamer to Fort St. John, B. C. Hired Indians there with pack ponies to take us over the Klondike trail to Laurier Pass, on head of Cypress Creek—a tributary of Half Way River. We picked up an Austrian at St. John who wanted to go as far as we went. Paid Indians fifty-eight dollars for privilege of going that far. His destination was two hundred miles farther on to the Ingenitra diggings on the upper Findlay. He started out from our camp walking, with his dunnage on his back. He never even reached Fort Graham, eighty miles farther on. I have heard since that he was killed by Sekani Indians fifty miles beyond our camp. I have never heard anything definite about that Austrian since. We were at Laurier Pass until October 25, when our cabin was burned to the ground. Fortunately, we had another camp with a little grub and one blanket. We hiked back again to Fort St. John with only seven matches, very little grub, and damn cold. Burned the last match, and ate the last bite of bannock thirty-five miles from St. John. Landed at Fort St. John, 10:30 p.m. We intended coming out to Edmonton, but ice was running in the Peace River and it wasn't safe to tackle it. Bought more supplies, made two toboggans, and came back again one hundred and sixty miles to Laurier Pass; motive power, the two Sweeneys. Came back to St. John in April, 1909. My brother Jim and I had one L of a time coming out and pulling our toboggan. Had to wait some time for ice to go out of the river. Built raft and came to Peace River Crossing. From there to Edmonton, and back to Montana. My brother died

319

there in 1912. I came here the following spring, and am here yet.

"Yes, I am still here," said Sweeney, "defending freedom of thought, and doing the best I can. It's hard these days to make any comments on the sweltering mass of humanity. If I could get somebody to publish my poetry, maybe that would be of some help. It costs money to publish poetry, and old Father Time never waits. My exit from this ball of mud may come before my financial condition improves. Here's a piece I wrote about the boom at Waterhole:

> *The boom is off at Waterhole,*
> *That boom that echoed to the pole*
> *Their big inflated bubble broke,*
> *Crooked schemes went up like smoke.*
> *Hard times hit them such a welt*
> *It made them slack below the belt—*
> *At time to dine they sit and stare*
> *Upon a scanty bill of fare.*
>
> *A shyster's sign it swings in sight,*
> *To guide you to the legal light;*
> *But until death you'll always rue*
> *The day you met that Irish Jew.*
> *For once within his cheap abode*
> *He'll skin you clean as any toad.*
>
> *They have an aviator there,*
> *When he talks the natives stare.*
> *Once by luck (or was it chance?)*
> *He saw the far-off coast of France.*
> *Right then and there he said a prayer,*
> *Vowed he never would go there.*
> *He never did, but just the same,*
> *They tacked Lieutenant to his name.*

They have an iron-burner, too,
He sports the name of Jake-a-loo,
Never washed, he's black as Hell,
What nation bore him, I can't tell.
A sawbones and a Man of Prayer
Likewise both are stationed there,
One trains your spirit to ascend—
The other hastens on your end.
One thing I know they both can do—
They fasten on your coin like glue.

A livery barn that's cold and dark
Old skates there from Noah's Ark;
Their rotten hay and musty oats,
Fragrance o'er the Mudhole floats;
They feed your team a wisp of hay
Turn your back, it's stole away!

O'er the bar they sell a swill
That comes from some Green Island still.
A cop, two bankers and their clerks
Are enrolled among these shirks.
Of this cull lumber they have made,
A something called a Board of Trade.

If their sin-buster he is there,
Their banquet opens with a prayer,
But e'er the shades of eve have fled,
They drink a toast to Baldy Red.
They spout of all they're going to do—
They'll fetch the railroad whizzing through.

Before snow flies, the trains will roll
Right into stinking Waterhole.
(When Vanrena's boom it comes,
We'll harbor none o' Mudhole's bums,
We'll meet 'em wi' a poplar club,
And knock them back to Beezlebub.)

Now to conclude, those pioneers
Have mostly gone to other spheres,
And in that bunch that have no pelf
Include yours truly, that's myself!

Which is Sweeney's comment on the Waterhole real-estate boom.

"People around here sometimes call me an atheist," Sweeney continued. "But that just shows how little they know about me. A fellow I know sets out to raise a garden. He doesn't take any particular care of that garden and shouts to the Lord to raise it for him. I don't do anything like that. I plant my garden in a good place and put a little fertilizer on it, and after a while I raise a good garden, a whole lot better than that other man's. He calls me an atheist. What do you think?

"One thing that does make me good and mad, though, are these fellows who set out to make a lot of profit out of the man who doesn't have anything anyway. I speak my mind about this whenever I get a chance, and as a result some people call me a communist—or worse. Well, what I've got is right here in this room—that, and my verses. I've always shared what I had with the other fellow, and if that makes me a communist, that's all right with me. I used to work on threshing rigs, and I'd get so mad—well, here's the verse I wrote about *that*.

In Heaven I never want a seat,
If I have got to shovel wheat.
To tell the truth upon my soul
In Hell I'd rather shovel coal,
To keep old Limbo good and hot
And burn the whole infernal lot,
That owns a damn old threshing rig
And tries to make their profit big.

322

Each time the griddle made a turn,
I'd make them wiggle like a worm—
The Dirty Measley Lousy ginks:
They're not one half as good as chinks.
Their hours are long, their pay is small,
No end unto their day at all.
You never need to have a bed—
No place to rest your weary head.

Go buy a lantern at the store,
For you have got no time to snore.
E're you have your supper downed
You hear again the whistle sound.
They blow it long, and loud and shrill
So you can find the threshing mill.
Enough is said, I'll cut my tale,
And very soon I'll hit the trail.

When we finally got up to go, Sweeney followed us out to the gate.

"Things will turn out all right," he said. "There's more good in man than evil. Things will be all right. But I wish you'd send me some Burns's poetry when you get back to Edmonton. That'll help *me* see things right, anyway."

I looked back when we were a long way off and Sweeney was still standing at the gate.

It's easy to remember John Sweeney, and possibly, coming generations leafing through many a yellowed scrapbook will think, *"I'm glad you were there to tell the tale, Sweeney!"*

V

Dunvegan

Leaving John Sweeney's place it's a fairly short drive to Dunvegan. For over a century Dunvegan was the best known fort on the Peace River, and its name appeared on every map of the north country, long after Dunvegan's importance as a trading post declined.

The first white man to visit Dunvegan was Alexander Mackenzie when, on May 11, 1793, two days out from his fort at the Forks of the Peace and Smoky on his journey in search of the Western Ocean, he was accosted by a band of Beaver Indians. Possibly the idea of a post on the site where Dunvegan now stands may have occurred to Mackenzie; but certainly David Thompson, the North West Company's surveyor, noted the spot as a suitable trading post location when he camped there eleven years later. The post was built finally in 1806 by Archibald Norman Macleod.

Dreams of yesterday, a ferryman, and a farmer inhabit Dunvegan today. Of the old fort nothing is left. The farmer lives in the old Hudson's Bay Factor's house. The church which Bishop Grouard built with so great an effort is now a warehouse. The sky-blue chancel is still there, though, decorated with stars cut from tin foil. Memory hangs like a veil over Dunvegan. Besides the long trading post history of Dunvegan and the history of the Catholic Mission, there is the story of John Gough Brick, the Anglican missionary. Mr. Brick came to Dunvegan in 1881, where he established a mission, and set out maple trees which are still standing. In fact, the Reverend Brick seems to have been almost as interested in farming as he was in religion. He raised some good wheat on the flats at Dunvegan, and later conducted a farm at Old Wives Lake, some thirty miles from Dunvegan where he raised the wheat that took a championship medal at the Chicago World's Fair in 1893.

There are hints that Reverend Brick was also interested in distilled spirits. I have heard one story which seems to prove this, but also seems to prove that distilled spirits may sometimes be used to offer a missionary a leg-up in his calling. Reverend Brick once came upon a gang of men who were resting after very strenuous labors. Seeing their condition, Brick knew that they needed encouragement. He happened to have a small keg of rum on his wagon, and this he freely opened for the men. After they had heartily partaken they were profuse in their thanks.

"Boys," said the missionary, "I don't want any thanks, but I *am* supposed to preach down at the river tomorrow, and if you all showed up, it would be a big help to me."

The boys showed up in a body, for this was a missionary they could truly appreciate. When he began to speak, Reverend Brick said, "Now, boys, I don't want you to *do* as *I do,* that would get you into a lot of trouble. But if you can *do* as *I say,* you'll be all right." He then gave them a thundering good sermon.

I was interested in the tales told me about the individualistic ferryman who used to run the Dunvegan Ferry. His name was Joe Bizzette. If, for some reason, Joe happened to dislike a traveler, or if he was not in the mood for ferrying, he might yell, "Go around!" And I think the story is certainly true that he kept a newly married couple sitting on the opposite bank all night, because he didn't happen to feel like bringing them across.

I have also heard at Dunvegan, tales about Scotchmen who were so stubborn that if they drowned they would float *up*stream; and I have received hints about a delightful mailman who wore a velvet coat and carried a silver horn which he would joyously blow to announce his arrival.

Regarding the hill at Dunvegan, I have heard a wondrous tale concerning a team and wagon and rawhide traces. A farmer who one time found himself without a suitable harness, cut some strips of rawhide and used them to draw the wagon. When he was about halfway up the Dunvegan hill a heavy rain came up, and the rawhide traces began to stretch and stretch. The horses reached the hilltop, but the wagon slowly slid back to the foot. The farmer didn't know what to do. Finally he solved the problem. He went up the hill, unhitched the team, and tied the traces to a couple of trees. Then he went home. The next day the sun came out and took up the slack in the rawhide. When the farmer returned he found his wagon at the top of the hill.

Possibly the best yarn concerning Dunvegan, however, is the story of the Dunvegan real estate boom. Dunvegan, being so well marked on the maps, was considered a likely spot by certain unscrupulous speculators for a wildcat land scheme. The more or less perpendicular banks of the Peace River were surveyed, marked off into lots, and thrown on the market.

In Edmonton, Winnipeg, Toronto, Montreal and Quebec, as well as in many English cities, posters were put up advertising Dunvegan as the coming metropolis of the continent. The posters showed four railway bridges across the Peace River, street cars, paved streets and handsome stone buildings. Apparently many bit, for I have heard of a number of cases of people visiting Dunvegan, some with their household belongings, with the intention of settling on their *property*.

The story was told me of one poor woman in Scotland who wrote to the Catholic priest at Dunvegan to "please investigate her lot," since she wanted to come right out to settle. The priest wrote back, "Dear Madam: I regret to inform you that last night my one cayuse fell off your property and broke his neck!"

Another lady appeared at Dunvegan one day, took a single glance at the surroundings, and broke into tears. She had invested her life's savings in Dunvegan real estate.

When a Toronto man came to Dunvegan to look over his purchase, he was informed in as kindly a manner as possible that his land had just the night before fallen into the Peace River.

Certain old-timers from the Peace Rivery Country have quite a bit of fun telling how they would saunter into an Edmonton establishment which carried a Dunvegan poster in the window and inquire about purchasing a lot. They invariably tell of the frantic haste with which the clerk shut up shop when he found out that *they were from Dunvegan!*

VI

❦

Fate's Fickle Fortune

THIS IS PROBABLY AS GOOD A PLACE AS ANY TO MENTION one of the slyest tricks of fate I have ever run across. I heard bits of this fabulous story from numerous persons in the Peace River Country, but I think it has been put into writing only once—in a curious little book called, *A Hatchet Mark in Duplicate,* written by the Reverend Alfred Garrioch, an Anglican missionary who sojourned at Fort Vermilion, Dunvegan, and other Peace River spots.

It all apparently began with an Englishman named Armson who panned gold in 1871 at Fort St. John in company with Nigger Dan Williams, Banjo Mike, and Twelve Foot Davis. As fall drew near, Armson was heard to say that he intended going south of the Peace River to trap. This he apparently did, taking with him his beautiful Blackfoot wife.

The wife, so the account goes, had but one imperfection. She had been chopping wood one day and had struck the second toe on her left foot, leaving a scar which extended from the toenail in the form of a ridge.

---

*Published by the Ryerson Press, Toronto, 1929.

The Armsons left Fort St. John in a dugout canoe, and Armson stated that in the spring they would return to the Saskatchewan, via Lesser Slave Lake and the Athabaska River. Instead of reappearing, however, the Armsons vanished and were not heard from again.

Less than a year later a Blackfoot Indian named Jean was paddling up the Peace in his dugout looking for beaver. Suddenly he saw a small raft floating down toward him, and to a stick on the raft was fastened a red rag. Jean paddled rapidly out and to his profound surprise, discovered a very young baby girl on the raft. He lost no time getting the child to shore, and found that she was in the last stages of starvation. He hurriedly boiled a duck that he had recently shot, made some soup, and fed the baby a few drops. Fortunately, a camp of Beaver Indians was close by, and Jean carried the baby to an Indian mother who nursed the child.

When they were examining the baby the Indians discovered a curious mark on the second toe of the left foot —a mark which one of the Indian women said was "older than the child!"

Jean left the child with the Beaver Indians, who soon broke camp, taking the baby with them. That was the last to be heard of this female Moses of the Peace for a long time.

Several years later the Reverend Garrioch chanced upon a couple from St. Paul, Minnesota, named Vinning. The couple had with them an extremely attractive young girl. The Vinnings confided to Garrioch that the child was not their own, but that she had been turned over to them by a free trader at Edmonton who said he got the child from some Indians up in the Peace River Country. The Vinnings had adopted the child and were raising her as their own.

It happened that not long after parting from the Vinnings, Garrioch encountered the Indian named Jean. In the course of their travels together, Jean told the missionary about finding the baby girl, a white child, on the raft. Garrioch immediately began to suspect that the Vinning's adopted daughter and the raft-baby were one and the same. He set out to discover where the child had come from.

He enlisted the help of a trapper named Sizerman, who eventually discovered the remains of an old trap-line somewhere south of the Peace River. He followed the marks of the old line until he came to the remains of a cabin, across which a large tree had fallen. Digging in under the tree he discovered two skeletons. One was lying on a bed. The other was on the floor beside the bed. Hanging on a projection of the cabin was a small notebook done up in a piece of skin. On the floor were remains of a child's rattle, parts of a moss-bag, and a shattered gun. There was, however, no child's skeleton present.

Sizerman carried the notebook to Garrioch, and after reading through it they reconstructed what had probably happened in the cabin. The Armsons had put up a comfortable cabin in the autumn of 1871 and had spent a profitable winter trapping, for Sizerman found the mouldering skins of many marten and beaver. Probably sometime in March a child had been born to Mrs. Armson, and soon afterwards Armson had had an accident with his gun, and infection had set in. He became more and more weak, and finally so weak that he could not provide food. The woman was unable to provide, and father, mother, and child were slowly starving to death. When it became apparent that Armson would not recover, Mrs. Armson staggered down to the banks of the river, made a simple raft, placed the child on it, and pushed it out into the current. She then returned to the cabin to die.

One item from Armson's diary explained the mark on the child's toe. "Born this day (March 31), a girl, perfectly formed and with vocal organs in fine working condition. It would seem that when Mrs. Armson's glancing hatchet hit her toe at the mining camp at Fort St. John she inflicted a hatchet mark in duplicate, for on the corresponding toe of her little daughter's foot there is the perfect replica of the scar of hers."

Another item in the diary stated: "May 15, 1872: I am dying—effects of accident. My first wife died in England, leaving a son, now five. Write to legal firm Blake and Barstow, London, England. Wife and babe weak from starvation. The Lord will provide."

Garrioch turned the memento of the tragedy over to the couple who had adopted the child—by this time a girl of eighteen. They called her Lily, and she was soon to be married to a handsome young man named Herbert Melvin, fresh over from England. The foster parents immediately cabled the legal firm, stating the facts, and asking for the name and address of the son Mr. Armson mentioned in his diary. The wire was shocking to all concerned. The firm wired back that the son's name was Herbert Melvin, and it was actually established that Melvin was Lily's half-brother!

VII

❧

A Notable Influence

At Beaverlodge i realized one of my ambitions when I spent a delightful evening with W. D. Albright, Superintendent of the Beaverlodge Experimental Station. For a good while now—about thirty-one years in fact—Mr. Albright has been dispensing useful information, common sense and a very real quality of inspiration to the Peace River people.

"At an early age," Mr. Albright told me, "I took in the fact that if Canada were to amount to anything as a nation she would have to multiply her three thousand mile breadth by some depth worth while. Otherwise a string of settlements along the International boundary, speaking the same language as the nation to the south, would inevitably become tributary to it in business, thought, culture, and eventually would be absorbed politically. With the best of good will toward the neighboring republic, from which most of my ancestors had come, I still wanted to feel that Canada had a future of her own. In order that she might have a cultural future she must broaden her physical basis; so it became an absorbing quest how far north Canada could be proven habitable and good.

"I always wanted to farm and many day dreams were indulged, planning such a future. I felt that there were neglected opportunities in Old Ontario, but mostly my thoughts turned to the newer regions. I read all the immigration literature I could get hold of relating to Northern Ontario and the Prairie West.

"When eighteen years of age I went to Manitoba on a harvest expedition and on my return a neighbor of Scottish extraction remarked: "So you have come back to Canada, have you?" She knew better, of course, but this chance question betrayed an habitual point of view which practically bounded Canada by Lake Erie on the south, the Niagara River on the east, Lake Ontario on the north and Hamilton on the west—Toronto a sort of outlying suburb and Ottawa almost beyond the pale. The other provinces were a remote land with which the Niagara Peninsula had little in common. Buffalo was the metropolis and the chief avenue of escape for ambitious youth, as Boston was for the "Bluenoses".

After he had put himself through the Ontario Agricultural College, Mr. Albright took a job as herdsman on a dairy farm. He didn't stay there long, however, because he very soon got an offer to come to Sussex, New Brunswick, as assistant editor of the *Maritime Farmer*. He hesitated for a long time, but one of his friends said to him: "If you go down there at journalism for a couple of years, it will be a couple more years of education, a couple more years of broadening out. If you go on the farm now, in spite of yourself you will narrow." Mr. Albright took the job. He was pretty nervous about it, too.

During the next ten years Mr. Albright was an editor,

but always he was looking ahead to the day when he should be able to own a piece of land. Eventually he bought a quarter-section at Beaverlodge in the Peace River Country and with very humble beginnings, settled right down to conduct the agricultural experiments for which the Beaverlodge Station has become famous.

The Beaverlodge Experimental Station has touched Peace River agriculture in many ways, but perhaps its greatest contribution has been to good citiizenship and homemaking. In 1917 a hired man abruptly put this question to Mr. Albright: "What is your greatest ambition in life?" Then answering himself he continued, "Oh yes, I know. You would like to breed a new wheat of high yield and good milling quality."

"I thought a little while," said Mr. Albright, "then I replied: 'No, I would not mind doing that, but its value to the farmer could be easily over-estimated. If it in-creased the profits of wheat growing the ultimate effect would be to shove up the price of wheat land. Society as a whole would benefit and land owners would profit, but the producer as a whole would receive little more than before. No, there is something I would rather do than that. I would rather show how good homes and good living conditions could be established in the Peace, for that is a benefit that would weave itself into the lives and characters of the people, and that no economic process could filch away'."

W. D. Albright is one man greatly loved in the Peace River Country. He has contributed much to the growing tradition of the region, and to him it has been a great satisfaction to watch the region develop from its pioneer stage to its present mature aspect. He has seen the experimental Sub-station develop from half a dozen crude plots of grain sown with four oxen and a drill, into a Station with from twelve to twenty employees and eighty acres of small plots.

"In the words of the late Theodore Roosevelt," said Mr. Albright, "I have always been able to say, 'I like my job'."

VIII

A Word to Epicures

IF YOU CONTINUE ON THE ROAD FROM BEAVERLODGE TO Dawson Creek you come eventually to Ma Brainard's place. It's a long log cabin facing a shining lake. You will often see people sitting by the lake, but usually they are not gazing at the scenery. More often than not they have that complacent, slightly dazed look that can only come after eating a wonderful and extremely bountiful meal; for Ma Brainard will feed any hungry and worthy traveler.

She runs a stopping-place in the hospitable and generous sense of that traditional Alberta word. In these days it is not uncommon to see army trucks, jeeps, and dull brown military sedans parked side by side with teams, farm trucks, and civilian cars, for majors, colonels, and generals shove each other to get a seat at Ma's big kitchen table.

The chief attraction, of course, is Ma herself. As you go into the kitchen, if she is not exchanging quips with someone at the table, she will glance at you and say: "Howdy. Take your hat in that other room and have a seat. Reckon I can scare up some grub, but don't push me. I'm too old."

Pretty soon there may be an empty seat at the table and you'll grab that. From that moment Ma's greatest concern is that you won't get enough to eat. You'll eat fried chicken, hot biscuits, a dozen kinds of vegetables, ten kinds of jellies and preserves—all home-canned, of course. After you have gasped your way through a huge slice of famous apple pie, Ma will say: "Doggone it! I forgot to give you any of my mustard pickle! And you ain't had any salad! Reckon I must be losin' my mind. Here. Try this."

If you have the strength you may ask Ma where's she's from. She'll tell you she's from North Carolina, but that was—Lord knows how far back. If you're not in a hurry to go, and if not too many folks come in to demand Ma's attention, she'll maybe tell you that she's lived in Alberta a long time; first down in the ranching country where her husband lost over seven hundred head of fine cattle in the big freeze of 1907. She'll tell you other stories, too, about herself. How she once served a meal for Sir Henry Thornton and his party, after which Sir Henry, who was a real appreciator of good food, wrote on her visitor's book: "To the author of the best meal I ever ate."

She'll possibly tell you that she got a letter from Sir Henry—after she fell off her barn a couple of years ago and broke her leg.

She probably won't tell you about *all* the famous people she's fed but take it from me, she's fed plenty of the great as well as thousands of plain, ordinary, food-lovin' folks. Without doubt she's the most famous cook in all of Alberta, and the Brainard stopping-house is one of the real traditions of the North Country.

IX

Peace River Town

MR. NORMAN SOARS IS LIBRARIAN AND RATION BOARD CLERK of Peace River. When we went into his little office he was very busy giving out permits to purchase ammunition. Watching the more or less steady stream of applicants, I realized how essential ammunition is still in the Peace River Country. The stories of the applicants were similar. One would say that the coyotes were bad around his place. Another might relate how a timber wolf was threatening his sheep. A third had been haunted by a particularly fierce hawk, and out his way the owls were gettin' troublesome.

Mr. Soars sized up each person quickly, said yes, or no, with authority. And there were lots more yeses than noes.

When there was finally a little lull in the procession, Mr. Soars got up and locked the door. "It's the only way I can get a minute's peace," he explained, "and I do want to have a chat with you. Are you interested in history?

"Here in Peace River we go back to the time of Alexander Mackenzie, the explorer. Mackenzie, you know, arrived at Fort Chipewyan in 1788. We owe the explor-

338

ation of the Peace River to his anxiety to solve the riddle of the Northwest Passage—thought he could reach the Pacific down the river that he believed emptied itself from Lake Athabaska into the Western Ocean, only to find himself in his birchbark canoe among the icebergs and whales of the Arctic. Called that river, The River Disappointment, but his partners in the North West Company spoke of it as the Mackenzie River and that name stuck."

"How did Mackenzie find out about the Peace?" I asked.

"While he was on this trip down the Mackenzie, he encountered an Indian who described to him the course of the Peace River which flowed down from the mountains and gave him the idea that these mountains might be crossed to reach the Pacific. He must have determined then to make the trip, but with typical Scottish foresight he first made a trip home and studied surveying and secured a sextant, compass, and other surveyor's instruments.

"But Mackenzie wasn't the first man to travel up the Peace. Some thirty years ago there was an interesting legend extant which told about the first white man to travel up the Peace. His name was Jean Baptiste St. Germain. Jean Baptiste is supposed to have rescued an Indian girl abandoned by her tribe and married her.

"From this union sprang the numerous tribe of St. Germains that still inhabit the country. The story is borne out, too, to some extent by one of Mackenzie's letters in which he speaks of sending a party of men ahead to locate a post, in charge of his assistant, St. Germain. It may well have been this same St. Germain whom he sent from Fort Chipewyan in the spring of 1792, to select a camping ground as far up the Peace as he could get in time to build a fort by fall. Mackenzie followed the party and arrived at the site they had selected in November, 1792, only just ahead of the ice. Here he spent the winter, building the fort and making plans for his search for the Northwest Passage. You see, in the development of this country, the building of that little fort at the forks is of the utmost importance, for it was here that Mackenzie made a garden that became famous throughout the entire north. This garden was the first attempt to raise food stuffs in the Peace River Valley."

There was a knock at the office door, and Mr. Soars glanced toward it nervously. The knocking continued for a while, then, when it stopped, Mr. Soars continued, "In 1929 we put up a marker across the river from Mackenzie's old fort. Had to put the marker across the river because the road runs up that side."

He rummaged around in the pile of papers on his desk and brought out a copy of the *Peace River Record* for October 30, 1942.

"Here's something kind of interesting, amusing too. Don't know who wrote it, or maybe I won't say. Read it."

He handed me the paper and I read the following little epic which is neither prose nor free verse, but is good, because the Peace River folk feel they've been neglected ever since Alexander Mackenzie discovered 'em. Here it is.

MACKENZIE, HERE WE COME! or
LOOK WHAT YOU DID, ALEXANDER!

Almost exactly one hundred and fifty years ago
(On November the first to be exact)
Alexander Mackenzie arrived here.
He had heard about the Peace River Country,
And decided that it was time he discovered it.
And his first act on arriving
Was to gather the inhabitants together
And, having first fortified them with Rum Punch
(Composed of Rum and Coca-Cola),
He made them a speech
In which he informed them that they were
A race of sturdy pioneers
And that their inland empire was a heritage
Of vast potentialities.
After which he traded them out of their fur
And went on and discovered the Pacific Ocean.
(A fact that is generally ignored
By the American historians,
Who prefer to think that Lewis and Clark came first,
Though they were twelve years later.)
And ever since that day
We, who have been sitting here,
Waiting for something to happen,
Have been subjected
To an intermittent stream
Of distinguished visitors
Everyone of whom arrived ready and willing
To make a speech.
The same speech.
On the least provocation they would rise to their feet
And, adopting a patronizing attitude
They would shoot off the same old platitude,
All about our vast potentialities.
But they never did anything about it.
And so it is with feelings

Of amazement and delight
That we find in our midst
A group, bunch or gang
Of distinguished strangers—
(Tall, Dark and Handsome*)
Who come unprepared and apparently unwilling
To make speeches
About our vast potentialities
But are evidently prepared
To do something about it.
We should feel grateful
To a thoughtful and paternal Government
That has equipped them,
Each and every man,
Not with speeches,
But with ten-wheeled trucks
And at least fifteen pairs of breeches,
And peeps and beeps and jeeps
And even jeep-dogs.
And so the least we can do
Is to get out the whitewash and a brush
And chalk a welcome on the mat!

"The Negroes were fine," said Mr. Soars, "everybody liked 'em here."

There was a terrific banging at the door, and outside a voice bellowed, "Mr. Soars! Mr. Soars! We know you're in there! Please, Mr. Soars, I need some shells!"

"That is the way it always is," sighed Norman Soars. "Somebody's always after something. Oh, well, I'll have to let 'em in. You'll get good stories here. Doggone it! I could tell you some myself if I had time."

He went to the door and jerked it open. "Come in, boys!"

---

*Referring, of course, to the American Negro troops quartered at Peace River town.

X

A Northern Giant

ONE OF THE GREAT VIEWS OF THE WORLD IS THE VIEW FROM the top of the valley above Peace River town. The Peace River received its name when the Crees, Beaver and Slave Indians entered into a lasting peace pact; and the atmosphere of peace seems to dominate the whole vast panorama.

Looking upriver there is a great softness in the sky and the land. The hills are gentle. The mountain waters of the Peace join the waters of the Smoky—together they rush north; toward Vermilion; toward the northern sea.

In this gentle atmosphere of peace it is easy to understand the spirit of good-fellowship and faith imaged in so many of the northern tales. I could believe the tale of the pioneer who left his watch hanging on the branch of a tree while camping on the trail. It was two or three weeks before he could get back to the same spot, and, of course, he thought the watch would be missing. But when he returned he found the watch hanging exactly as he had left it, and what is more, it was running! Someone had come along and wound it for him.

On this height above the Peace a sentinel stands guard.

343

This sentinel is the monument to Twelve Foot Davis, the prospector and trader who, more than any other, seems to symbolize the generosity and faith of the country.

On a quiet November morning we climbed the hill to Twelve Foot's grave. When we reached the rough rails surrounding the stone, a gentle wind sprang up, and in its whisper we seemed to hear the tale of this man whose name has become a Peace River legend.

Twelve Foot Davis was not a giant as many believe. He was, in fact, not even a large man. Through the legends he has become a true giant, although totally unlike Paul Bunyan. For Paul performed miraculous deeds through his strength and size, while Twelve Foot performed only deeds of generosity and kindness.

Twelve Foot Davis got his name in this way. In 1849 he followed the gold rush to California and later moved on up to the Cariboo Creek gold mining district in British Columbia. After he had arrived there and had had a chance to look over the claims that had been already staked, the thought struck him that two of the claims covered too much ground. So one dark night he carefully stepped off the areas of the two claims, and found, sure enough, that they covered *twelve feet* too much territory. He staked on this twelve foot strip for himself and took out $20,000 worth of gold, much of which he probably gave away.

When the gold played out he turned his attention to the fur trade and became a free trader in competition with the Hudson's Bay Company and other large concerns. His reputation for fairness was unquestioned and he traded with the Indians sucessfully for over twenty years. The

Indians called him The Wolf because of his ability to travel long distances, heavily laden, and with very little food.

Davis was a famous cook, and his specialty was pumpkin pie. This might be explained by the fact that he was born in Vermont; at any rate, his "punkin'" pies were known far and wide in the Peace River Country. He was never known to turn anyone away from his cabin, and any traveler could be certain of a meal at Twelve Foot's place.

He was no fool, though. Very industrious himself, he expected industry from those around him. On one trip up the Peace with a party, he purchased all the watches in the whole outfit, so none could tell the time and might, therefore, work longer hours.

Davis feared that he would die a pauper. He dreaded this fate more than anything, but like so many heroes his greatest good was his greatest evil. He simply gave too much away. When at last he came to die, he had nothing.

When he was on his deathbed at Grouard, he was asked by a lady missionary whether he feared to die. Davis answered, "Why should I be afraid to die? I never kilt nobody, I never stole from nobody, and I kept open house for travelers all of my life. No, ma'am, I ain't afraid to die."

One thing Davis loved more than anything else was the beautiful view from the top of the Peace River valley above Peace River town. He often told his friend, Colonel Jim Cornwall, that he wanted to be buried on the hill looking up the mighty valley where the Smoky flows into the Peace.

345

And after Davis died, Cornwall kept his promise. He took up Davis' bones and had them carried to the new grave overlooking the valley Davis loved so much. Jim had a stone made for his friend in the form of a tree trunk and on this stone you may read the legend:

"H. F. Davis, born Vermont 1820. Died at Slave Lake 1893. Pathfinder, Pioneer, Miner, and Trader. He was everyman's friend and never locked his cabin door."

No better commentary on the friendliness of the North Country is needed.

XI

❦ ❧

Assorted Episodes

AT PEACE RIVER TOWN I HEARD MANY TALES. THE PEOPLE told me about Charlie Roberts, the magistrate, who was once faced with such a curious legal problem. A townsman stole a dugout canoe to cross the Peace River. The owner of the canoe apprehended the borrower and hauled him before Charlie Roberts, who had the reputation of "making the punishment fit the crime." Charlie remanded the prisoner for a couple of hours until he had a chance to study up the law on the case. The only thing he could find in the books that seemed to apply, was "piracy on the high seas." The penalty was "death by hanging." This stumped Charlie, but since it was in the books, the only way out seemed to be to hold to the letter of the law. True, the punishment seemed a bit drastic, even in a country which believed in hanging the accused first and trying him afterwards. A jury assembled, and after some heated arguments pro and con, the jury finally agreed that the man was guilty but recommended that he be fined ten dollars and a bottle of whisky which he happened to have in his possession. The culprit always felt that if he hadn't happened to have any whisky, he'd have been hanged.

The independence and initiative of the country appears in the famous folktale about a Mounted Police Inspector and his curious journey with a man's head.* A murder had been committed at Pouce Coupe. When the Inspector arrived on the scene the weather was bitterly cold, the snow deep, and it was entirely impossible to remove the body. Since the man had been struck on the head, the Inspector did the only thing possible. He removed the man's head, put it in a bag, and set off with the specimen for Edmonton. When he arrived at the coroner's office he opened the sack, displayed its contents to the astonished official, and asked, "Doc, what killed this man?"

The coroner gazed for a moment and then muttered, "Good God, Inspector, this fellow died of decapitation!"

At Peace River we heard about the little squatter settlement on the edge of town with the fascinating name of *Moccasin Square Garden,* and where it is said that scarcely a child knows its own father. I heard of one family belonging to a versatile lady named *Buckskin Annie,* which had no fewer than six children, each one of the six combining different bloods. Italy was represented, as well as China and England. Needless to say, Scottish blood was present.

It was with a great deal of pleasure, too, that I encountered at Peace River a tale about Nigger Dan—the same Nigger Dan of whom I heard at High River. Dan was still illustrating his complete independence in the Peace Country, just as he had in the south. Dan had run afoul

*There are different versions of this tale and this may not be the authentic one.

of the interests of the Hudson's Bay Company, and refusing to be daunted, had declared in writing on a tree that he would not be trodden underfoot by any *man*, except Her Majesty, Queen Victoria. It seems strange that Dan should have finally been brought to trial at Edmonton in the name of Her Majesty, charged with having aimed at and discharged a gun at the person of a man named James McKinlay.

Knowing as I did that Dan was a dead shot, I was puzzled at McKinlay's escape. But the trial was a complete vindication of Dan's markmanship.

McKinlay charged that Dan said to him one day, "I'll fix you!" and without any further conversation, entered his cabin and re-appeared with his rifle which he presented muzzle first at McKinlay and pulled the trigger. According to McKinlay the bullet whistled close to his ear.

Dan was defended by a character named Banjo Mike who happened to be in Edmonton, and who, like Dan, had no love for the Hudson's Bay Company.

Banjo Mike asked McKinlay a few pertinent questions.

"You could hear Dan Williams distinctly?"

"Yes."

"You know for certain that his words 'I'll fix you' were addressed to you?"

"Yes."

"Were you standing in front of the house, or at the side of it?'

"In front of it."

"Did the bullet strike the house?"

"I don't know."

349

Banjo Mike then addressed the jury. He pointed out that the words "I'll fix you" might have meant most anything. As he suggested, perhaps Dan had been having trouble with his gun, and the words were addressed to the gun. Who knows? He also pointed out that Mr. McKinlay had said that the bullet whistled close to his ear. "Gentlemen, anybody who knows anything about bullets will tell you that it's impossible to know from the sound whether a bullet is a foot, or a yard, or ten feet, or ten yards away. Also the plaintiff admits that he was standing *in front of his house,* yet he does not know whether the house was hit. I leave you to decide this point, Gentlemen. But this much I do know, as so many others know, that Dan Williams at a distance of one hundred yards, can take the eye out of a jackrabbit at every pop. Gentlemen, had Dan Williams the slightest intention of harming Mr. McKinlay, he would not be here today to amuse you with his little story."*

Nigger Dan was one of the famous "strong men" of the North. So gigantic was his frame that no suit the Hudson's Bay had for sale would fit him. Special clothing had to be made for Dan out of sacks. And his strength was phenomenal. One time the Hudson's Bay men were trying to raise a large flagpole in front of the post at Dunvegan. The pole was too heavy and it kept slipping back to the ground. Nigger Dan happened to come along. He motioned the men aside, got a firm grip on the pole, and raised it upright by himself.

Dan was more than equal of a team of oxen. A heavy

*You may read a full account of this incident in *A Hatchet Mark In Duplicate,* by Rev. Alfred Garrioch, Ryerson Press, Toronto.

cart was stuck fast on the Dunvegan Hill. The oxen couldn't seem to pull it loose. Dan simply took the oxen off the cart and pulled it loose by himself.

At the little white Catholic Mission which faces the broad Peace, we were greeted by a pleasant young priest who took justifiable pride in showing us the famous painting by Bishop Grouard. Bishop Grouard and Father Husson built the church which still stands, though abandoned, at Dunvegan, many miles up the river from Peace River town. When the two priests decided to secure logs to build their church, the river was already frozen over. Happily a thaw came to break the ice and free the river. They engaged *un bon Castor,* a Beaver Indian, and took a boat three days travel up the river where they cut the logs, rolled them down to the water, built their raft which they floated back to the mission, and there spent the winter cutting the logs and sawing the lumber by hand. The following year the church was completed, and wishing to embellish it, Bishop Grouard decided to paint *Notre Seigneur mort sur la croix.* The good Bishop, however, had no canvas, so he commissioned an Indian hunter to secure him an unblemished moose-hide. This was finally provided, and after being tanned and stretched, made a fine surface on which to paint. The Bishop then colored in the figures of Christ on the cross, and Joseph and Mary.

The Bishop was very proud of his work. The painting found its way to Grouard, and after the mission there was abandoned, to Spirit River, and finally to the mission at Peace River where it hangs today. It's well worth seeing.

351

I have been puzzling ever since I saw the picture over the problem of the paints. What did Bishop Grouard use for colors?

As we left Peace River town and drove upriver toward Mackenzie Cairn, I kept looking back. Far away, touched by the morning sun, I could see the Twelve Foot Davis stone, thin and straight, keeping sentinel watch above the valley.

XII

❧ ❧

Boucher's Message

FRED BRICK IS ONE OF THE OLDEST LIVING PEACE RIVER
pioneers. He is also a son of the famous John Gough
Brick who set out maple trees at Dunvegan, raised championship wheat, and preached mighty sermons.

Fred has returned now to his Edmonton home, and
when I went to see him, an event occurred which shows
that spirit of thoughtfulness so deeply implanted in the
pioneers is still remembered in the Brick household.

Fred has a little black cocker spaniel. I was flattered
by the dog's attention, and when I left, he followed me
out to the street. Somehow my wallet slipped out of my
pocket and fell on the sidewalk. When I had gone, the
dog carefully picked up the wallet and carried it to his
master who made a trip clear across Edmonton to return
it to me.

While I was visiting with Mr. and Mrs. Brick, I asked
Fred what experience in the Peace River Country he
especially remembered. Without hesitation, he said he
remembered a particular trip he made up the Peace from
Fort Vermilion with an Indian named Boucher.

I was trading in the North in partnership with my
brother, Ally. (Ally was later a member of the Alberta

353

Legislative Assembly and is said to have driven a team of moose to the meeting in Edmonton.) Along about the middle of April, 1894, this Cree Indian, Boucher, and I loaded a raft with goods at Peace River and floated down to Vermilion, three hundred miles. We then loaded the goods onto pack horses, went one hundred miles west to Hay River, traded for furs, returned to Vermilion, packed up the furs, put them into a large canoe and started the long hard journey upriver to Peace River Crossing. It was no easy trick poling a heavy canoe up the swift Peace, but Boucher was a wonderful canoeman. He could handle with the greatest ease the twenty-five foot birch pole used to move the canoe, and he had a technique few men could duplicate. He would stand in the canoe and holding the pole at the center, would roll it over and over, shooting the canoe ahead so fast the bow would sometimes stand clear out of the water.

It was then the twentieth of June. Nobody had come downriver that season except myself. At that time there was no mail coming into the country. It was a land of utter loneliness and rarely heard the sound of a human voice.

On June twentieth, about three in the afternoon, Boucher suddenly stopped poling. He said to me, "Boss, I've got to go ashore."

"It's not time to eat. Let's travel!"

But Boucher replied, "No, I've got to go ashore."

So we turned the canoe into the bank. Without saying another word, Boucher climbed the bank, made himself a smudge fire to keep off the mosquitoes, and sat down with his back against a spruce tree.

I didn't know what to think. Boucher had been a wonderful worker—a companion. He was also rather remarkable in that he could speak in Cree, Chipawayan, Beaver, English, and French. I would have trusted him with anything, but I could think of no reason for his strange behavior.

However, I went about the task of building a campfire, boiling water for tea, and fried up a bunch of eggs—may sound strange to you that we had eggs. Well, they were given to me by Mrs. Lawrence of Vermilion, the earliest settler there. You can bet I packed 'em carefully. Eggs were a real luxury.

When I had dinner ready I called to Boucher to come and eat.

"I will not eat," said Boucher.

"Are you sick, Boucher?"

"No."

"Then what's the matter?"

"You wouldn't understand."

Boucher just stared into his fire. I couldn't get another word out of him. I saw the Indian wouldn't move any farther that night, and I knew we must camp. I went to the canoe, brought the bed rolls, and sticks for the mosquito bar. I fixed my own bed and had begun to fix Boucher's bed, when he said, "I will not sleep tonight."

Well you can bet I was becoming more and more puzzled. Never before had Boucher behaved like that. However, I cooked supper, prepared my blankets, and went to sleep. I didn't sleep well, since I was worried about Boucher, and I kept waking up. Whenever I awoke I saw Boucher in the same position—just squatting beside his fire.

"I got out of bed at four o'clock, built a fire, cooked breakfast and called to Boucher to come and eat.

"I will not eat," said Boucher.

By this time you can bet I was mighty worried. I went over to Boucher and said, "Boucher, what's the matter?"

"You wouldn't understand."

I couldn't get another word out of him. I took the situation as philosophically as I could, completed my breakfast and, since I was very tired, went back to bed. I slept until late in the forenoon.

At noon I fixed grub and called Boucher again, but the Indian only shook his head.

Well, I was beginning to think we were marooned on the banks of the Peace for good, but about two o'clock that afternoon Boucher got up. Without saying a word to me he fixed himself something to eat. When he had finished he grunted, "Let's travel."

While we were packing up I asked, "Boucher, what was the reason for this delay?"

"You wouldn't understand," said Boucher, but he got a good look at my face and pretty soon he continued, "I was getting a message, Boss. Last night a baby girl was born to my wife, and the child lived two hours."

Well, can you wonder that I thought Boucher had gone crazy? There we were, about half way between Fort Vermilion and Peace River Crossing. Not a soul had passed that way but ourselves all season. There was no mail, no telegraph. Yet here was this Indian claiming to have had a message from God-knows-where that he was the father of a baby girl that had lived two hours.

"Boucher, have you gone bats?"

"We will travel," replied Boucher.

Well, sir, we did travel that afternoon. Boucher worked like a madman! At times he poled so hard and so fast that I feared the canoe might burst apart. He refused to stop for supper, and poled until ten o'clock that night. At ten o'clock we went ashore and made camp. But Boucher hardly slept and was eager to start at three the next morning. Boucher worked like a fiend! That day we made a day and a half of ordinary upriver travel—about thirty-five miles. If you think that's not good traveling, try poling a heavy canoe up the Peace sometime. The next day we made the same distance. In the afternoon, the following day, we passed a place where an old half-breed named Pat Wesley lived. Wesley came out of his shack as we went past, and I called to him, "Hey, Wesley!" The old fellow came down to the shore and we turned in.

"Wesley," I asked, "what's the news?"

"No news," said Wesley, "nothin's happened."

"Boucher," I said, "that was a dream you had. You see, nothing's happened."

"Boss," replied the Indian, "you don't know what you're talking about. That message came to me, and it must be true."

Well, about five miles above the Wesley place we met some men taking out logs. I called to them.

"Anybody been born, died or married?"

"Haven't heard of anybody."

This time I just looked at Boucher and didn't make any remarks. We got to within seven miles of Peace River and were poling the canoe under a cut bank when we heard somebody call out to us from the bank above. I looked up and saw my brother. He was holding the reins of a saddle horse in his hand.

Boucher ran the canoe ashore, and Ally came down the bank. Boucher and I got out of the canoe, built a fire, and put the kettle on. After a while Ally said, "Boucher, I have bad news for you."

"I know," replied Boucher.

"You know," asked Ally, "that three nights ago a baby girl was born to your wife, and that the child lived only a few hours?"

"I know when it happened," replied Boucher. "I told the Boss, but he laughed at me. If you don't mind, I'll take your horse and go on home."

Well, Boucher took the horse and rode away. Ally and I poled the canoe on home. But I've wondered ever since about that message Boucher got in the night. There are strange things in the North. Stranger things than anybody knows about . . .

Epilogue

Johnny Chinook's everywhere. Might be living right in your house. Might be down at the general store or out in the milking barn. He's in every town and on almost every farm. Great fellow! Look Johnny up. Get him to talk. Won't be much trouble. Just tell him you've heard he was present at such or such an event, or that he had a narrow squeak once from a b'ar or a mountain lion. That ought to do the trick.

Last time I saw Johnny was just after I'd finished writing the last story. I'd just closed my typewriter when the door opened and there stood Johnny looking at me very accusingly.

"So," said Johnny, "you're going to stop. Seems to me you missed a lot o' good yarns. How about the Mormons down at Cardston? Yeah, and how about some of those good mountain tales? And how about—"

"Later, Johnny," I said. "You can't tell 'em all. Let's save a few."

"All right," muttered Johnny, "if that's the way you feel, guess I'll be on my way. Got plenty to do!"

"Where you bound, Johnny?"

"Goin' north. <u>Way</u> up north. There's a country!

Big—it's so big no man's got the eyes to see all o' it. And stories! Got plenty o' yarns to make. Alaska Highway, Canol Project and a future that'll be full o' land booms and gold strikes and Lord knows what. There's a country for giants! Well, be seein' you again—sometime!"

Johnny was gone. I got up and looked out my window. The Alberta countryside was hidden in deep twilight. But I thought I saw Johnny, and he was heading north. He was going fast, too. Not ordinary steps like I'd take, but big steps, twenty, thirty, forty miles at a crack. Steps like a giant's.

"Goodbye, Johnny," I called, "I'll be seeing you. Goodbye, Johnny Chinook."